Leaves of Faith:
The World of Jewish Learning

Leaves of Faith:
The World of Jewish Learning

VOLUME I

by
Rabbi Aharon Lichtenstein

KTAV PUBLISHING HOUSE, INC

Library of Congress Cataloging-in-Publication Data

Lichtenstein, Aharon.
Leaves of faith : the world of Jewish learning / by Aharon
Lichtenstein.
v. cm.
Includes bibliographical references and index.
ISBN 0-88125-667-6
1. Judaism--Study and teaching. 2. Jewish learning and scholarship.
3. Rabbinical literature--History and criticism. 4. Jewish religious
education. I. Title.
BM70.L49 2003
296.6'8--dc21
2002156791

Manufactured in the United States of America

Published by
KTAV Publishing House, Inc.
930 Newark Avenue
Jersey City, NJ 07306
Email: info@ktav.com

To Tovah:
With Appreciation and Admiration

Contents

Preface

The essays herein collected – some previously published, others appearing initially – were written over a span of four decades, and for significantly different audiences. They delve into a wide range of topics of moment – and, hopefully, of interest – to thinking, concerned, and committed Jews, whether from the specific Torah world or from broader circles.

In character and tone, they range from the expository through the hortatory to the forensic – although not, I trust, the belligerent. As regards themes, they include presentations and analyses of the substantive content of areas of Torah as well as probing of some of its halakhic and hashkafic frontiers, at the point of intersection with other spheres. Multifaceted in some respects, almost monochromatic in others, they are bound by an overarching concern to explore and express Torah content and values.

Given the character of the format – and, quite possibly, my own proclivities – none of the pieces presumes to be exhaustive. While they draw, to varying degrees, upon a range of resources, they are not, strictly speaking, scholarly. They are, rather, manifestations of the inner spirit, striving to attain *amittah shel Torah*, and yet imprinting a personal stamp; addressing some issues with certitude and passionate conviction, others with a sense of quest, still others, in a process of groping and grappling. I trust, however, that they will be viewed, collectively, as presenting the respective cores of their subjects; and that, as such, they will stimulate thought and discussion.

Some of the pieces are clearly dated – and, if written currently, would differ somewhat, with respect to either form or substance, and possibly both. The treatment of hesder, for instance, focused upon confronting the rejection of army service for *Bnei Torah* in favor of exclusive learning. In today's climate, the balance probably requires reverse redress, rebuttal of those who minimize, if not denigrate, the importance of intensive Torah study in favor of full-term military service. Or again, the hesped of the Rav ל"צז, may appear rhetorically stilted, reflecting not only the almost inevitable price of translation, but also the circumstances of its delivery. Nevertheless, rather than tinker via scissors and paste, or computer-driven, revision, I have – especially, as regards previously printed pieces – generally preferred to honor the integrity of the original and let the text stand as is. I hope I have decided wisely, but, obviously, this is the reader's call. In any event, I can state categorically that I have included nothing I regard as outdated. I have not sought to present a record of past ruminations but, rather, have set down an attempt at serious grappling with relevant concerns.

Likewise, I have, albeit somewhat reluctantly, waived rigorous uniformity, either substantive or technical – presenting, for instance, both the primary Hebrew text or terminology in some places, only one of the two in others. With regard to previously published essays, in particular, presumed differences in readers' sophistication and commitment, as reflected by the diversity of venue, were, initially, taken into account, and a measure of differentiation has here been retained. In this respect, too, I hope internal coherence will compensate for any lack of comprehensive consistency.

In conclusion – in truth, the point of departure – *shevah v'hoda'ah*, praise and thanksgiving to the *Ribbono shel Olam* who has cast my lot among denizens of the *bet midrash*; among those privileged to experience the exploration and explication of Torah as their primary lifelong concern. May He continue to bless me and my family with the strength and the wisdom to confront this wondrous challenge.

At the human plane, my broader indebtedness – to my parents, family, mentors, associates, students – is beyond present enumeration. In this context, I will content myself with thanking those more or less directly responsible for these volumes: catalysts from various quarters – most prominently, of Yeshiva University's Orthodox Forum – who have stimulated the writing of many of these essays; Mr. Terry Novetsky, who has prodded the process of their publication; and the leadership of Ktav Publishing – most notably, Mr. Bernard Scharfstein, its president, and Dr. Yaakov Elman, as editor – who have helped weave a collection of occasional discourses into a book.

Finally, my deepest personal appreciation – inadequate though the term be, in this relation – is encapsulated within the dedication. That lies, however, beyond words, among "thoughts that do often lie too deep for tears." May Yotzer Ha'Adam enable us to share and sustain each other, in good health and joyful spirit, for many years to come.

Aharon Lichtenstein

17 Elul 5762
Jerusalem

Chapter 1

Why Learn Gemara?

Early in his essay, "Why Should I Be Moral?" F. H. Bradley takes issue with the usual formulation of its topic. "But here," he observes, "the question seems strange. For morality (and she too is reason) teaches us that, if we look on her only as good for something else, we never in that case have seen her at all. She says that she is an end to be desired for her own sake, and not as a means to something beyond. Degrade her, and she disappears; and, to keep her, we must love her and not merely use her."[1]

The question, that is, seems not only strange but unethical. The implication that morality can be subservient to any other end contravenes the essence of ethical idealism. Analogously, the quest for a raison d'être par excellence for Torah study may be regarded as an anti-Torah initiative. Hazal, we recall, incorporated the aspiration that Torah be learned *lishmah* into the central *birkat Ha-Torah*, the blessing over Torah study recited daily by an observant Jew. In one sense, to be sure, the query is perfectly in order. We use the term "why" in two distinct modes. At times, we ask it with respect to a phenomenon we fully accept (if indeed it requires acceptance), but whose causal base we seek to discover. We might ask why Wilson entered the First World War or why rainbows only appear after rain. Alternatively, however, we pose the question in a spirit of challenge and demand, perhaps even of reproach, on the implicit assumption that at some level, the reality ought to be different, and requires vindicating exposition. A mother who wants to know why her adolescent daughter's room is so messy is not seeking information; she is remonstrating. The taxpayer who asks why his bill is higher than his neighbor's is, in effect, challenging the assessor; and he is demanding relief rather than reasons. Sadly, however, "Why learn gemara?" is asked by many of its students today, explicitly or subliminally, in both senses, even in certain segments of the yeshiva world.

What is even more disturbing, many find no satisfactory answer. Of these, some drop out, others plod on, but both groups cry out for some response. Perhaps someone like myself, steeped from childhood in the world of Abbaye and Rava, passionately devoted to exploring and explicating it, is not equipped to provide the response. Camus apart, what would we answer if asked, "Why live?" But then again, perhaps it is precisely those who have never truly wrestled with the issue who are best suited to allay such concerns.

Like Mah Nishtannah, this simple single query is reducible to at least four distinct questions. First, why study extensively at all, rather than do something more productive or enjoyable? Second, if intellectual pursuit, must it be Torah? Third, assuming that one is committed to *talmud Torah*, ought not priority be assigned to scriptural *devar Torah* or even to *mahshavah*? Finally, allowing for the primacy of Halakhah, why focus upon gemara, relatively arcane and abstruse, rather than upon Mishnah, *Mishneh Torah*, or *Mishnah Berurah*? For my present purposes, however, I shall assume an audience impervious to Philistinism and normatively committed to Torah study – and hence unperturbed by the first two issues. I shall focus, therefore, upon the last two questions, distinct and yet interrelated, of the centrality of Halakhah and gemara, respectively.

The preeminence of the study of Halakhah is indeed surprising, if not anomalous. *A priori* – and certainly, in light of comparisons with the derivative and kindred Christian and Islamic cultures – one would have expected primacy to be assigned to other areas. These might include such disciplines as theology and philosophy, grounded in the critical issues of religious thought, or scriptural and liturgical texts, which presumably stir passions and elevate the soul. With reference to general education, particularly in the vein of וכל בניך לימודי ה', whether on the adolescent or the adult plane, we might have assumed that it would be oriented to the existential and experiential needs of *homo religiosus*, and that institutions of learning would be tailored accordingly. Who but a scholarly legist would wrinkle his brow over the niceties of canon law or the sharia?

Nevertheless, our traditional emphasis upon the study of Halakhah is thoroughly understandable. It is fully consonant with the nature of Jewish religious experience and rooted in our collective existence. Without doubt, the Jew, like other people, confronts the *Ribbono shel Olam* as redeemer, benefactor, and judge. Primarily, however, he encounters Him as commander. Jewish sensibility is pervasively normative. The Jew is, first and foremost, a summoned being, charged with a mission, on the one hand, and directed by rules, on the other. The message addressed to him ranges from the comprehensive to the minute; but whatever its scope, it is normative in character.

In one sense, Judaism has brought this perspective to bear upon universal human existence. Moreover, it has done so even with reference to presumably neutral areas. The point is strikingly illustrated by a sequence of several *pesukim* in Bereshit. Having concluded the account of the creation of man with the statement that he was positioned in Eden לעבדה ולשמרה, "to till it and to superintend it," the Torah continues: ויצו ה' א‑להים על‑האדם לאמר מכל עץ‑הגן אכל תאכל. ומעץ הדעת טוב ורע לא תאכל ממנו כי ביום אכלך ממנו מות תמות. (Bereshit 2:15–16), "And the Lord God commanded the man, saying, 'Of every tree of the garden thou mayest freely eat; but of the tree of knowledge of good and evil, thou shalt not eat of it; for in the day that thou eatest thereof thou shalt surely die.'" *Prima facie*, the command relates only to the prohibition against eating from the tree of knowledge, with all other trees remaining beyond the pale of command. And yet the license to partake of them is subsumed under *va-yezav* in order to emphasize that such indulgence is not the exercise of some natural right within a normative vacuum, but the subject of express permission granted by a commanding Taskmaster, whose directives relate, albeit in different ways, to the plane of *reshut* as well as that of *mizvah*.

Nevertheless, both quantitatively and qualitatively, the normative aspect figures far more prominently in Jewish existence; and this with respect to the realm of *mizvah*. The normative realm is, of course, the very stuff of Halakhah. Small wonder, then, that study of Halakhah, defined by Hazal as the quintessential *devar Hashem*,[2] has figured so prominently in collective *talmud Torah*.

On Hazal's view, this relation to Halakhah lies at the heart of our covenantal existence. On the basis of a fine inference from a command issued to Mosheh Rabbenu after the reconciliation culminating in the issuing of the second *luhot*, Rav Yohanan states:

לא כרת הקב"ה ברית עם ישראל אלא בשביל דברים שבעל פה שנאמר, כי על פי הדברים האלה כרתי אתך ברית ואת ישראל (גיטין ס)

The Holy One, blessed be He, established a covenant with Israel only due to the oral matters, as the verse states, "For on the basis of these words I have established a covenant with you and with Israel."[3]

These "oral matters" are essentially halakhic. Whereas the written text is an amalgam of the literary and the legislative, with narrative and normative sections interlaced, *Torah she-be'al-peh,* whether as interpretation or as accretion, is overwhelmingly halakhic. And it is this component that Rav Yohanan defined as the basis of our covenantal relation to the *Ribbono shel Olam*.

A well-worn midrash, familiarized by the opening Rashi on Bereshit, goes remarkably further:

אמר רב יצחק: לא היה צריך להתחיל את התורה אלא מהחודש הזה לכם שהיא מצוה ראשונה שנצטוו בה ישראל ומה טעם פתח בבראשית.

Rabbi Yitzhak stated: The Torah ought to have begun with "This month shall be unto you," which is the first *mizvah* that was commanded to Israel. Why does it open, then, with "In the beginning"?[4]

The answer – that this opening, and the entire first quarter of the Torah, was incorporated for forensic purposes, in order to fend off Gentile critics by providing the legal, moral, and theological rationale for our occupancy of Eretz Yisrael – has radical implications. Clearly, Rabbi Yitzhak assumed that Torah, as guide and directive, is intrinsically confined, by definition, to Halakhah.[5] Whatever else is included – cosmology, history, philosophy – requires an ancillary rationale. This startling thesis troubled the Ramban, who modified it with the suggestion that the thrust of the inference was that nonhalakhic elements, while essential, could have been encapsulated in the text in general outline, with their amplification to be transmitted orally for the cognoscenti.[6] Rashi, however, presumably accepted the thesis in its bald form; and at the very least, we are left with Rabbenu Bahye's formulation:

> והכוונה לומר כי כיון שהמצות הם עיקר התורה לא היה ראוי להיות פתח דבריה של
> תורה כי אם במצוה.

The intent is that inasmuch as the *mizvot* are the main part of the Torah, it should have opened with nothing else.[7]

The emphasis upon the study of Halakhah has these objective and subjective aspects. The Rav זצ"ל, in the early sections of *Ish Ha-Halakhah,* understandably focused upon the former. Drawing upon an analogy to mathematical thought, he portrays halakhic man as building a comprehensive ideal construct that serves, *inter alia,* as a theoretical model for a correlative halakhic order relating to every aspect of mundane reality. To this end, he cites a striking comment from the Tanya:

> כשאדם מבין ומשיג איזה הלכה במשנה או בגמרא לאשורה על בוריה הרי שכלו תופם
> ומקיף אותה וגם שכלו מלובש בה באותה שעה והנה הלכה זו היא חכמתו ורצונו של
> הקב"ה שעלה ברצונו שכשיטעון ראובן כך וכך דרך משל ושמעון כך וכך, יהיה הפסק
> ביניהם כך וכך, ואף אם לא היה ולא יהיה הדבר הזה לעולם לבוא למשפט על טענות
> ותביעות אלו מכל מקום מאחר שכך עלה ברצונו ובחכמתו של הקב"ה שאם יטעון זה
> כך וזה כך יהיה כך הפסק כך הרי כשאדם יודע ומשיג ותופס ומקיף בשכלו רצונו וחכמתו
> של הקב"ה דלית מחשבה תפיסא ביה.

When a person properly and soundly understands and grasps any Halakhah from the mishnah or the gemara, his mind grasps and comprehends it – and at the same time is enveloped by it. For this Halakhah is the wisdom and will of the Holy One, blessed be He, as it has been established by His will that, for instance, when Reuven shall claim such-and-such, and Shimon such-and-such, that the decision shall be such-and-such. And even though it never has and never shall come to pass that such a case, with respect to these claims and demands, shall be adjudicated, nevertheless, since it is the divine will and wisdom that if one shall contend such, and the other such, the decision shall be such, [then] when one knows and grasps this decision with his mind as a Halakhah set forth in the Mishnah, the gemara, or the *poskim*, he grasps and seizes upon and comprehends with his mind the will and wisdom of the Holy One, blessed be He, who is beyond [human] thought.[8]

The prospect is exhilarating, the claim possibly audacious; and yet, in a sense, the Rav's approach is limited in scope. The demiurgic enterprise is clearly the provenance of master-builders, and it is of them that the essay speaks. Can its categories be readily applied to an adolescent struggling to master recalcitrant texts, or even to the average Kollel student wending his way through Yoreh De'ah? On the subjective plane, however, the experience of hearing the magisterial commanding voice and of responding to its normative call is open to all. Given the requisite intellectual commitment and emotional relation, every student of Halakhah is exposed once again to his Master's commanding presence. Each page is a potential source of regenerative Antaean return to Sinaitic roots.

The point is amply illustrated by a singular exposition of the Rambam, drawn, perhaps surprisingly, from Hilkhot Hagigah. Explaining the *mizvah* of *hakhel*, he writes:

מצוה עשה להקהיל כל ישראל אנשים ונשים וטף בכל מוצאי שמטה בעלותם לרגל ולקרות באזניהם מן התורה פרשיות שהן מזרזות אותן במצות ומחזקות ידיהם בדת האמת.

It is a positive commandment to convene all of Israel, men, women, and children, at the conclusion of the Sabbatical year, when they make their festival pilgrimage, and to read in their ears, from the Torah, portions that quicken them with respect to *mizvot* and which strengthen them with reference to the true faith.[9]

Subsequently, he enumerates the portions to be read – all from Devarim:

מהיכן הוא קורא מתחילת חומש אלה דברים עד סוף פרשת שמע ומדלג לוהיה אם שמוע וגו' ומדלג לעשר תעשר וקורא מעשר תעשר על הסדר עד סוף ברגכות וקללות עד מלבד הברית אשר כרת אתם בחורב ופוסק.

From where does he read? From the beginning of the humash of Devarim until the end of the portion of Shema [1:1–6:9]; he then skips over to the portion of *Ve-hayah im shamo'a* [11:13–21]; and he skips to *Asser te'asser* [14:22–27], and he reads, consecutively, from *asser te'asser* until the conclusion of the Blessings and Curses, i.e., until "Apart from the covenant which He had made with them at Horeb," and then he stops [14:22–28:69].

Given the purpose posited by the Rambam, this list may seem surprising. The inclusion of the earlier and later segments is self-evident, as they deal directly with major theological cruces and the fundamental covenantal relation of *Knesset Yisrael* and the *Ribbono shel Olam*. By far the largest item, however, is the section from *asser te'asser* until the Blessings and Curses – roughly, the middle third of Devarim, and unquestionably its halakhic core. Are detailed accounts of the laws concerning tithes, firstling sacrifices, judicial appointments, and pawnbroking the optimal vehicle for quickening observance and reinforcing commitment? But that is precisely the point.

The Rambam's view is elucidated and sharpened in a subsequent Halakhah, in which he explains how *hakhel* is to be experienced.

וגרים שאינם מכירין חייבין להכין לבם ולהקשיב אזנם לשמוע באימה ויראה וגילה ברעדה כיום שניתנה בו בסיני. אפילו חכמים גדולים שידועים כל תורה כולה חייבין לשמוע בכוונה גדולה יתרה ומי שאינו יכול לשמוע יכוין לבו לקריאה זו שלא קבעה הכתוב אלא לחזק דת האמת ויראה עצמו כאילו עתה נצטוה בה ומפי הגבורה שומעה.

> And strangers who are not knowledgeable are obliged to prepare their hearts and bend their ears to hear, with tremor and fear, and with joy in trembling, as on the day that it [i.e., the Torah] was given at Sinai. Even great sages, who know all of the entire Torah, are obligated to listen with very great interest. And whosoever cannot hear shall attune his heart to this reading, for Scripture has instituted it only in order to strengthen the true faith. And he should envision himself as though he had just now been commanded it, and as if he were hearing it from the Almighty.[10]

Admittedly, perhaps neither the tremor nor the joy is felt with such force upon opening a gemara or a *Shulhan Arukh*. We are dealing, after all, with a septennial event. And yet, as a testimony to the direction in which proper study of Halakhah can and should lead, the Rambam's formulation is impressive.

Realization of this potential is often predicated upon faith. And this in two senses. First, there must be faith – not mere verbal assent to dogmatic propositions, but genuine conviction and relation – in the *Ribbono shel Olam* and in Torah as His word. Contact with Him and with it must be sought and appreciated as a critical desideratum. Second, there should be a measure of faith in oneself – in personal readiness and openness to let the power of divine law instill, directly or osmotically, both knowledge and love. It is the weakness of this dual faith which lies at the heart of much of the malaise concerning intensive learning of Halakhah and gemara.

This, in turn, raises the question – critical in its own right, independent of our topic – of how the necessary faith can be intensified. With an eye to the dying David's counsel to Shelomoh – ודע את א׳לקי אביך ועבדהו בלב שלם ובנפש חפצה (Divrei Ha-Yomim I 28:9), "Know thou the God of thy father, and serve Him with a whole heart and with a willing mind" – one may suggest, with the utmost brevity, two directions. The first, in our context admittedly somewhat circular, is through deepening and enriching the study of *devar Hashem – zeh Halakhah.* Obviously, however, this approach presupposes a degree of sensitivity lacking in many, and hence is not always applicable, even to a committed populace. The second, then, is a range of intellectual and experiential elements that can speak more directly to a questing Jewish soul. The need, at times, for the latter, whether as complement or substitute, was recognized by no less ardent an advocate of halakhic study than Rav Hayyim Volozhyner, and that recognition is surely far keener today. Nevertheless, this is still radically different from any overall questioning of the spiritual value of the intensive study of Halakhah.

The implications for setting the priorities in Torah education are clear. To be sure, aggadah, too, is an integral aspect of *Torah she-be'al-peh.* As students or educators, we are mindful of the Sifre's admonition:

שלא תאמר למדתי הלכות די לי ת״ל כי אם שמור תשמרון את כל המצוה הזאת – כל המצות למוד, מדרש, הלכות ואגדות וכן הוא אומר למען הודיעך כי לא על הלחם לבדו יחיה האדם כי על כל מוצא פי ה׳ יחיה האדם – אלו הלכות ואגדות.

Lest you say, "It is sufficient that I have learned halakhot," Scripture states, "For if ye shall diligently keep the whole of this commandment." "The whole of this commandment": learn midrash, halakhot, and aggadot. Likewise, it is stated, "That He might make thee know that man doth not live by bread only, but by every thing that proceedeth out of the mouth of the Lord doth man live": these are halakhot and aggadot.[11]

The study of aggadah is vital both as an essential facet of Torah per se and as a stimulus to religious commitment. רצונך שתכיר מי שאמר והיה העולם, למוד הגדה שמתוך כך אתה מכיר את הקב"ה ומדבק בדרכיו "If you wish to know Him who spoke and the world came into being," the Sifre counsels subsequently, "study aggadah, for thence you know God and cleave unto His ways." And, of course, a significant segment of Shas is accordingly composed of aggadic materials.[12]

Nevertheless, the primary thrust of *Torah she-be'al-peh,* far more than of written Torah, is clearly halakhic, and the normative imprint is broad and deep. Hence, its study constitutes an encounter with its magisterially commanding Giver even more than with the Creator of the cosmos.

We have heretofore focused upon doubts concerning the study of Halakhah. A second dragon remains to be slain, however. Why gemara? Why not, one repeats, Mishnah, *Mishneh Torah,* or the *Mishnah Berurah?* Why the convoluted dialectic of intermediate texts, and why not the alpha and omega of *Torah she-be'al-peh,* either its pristine core or current psak?

The question is exacerbated by the difficulty entailed in learning gemara. This was already recognized by Hazal.

אמר רבי זירא אמר רב: מאי דכתיב כל ימי עני רעים – זה בעל גמרא, וטוב לב משתה תמיד זה בעל משנה.

Rabbi Zera said in the name of Rav: What is it that is written, "All the days of the poor are bad"?[13] This refers to a person of gemara. "But he that is of a merry heart hath a constant feast." This refers to a person of Mishnah.[14]

As the Rashbam explains, the privation of the *ba'al* gemara derives from the strain entailed in mastering halakhot and their attendant difficulties: שממית עצמו לכוין הלכות ולתרץ הוויות.[15] "He kills himself in order to get the halakhot right and to resolve cruces." In the post-talmudic era, however, far more rudimentary obstacles abound. Simply coping with an unwieldy, rambling, allusive, and convoluted text began to pose a formidable chal-

lenge. Consequently, much of the literary energy of the Gaonim and the
early Rishonim, from the *Ba'al Ha-She'iltot* to Rashi and the Rashbam, was
devoted to surmounting these obstacles, to bringing the gemara and its
contents within reach of a wider audience – whether through systematiza-
tion, contraction, explication, or recourse to simpler Hebrew.

Both the difficulties and the efforts to overcome them were noted by
one of the most prominent of the Ramban's disciples, Rav Aharon HaLevi.
Sketching the background for his commentary on the Rif's redaction of
several massekhtot, he writes:

וגם עליה (=המשנה) יצאו עסקים סברות רבות ודקדוקים נבנה עליה התלמוד הבבלי
שהם מים עמוקים דברים נעלמים וארוכים עד שקראוהו חכמים מחשכים ורוב הרוצים
להכנס מצאו דלתותיו נעולות זולתי יחידים בדורות סגולות... והתלמידים יעפים יצאו
דחופים תחלוש דעתן מרוב המשא והמתן ואני בראותי כי היגיעה רבה והגמרא סוגרת
ומסוגרת ואין יוצא ואין בא חברתי ספר קראתיו כור הקודש על דרך הגמרא... ועם
כל זה דרכי התלמוד נעלמים בחותם צר סתומים וכל הדברים יגיעים ואין הכל זוכים
להיותם יומם ולילה קבועים ומפני טרחות הזמן למדים תורה לשעות ולרגעות ויש רבים
צריכים דברים קצרים ופסקים מסודרים ישאו חן בעיניהם יאירו כספירים.

And upon it [i.e., the Mishnah] many claims were made, numerous thoughts
and fine inferences out of which was built the Babylonian Talmud, which
is deep water, consisting of obscure and lengthy matters, to the point that
the sages denominated it as "[a place of] darkness." Most of those who have
sought to enter have found its gates shut, except for individuals in favored
eras.... And students venture forth both fatigued and pressured, their thoughts
sapped by the extensive dialectical discourse. So when I noted that the labor
was great and the gemara [nevertheless remained] closed and shut, access
and exit being generally barred, I composed a [commentary] work called
Nezer Ha-Kodesh, following the order of the gemara.... And yet the ways of
the Talmud are obscure, closed with a tight seal, and its matters are wearying,
and not everyone is fortunate enough to have fixed daily and nightly periods
[i.e., of Talmud study], and, because of their temporal travails, [most] learn
Torah by hours and moments, and many need short summaries and orderly
codes, such as find favor in their eyes, like radiant sapphires.[16]

For the average modern student, these problems have, if anything,
worsened – all the more so because the gemara's sequence and syntax are

so different from his usual well-groomed intellectual fare. Why, then, the yeshiva world's continued commitment to gemara?

In response, I believe we may single out at least four distinct and yet confluent factors. The first is its status as a primary – in a sense, in the world of *Torah she-be'al-peh*, as *the* primary – text. On the one hand, in contrast with much of Mishnah, the gemara is not a compendium of inchoate factual or normative data. It is the arena within which raw material is analyzed and molded, within which bare bones are fleshed out and information transmuted into knowledge. On the other hand, at no point does it convey a sense of systematized accretion or summary digest. On every *daf*, one feels the freshness of virgin birth, the angular edge of rough terrain plowed and yet unplowed, the beck of meandering paths charted and yet uncharted. There is nothing distilled, nothing lacquered. The sense of challenge and concomitant invigoration is pervasive.

Contact with the terra firma of primary texts is of significant educational and intellectual value in any serious discipline – and, by and large, sorely lacking in the current academic climate. How many law students have ever seen Justinian or Coke – or, for that matter, surveyed *Marbury vs. Madison*? It is incalculably important, however, with respect to *talmud Torah*, whose study is enjoined as a religious experience rather than as a mere intellectual exercise. On the experiential plane, recourse to secondary or tertiary texts may simplify; but it almost certainly dilutes.

Relation to the primary source is felt not only with respect to the text or its content. It is felt, in a personal vein, with regard to Hazal. To open a gemara is to enter into their overawing presence, to feel the force of their collective personality – and not as in a historico-critical mode, in order to pass judgment upon them, but so as to be irradiated and ennobled by them. It is to be exposed, with a sense of intimacy, not only to their discourse, exegesis, aphorisms, or anecdotes, but to themselves – at once engaging and magisterial, thoroughly human and yet overwhelming. To be sure, a sense of access to its masters could be attained from the texts of any given period. Intensive study of medieval *poskim* or of the *Shulhan Arukh* and its appendages would link us to the worlds of the Rambam and the Rama, respectively. But the gemara is clearly special. This is due, in part, to its structure as an arena within which the mind encounters a panoply of personages spanning successive generations. Primarily, however, it is attributable to Hazal's unique stature. On the textual plane, they are, in a real sense, the alpha and omega of Halakhah, both primal fount and ultimate authority. We acknowledge them by dint of their being, with an eye to Justice Jackson's distinction, both final because right and right because final; by virtue of the conjunction of their distinctive greatness and their historical position. For an aspiring *ben Torah*, linkage with them has particular significance; and it is best attained by learning gemara. Mishnah, which precedes, is relatively sparse and tentative; and whatever follows is relatively ancillary. It is not a question of limning biographical portraits. We obviously know far more of the Rama's *curriculum vitae* than of Rava's. At issue is feeling the pulsating presence of our masters in the primal forge of *Torah she-be'al-peh*.

This point dovetails with a third factor, the substantive nature of gemara. We are accustomed to distinguishing between *Torah she-bi'khtav* as a fixed datum – graven in stone, inscribed upon parchment, its sanctity invalidated by the accretion or deletion of a single letter – and *Torah she-be'al-peh*, sinuous, efflorescent, developmental. *Asher natan lanu Torat emet*, "Who has given us a Torah of truth," explains the *Tur*, refers to the former, while, *ve-hayyei olam nata betokheinu*, "and eternal life He has implanted within us," refers to the latter.[17] There is a further and parallel distinction pertaining to Mishnah and gemara within the world of *Torah she-be'al-peh*. Defining the respective terms, Rashi explains, "Mishnah: as they [i.e., the texts] are formulated with no reason set forth in them." Gemara, by contrast, he identifies with *hokhmah*, explaining that it expounds: סברת טעמי המשנה ולהבין שלא יהיו סותרות זו את זו וטעמי איסור והיתר והחיוב והפטור והוא נקרא גמרא "the rationale of the Mishnah's reasons, [enables us] to understand them in such a manner as to not contradict one another, and the reasons for what is proscribed and licit, obligatory and exempt."[18]

As such, it was defined by Hazal and the Rishonim as a reliable guide to practical observance, "the rationale of the Mishnah's reasons, from which instruction issues forth."[19] Comparably, the Rambam contrasts the term *Torah she-be'al-peh* – in his usage, the equivalent of Mishnah – as denominating a delimited corpus, with its elucidation and analysis in gemara. The student of the latter is actively engaged in an intellectual enterprise, both analytic and synthetic.

יבין וישכיל אחרית דבר מראשיתו ויוציא דבר מדבר וידמה דבר לדבר ויבין במדות שהתורה נדרשת בהן עד שידע היאך הוא עיקר המדות והיאך יוציא האסור והמותר וכיוצא בהן מדברים שלמד מפי השמועה. וענין זה הוא הנקרא גמרא.

He shall understand and perceive a conclusion from its inception, will extract one matter from another and compare one to another. He shall further understand the hermeneutic principles through which the Torah is expounded, to the point that he will apprehend the essence of these principles and how to extract the prohibited and the licit, and the like, from matters he has learned from the tradition. And this subject is that which is called gemara.[20]

In a word, Mishnah is the given *Torat emet* of the oral tradition, gemara, its implanted *hayyei olam*.

The ramifications for personal *talmud Torah* are obvious – and far-reaching. Relatively speaking, the study of Mishnah per se is passive, at times even submissive; that of gemara is vibrant. To open a *sugya* is to gain access to a world in ferment. It is to enter a pulsating *bet midrash*, studded with live protagonists; to be caught up, initially as witness and subsequently as participant, in a drama of contrapuntal challenge and response, of dialectic thrust and parry; to be stimulated by the tension of creative impulse; to be charged by the *Sturm und Drang* of *milhamtah shel Torah*. Once formidable textual barriers are surmounted, one is animated by a sense of movement and anticipation. Very little is pat. Learning becomes, in great measure, a quest for a captivating but frequently elusive truth that must be sought, and at times molded; and the student of gemara – alongside amoraim, Rishonim, and Aharonim – is privy to the process and part of the process. Gemara is quintessential *hayyei olam*; that is the crux of the difficulty and the glory of its study.

Admittedly, the term "gemara," as derived by Rashi and the Rambam, need not refer to a specific text. It denotes a mode of study that is presumably also applicable in the course of learning Mishnah; and conversely, one could certainly transmute the Talmud into a clearly defined textual corpus, to be mastered and integrated as such. Nevertheless, there is a clear correspondence between the respective concepts and the texts. The apodictic character of a code encourages one intellectual mode, and the expansive record of its analysis and interpretation stimulates another. A context within which anecdote and proverb jostle with rigorous textual and legal analysis; within which the excitement of confrontation takes precedence over the lucidity of exposition, discourse over conclusion, debate over resolution – such is the fabric of the gemara. Hence, it exudes vitality and imposes a charge upon its students. More often than not, a *sugya* "ends," as T. S. Eliot said of Henry James's novels, like life itself: unfinished. Hazal themselves perceived the Bavli as a potpourri; and there is no question but that its structure can be the cause of frustration and confusion. "'He has placed me in darkness like the world's dead'" במחשכים הושיבני כמתי עולם – "this," commented Rav Yohanan, "refers to the Babylonian Talmud" (Sanhedrin 24a). Its very amorphousness also serves as a source of challenge and fascination. These are not, to be sure, ends in themselves. We fasten upon gemara not out of a quest for intellectual stimulation, but out of cleaving to *devar Hashem*. But to the extent that we are gripped and animated by its vitality, the stimulus attains religious significance.

This, in conclusion, brings us to the fourth element. Traditionally, *yahadut* has stressed that *talmud Torah* is not to be perceived as a purely intellectual pursuit. It constitutes, rather, a dialogic encounter with *Ribbono shel Olam*. This is a truism of the yeshiva world and axiomatic to the existence of every serious *ben Torah*. Clearly, however, the nature of the encounter is a function of the character of one's learning. When Rav Halafta Ish Kefar Hananyah spoke of the immanence of the Shekhinah in this context, he focused upon its presence among those who are *yoshevim ve-osekim ba-Torah*, "those who are sitting and engaged in Torah"[21] – not simply studying Torah but caught up by it. To the extent that one is more deeply and intensely involved, insofar as one's being is more fully charged, he is more powerfully engrossed by the encounter, and presumably worthier of divine grace.

This engagement is optimally provided by gemara qua both text and method. As opposed to the relatively more passive nature of Mishnah, the dynamic character of gemara vibrantly energizes the student. The activated self is then more open to a more intensive relationship, religious as well as intellectual. I grant that the reverse is sometimes true. Rather than reinforce the dialogic element, *milhamtah shel Torah* may become a diversionary substitute for encounter. Properly pursued, however, the challenge of the enterprise can serve as a powerful engine to profounder *kabbalat pnei Ha-Shekhinah*.

On a practical plane, admittedly, much of the foregoing is not always applicable. Whatever the ideal priorities may be, we cannot be oblivious, in planning and implementing educational policy, to the differential concerns of varied populations. There are students who are turned off by the niceties of halakhic discourse and who thirst for the more direct confrontation with gut existential issues afforded by *mahshavah* or aggadah. Moreover, for some this is no mere predilection. The sustenance, or even the very continued existence, of their religious commitment may hinge, genuinely and perhaps desperately, upon dealing with these issues *in extenso* and in depth. Others, while attuned to a normative wavelength, may find the formidable barriers entailed in learning gemara virtually insuperable. Surely, it is arguable that for a certain student population – in some cases, sufficiently exposed to gemara to resent it but not given the wherewithal to appreciate it – a Mishnah-oriented curriculum would be preferable.[22] At the other end of the spectrum, there are segments of the Torah world for whom the primacy of gemara is so securely established that they suffer from a reverse imbalance – a paucity of experiential encounter which may result in spiritual dessication; and were I addressing them, I would present a very different thesis. We ignore these elements at our peril. Nevertheless, it is important that ideal traditional priorities be understood and defined, so that we can perceive which course to prefer and, optimally, encourage.

"Why learn gemara?" Would that the question did not arise, we might respond, at least not in its currently prevailing form. Would that the amalgam of confusion, drift, discouragement, and frustration that frequently animates groping students were not part of our educational scene. Inasmuch as these elements do lamentably exist, however, they need to be forthrightly addressed, so that *rabbanan* and *talmideihon* alike would be better equipped to cope with them.

Finally, in a more positive vein, the question may also be asked by *Bnei Torah* who are fully committed, intellectually and emotionally, to the study of gemara, and yet seek to define the basis of their aspiration. Even when there is no felt need for an apologia or raison d'être to shore up personal learning, a richer understanding of its import may very well enhance it. For those who are fortunate enough to experience the power and glory of *havvayot de-Abbaye be-Rava,* there may still be benefit in a more perceptive insight into how and why they are, preeminently, *hayyenu ve-orekh yameinu.*

Notes

1. See his *Ethical Studies* (New York, 1951), p. 3.
2. See Shabbat 138b. It should be noted, however, that the gemara there also applies the term to prophecy and, much to Rashi's surprise, to eschatology.
3. Gittin 60b.
4. Bereshit 1:1. The midrash appears in several places. See the note in A. Berliner, *Rashi al Ha-Torah* (Frankfurt, 1905), p. 424.
5. See, however, in contrast, Midrash Tehillim 78:1:

   שלא יאמר לך אדם אין אין מזמורות תורה אלא תורה הם ואף הנביאים תורה לפיכך משל האזינה עמי תורתי ולא הדברות בלבד אלא אף החידות והמשלות תורה הם וכן הקב"ה אמר ליחזקאל בן אדם חוד חידה ומשול משל וכן שלמה אמר להבין ומליצה דברי חכמים וחידותם.

6. "ויש לשאול בה כי צורך גדול הוא להתחיל התורה בבראשית ברא אל־קים כי הוא שורש האמונה ושאינו מאמין בזה וחושב העולם קדמון הוא כופר בעיקר ואין לו תורה כלל" (בראשית א:א).

   See also his *derashah*, "Torat Hashem Temimah," in *Kitvei Ha-Ramban* (Jerusalem, 1963), 1:144–50.
7. From the introduction to his commentary on the Torah, in *Rabbenu Bahye: Be'ur al Ha-Torah,* ed. Rabbi C.B. Chavel (Jerusalem, 1982), p. 12.
8. Cited from *Likkutei Amarim,* chap. 5, in איש ההלכה – גלוי ונסתר (Jerusalem, 5739), p. 33. It may be worthy of note that in the sentence preceding the citation, the Rav points in another direction: גם בעל ההלכה וגם המתימטיקאי חיים בחתום אידיאלי ונהגים מזיו יצירתם. This formulation focuses upon the gratification of the creative mind rather than the religious impulse of the questing soul.
9. Hilkhot Hagigah 2:1.
10. Hilkhot Hagigah 3:6.

11. Sifre, Ekev 12, on Devarim 11:22. In this context, as in many others in Hazal, the term "midrash" does not have its later homiletic connotation, but refers to hermeneutic exegesis.

12. Ibid., sec. 13.

13. The Jewish Publication Society version renders רעים as "evil." This seems to me to be excessively sharp. In any event, it is certainly inconsistent with the gemara's discussion in this context, and I therefore prefer the milder epithet, "bad."

14. Bava Batra 145b. The citation is from Mishlei 15:15.

15. Bava Batra 145b, s.v. זה בעל גמרא.

16. *Pekudat Ha-Levi'im* (reprinted, Jerusalem, 1962), p. 11.

17. Orah Hayyim 139. Cf., however, *Sefer Ravyah* 1:181, who argues that *ve-hayyei olam* refers to שאר מצוות וגמילות חסדים שישראל עוסקים בהם תדיר, and rejects the view that the phrase refers to Torah, as in that case it would be redundant. See also *Beth Ha-Levi al Derush u-Milei de-Aggadata*, p. 130, who regards the *berakhah* before Keri'at Ha-Torah as referring to the Written Torah, and that which follows as referring exclusively to *Torah she-be'al-peh*.

18. Bava Mezia 33a, s.v. mishnah and *she-limmedo hokhmah*. Here Rashi speaks of gemara as dealing with both primary and secondary questions, i.e., with the exposition of rationale as well as the resolution of contradiction. Subsequently (ibid., s.v. gemara) he emphasizes the latter.

19. Rashi, Berakhot 5a, s.v. *zeh* gemara. See, however, Bava Batra 130b.
    It should be emphasized, however, that in some contexts the term "gemara" is juxtaposed to "sevara." In these, it refers to the base material of tradition, as opposed to its analysis and interpretation. See, e.g., Sanhedrin 36b.

20. Hilkhot Talmud Torah 1:11.

21. Avot 3:6. Cf., however, ibid. 3:2, which speaks, more amorphously, of the mediating presence of Torah: אבל שנים שיושבין ויש ביניהם דברי תורה שכינה ביניהם.

22. I have dealt with some of these issues in במשוך היובל: חמשים שנה למדרשית נועם. (Tel Aviv, 5756), pp. 160–67.

Chapter 2

The Conceptual Approach to Torah Learning: The Method and Its Prospects

To the average *ben yeshiva,* the very thought of a methodology of learning is, at best, a two-edged sword. On the one hand, he finds it alluring. On the objective plane, it holds out the promise of greater rationality and order, not to mention approximation to truth – values much sought and appreciated; and subjectively, it elicits the hope of a more efficient and effective direction of his most cherished activity. And yet he senses a discordant note. Its unfamiliarity is threatening, its pursuit potentially unsettling, and its occasionally technical formulations jarring. Moreover, the perception that a systematic impulse characterizes the academic community, which the budding *talmid hakham* possibly suspects, only intensifies the discomfiture.

There are, however, deeper and more genuine roots for the ambivalence. These relate, primarily, to anxiety over the loss of passion and the jading of awe. Concern that efficiency will be attained at the expense of reverence touches a raw nerve. A *bet midrash* is not a shoe factory, and its occupants are not indentured to the bottom line. It is the epicenter of their existential orbit, and their study there is animated by a simple petition: גל עיני ואביטה נפלאות מתורתך, "Open Thou mine eyes, that I may behold wondrous things out of Thy law" (Tehillim 119:18).

In this respect, the ambivalence is analogous to the Romantics' reservations (one recalls Watts-Dunton's designation of the movement as

19

"the renascence of wonder") about speculative thought. "Do not all charms fly," asked Keats,

> At the mere touch of cold philosophy?
> There was an awful rainbow once in heaven:
> We know her woof, her texture; she is given
> In the dull catalogue of common things.
> Philosophy will clip an angel's wings,
> Conquer all mysteries by rule and line
> Empty the haunted air, and gnomed mine
> Unweave a rainbow

(*Lamia*, II, 229–237)

It is exacerbated, however, by two disparate and yet complementary factors. First, one senses that at stake is not just mystery but sacred mystery, its apprehension to be accompanied, consequently, with tremor no less than with wonder. This, on the view of R. Matya b. Harash, was the thrust of the summons to Mosheh Rabbenu at Sinai, לא בא הכתוב אלא לאיים עליו כדי שתהא תורה ניתנת באימה ברתת ובזיע שנאמר עבדו את ה' ביראה וגילו ברעדה,[1] "The purpose of the Scripture here was to inspire him with fear, so that the Torah be given with fear, with trembling, and with sweat, as it is said: 'Serve the Lord with fear and rejoice with trembling' (Tehillim 2:11) and its echoes have reverberated for posterity. Second is the visceral quality that Hazal ascribed to *talmud Torah*. In characterizing it, they resorted to metaphors relating to the most elemental of physical and psychic experiences:

> א״ר שמואל בר נחמני מאי דכתיב אילת אהבים ויעלת חן וגו, למה נמשלו דברי תורה לאילת לומר לך מה אילת רחמה צר וחביבה על בועלה כל שעה ושעה כשעה ראשונה, אף דברי תורה חביבין על לומדיהן כל שעה ושעה כשעה ראשונה. ויעלת חן שמעלה חן על לומדיה דדיה יריֵיך בכל עת למה נמשלו דברי תורה כדד? כל זמן שהתינוק ממשמש בו מוצא בו חלב אף דברי תורה כל זמן שאדם הוגה בהן מוצא הוגה ממשמש בו מוצא בו חלב אף דברי תורה כל זמן שאדם הוגה בהן מוצא בהן טעם.

R. Shmuel bar Nahmani said: What [is the meaning] of the [biblical verse]: "Loving hind and graceful roe," etc. [Mishlei 5:19]? Why were the words of Torah compared to a hind? To tell you that as the hind has a narrow womb and is loved by its mate at all times as at the first hour of their meeting, so it is with the words of the Torah. They are loved by those who study them at all times as at the hour when they first make their acquaintance. "And a graceful roe?" Because the Torah bestows grace on those who study it. "Her breasts will satisfy you at all times" [Mishlei 5:19]. Why were the words of the Torah compared to a breast? As with a breast, however often the child nurses, it finds milk in it, so it is with words of Torah. As often as a man studies them, so often does he find relish in them.[2]

Would one expect an infant to suck by the book? A bridegroom to make love per his manual's instruction?

These reservations are neither idiosyncratic nor novel. Indeed, on one view, they were expressed by one of the early amoraim:

אמר עולא מחשבה מועלת אפילו לדבר תורה שנאמר מפר מחשבות ערומים ולא תעשינה ידיהם תושיה.

Thought affects even words of Torah, as it is said, "He abolishes the thought of the skilled [i.e., scholars], lest their hands perform nothing substantial."[3]

Rashi explains, as a possible interpretation:

ל"א מחשבה שאדם מחשב כך וכך תעלה בידי מועלת להשבית הדבר שאין מחשבתו מתקיימת אפילו לדבר תורה כגון האומר עד יום פלוני אסיים כך וכך מסכתות בגירסא.

Another interpretation: [The] thought that a man calculates, that such-and-such will I succeed in, is effective in negating the matter that his thought is ineffectual – even for matters of Torah, as when one says: "I will complete such-and-such [number] of tractates in reciting by this date."

Nevertheless, the benefits of a modicum of planning are so self-evident that hardly a *maggid shi'ur* opens a *zeman* without at least the equivalent of a tentative syllabus. And concern over *mahshavah mo'elet* is presumably allayed by Rabbah's qualification:

אמר רבה אם עוסקין לשמה אינה מועלת שנאמר רבות מחשבות בלב איש ועצת ה' היא תקום עצה עצה שיש בה דבר ה' היא תקום לעולם (שם).

Rabbah said: "[But] if they study [Torah] for its own sake, [such study is not adversely affected, as it is said, "There are many thoughts in a man's heart, but the counsel of the Lord, that shall stand."

Spirit and motivation are the key. Where these are truly religious, the claims of productivity and spontaneity can be reconciled; and the votary of Torah can enter its forests both in order to traverse them and because the woods are "lovely, dark, and deep."

Analogously, while the specter that analysis of methodology will have a deadening effect upon vibrant learning cannot be precluded, it is not inevitable. Properly animated, a measure of goal-orientation conjoined with reflexive awareness – grounded not in the self-conscious proclivities of an "age of analysis" but in the joyful quest for mastery of Torah – can genuinely enhance one's appreciation of *devar Hashem* and the process of studying it. Knowledge of technique can improve performance in swimming without diluting, indeed, possibly stimulating, its joy; and so may it be with respect to *yam ha-talmud*. It is with this hope and in this spirit that the following remarks are presented.

Upon embarking on a discussion of the methodology of *talmud Torah she-be'al-peh*, we need to distinguish between two sets of issues, each of considerable practical significance, but nevertheless quite different in character and substance. We confront, on the one hand, questions of method, narrowly defined: how should topics be approached, texts read, terms defined, concepts analyzed? On the other hand, we are charged to deal with questions largely subsumed under educational, or possibly even pedagogic, strategy. These often relate to the "what" of learning no less than to the "how," with curriculum the core: the emphasis upon range and depth, respectively; to which *massekhtot,* or segments thereof, ought priority be assigned; is general *beki'ut* best attained by learning Shas *cum* Rashi, its digest in the Rif, or its systematic codex in the Rambam? Obviously, in many respects, how and what overlap. Determination of the extent to which the learning of Bavli and Yerushalmi should be interwoven involves a substantive, and not merely tactical, decision. Nevertheless, the areas can be distinguished. The choice of learning Bava Kamma, Berakhot, or Menahot is ordinarily determined by factors little related to how any of these is to be studied. Our focus here shall be upon the mode of learning as such, specifically with reference to the conceptual approach, while the educational aspects will only be dealt with marginally.

Methodology generally revolves around three primary foci. It designates or delimits the tools to be employed and the disciplines to be engaged. It determines what kind of intellectual and ideological solutions are suitable for the questions raised. First and foremost, however, it defines the questions, particularly the types of concerns to be assigned priority. While full mastery of a topic obviously requires the interactive application of a number of disciplines – and responsible advocates of any given approach can hardly afford to rely upon it exclusively – it is self-evident that almost no one is, in practice, desirous or capable of addressing all issues equally. And it is the choice of emphases that, more than anything else, defines a *derekh*.

This bears directly upon the presentation of the conceptual approach to *talmud Torah*. Upon opening a gemara, we are confronted with a dual task. We are charged with learning a daf, on the one hand, and a *sugya*, on the other. Or, to put it differently, we wish to learn the text and the subject-matter of the text. The distinction between *iyyun* and *beki'ut*, currently in vogue in the yeshiva world but with firm roots in Hazal, largely turns on this point.[4] At issue is not just the immanent antithesis of depth versus range. The heart of the matter lies in the definition of primary responsibility. One mode demands traversing a given text, regardless of how loosely related its components might be; the other, mastering a topic – largely by excising adventitious segments but, compensatorily, incorporating into one's learning relevant sections imported from elsewhere and organically engrafted.

Awareness of this distinction is meaningful with respect to a range of intellectual pursuits, but is particularly significant with respect to the learning of gemara. Books on history or geology are almost invariably organized thematically, so that the gap between text and topic, if any, is usually minimal. As any neophyte can attest, however, the meandering character of the gemara, especially the Bavli, generates a very substantial gap; hence, the far greater need for definition of the material of study and of its *telos*.

The distinction is reflected in various genres of sefarim.[5] *Mefarshim* are intrinsically geared to texts. *Sifrei mizvot*, by contrast, are oriented to topics; and so, for the most part, are *sifrei psak*. This obviously does not hold with respect to the overall world of *psak*, broadly defined. Of the triad cited by the *Bet Yosef* as his guiding lights, two, the Rif and the Rosh, pursue the course of the gemara, their conclusions constituting the final stage in the presentation and analysis of a given *sugya*; and a number of the central works of *hakhmei Ashkenaz* in this field – Ravan, Ravyah, *Sefer Ha-Terumah*, or, at an earlier stage, the cluster originating in Rashi's *bet midrash* – are, at best, haphazardly organized. Nevertheless, thematic structure certainly was the hallmark of the Sephardi tradition, and in this respect, it subsequently carried the day. The Rambam's *Mishneh Torah*, of course, bestrides all else, and it set the tone for the more constricted codices of the *Tur* and the *Shulhan Arukh*. However, the systematic impulse is also evident in classical texts – *Torat Ha-Bayit* and *Sefer Ha-Terumot*, both models of lucid exposition, fusing comprehensive presentation and trenchant analysis – emanating from the milieu of the Ramban; and that impulse has become fairly standard in *sifrei psak*.

Hiddushim, on the other hand, straddle intermediate ground. They generally follow the sequence of the gemara, and thus lack an overall organizing principle. Nevertheless, in the tradition of *ba'alei Ha-Tosafot*, while lacking a master plan, they strive to treat each major crux thematically – pulling together far-flung relevant texts, analyzing central terms, resolving presumed contradictions. The net effect is often an archipelago of islands that need to be melded into a continent; and it serves to highlight awareness of the importance of the distinction between study of texts and mastery of their subject-matter. Hence, in charting the course of one's *talmud Torah*, the need to determine emphases and establish priorities.

The significance of this distinction is not confined to the choice and organization of material. It relates, equally, to the mode of dealing with it; and it serves, consequently, as a point of departure for delineating the conceptual approach to *lomdut*. This approach, virtually by definition, is oriented to working around the exposition of themes rather than the explication of texts; and it does so with an eye to probing their ideational content rather than limning their bare presentation, even if systematic and comprehensive. It takes its cue from the opening thrust of the plaintful plea incorporated into the *berakhah* of Ahavah Rabbah, designated by Hazal[6] as a halakhic variant of *Birkat Ha-Torah*: אבינו אב הרחמן המרחם רחם עלינו ותן בלבנו להבין ולהשכיל. "Our Father, merciful Father, He who has mercy have mercy on us, and place in our hearts to understand and to comprehend." And it is mindful of the fact that the Rambam used this very formulation in defining gemara:

ושליש יבין וישכיל אחרית דבר מראשיתו ויוניא דבר מדבר וידמה דבר לדבר ויבין במדות שהתורה נדרשת בהן... וענין זה הוא הנקרא גמרא.

And of the third [of a man's time devoted to Torah study] he should [strive] to understand and comprehend the end of a matter from its beginning, and differentiate a matter from a matter, compare one thing to another, understand the principles by which the Torah is interpreted... and this matter is what is called gemara.[7]

Gemara, thus succinctly defined as a mode, is the heart of the conceptual approach to Torah; and it is no accident that gemara, constituted as a corpus, stands at its epicenter.

In practice, upon opening a *massekhet,* the inquiring student embarks upon an enterprise whose resolution, if successful, will provide him with answers to questions about a given phenomenon – leading, in turn, to mastery of a broader area. From Hazal down, the Torah world has concerned itself with two kinds of questions that, for our purposes, I will designate as primary and secondary. The first category consists of points to be determined as part of any attempt to acquire the relevant data, raw or sophisticated, requisite for knowing a given phenomenon. These include issues of source (מנא הני מילי, מנלן); of scope as regards persons, objects, or circumstances; of rationale in light of general principles (מאי טעמא); or of definition, not simply lexicographic but jurisprudential. And it includes, further, their interaction – source, scope, and character often being closely and functionally related. Such questions are sometimes difficult to answer, but fundamentally they do not constitute difficulties. They are not conceived as problematic, nor are they generated by accident or crisis. They are intrinsic, an immanent aspect of any serious learning endeavor, and neglecting them reflects superficiality and sloth.

Concurrently, the student of Torah expends much energy upon

a second set of questions, which do arise as a matter of accident. These revolve around contradictions, and they occupy a prominent place – far greater than in most comparable disciplines, in the world of *talmud Torah*. Perceived contradiction is, to be sure, the stuff of which much intellectual discourse, legal or philosophic, is made. However, its position is obviously amplified in a system grounded upon reverence for sacral authority and veneration for the masters of a tradition. Confronted by apparent discrepancies between divergent texts, the secular jurist may be inclined simply to dismiss one. The *ben Torah*, however, while acknowledging the possibility of irreconcilable conflict, is determined to strive for resolution; and to that end, he is prepared to devote much effort and to exercise considerable ingenuity.

The contradiction may vary. It may be between two equally authoritative texts, as between two baraitot or two pesakim of the Rambam. Alteratively, it may pit unequal dicta – an amora against a mishnah, a rishon against a gemara. It may be direct or circumstantial, as when the gemara states that only one of two propositions can be derived from a given *pasuk*, and the Rambam nevertheless cites both. In all these cases, however, one is not dealing with intrinsic tasks but with accidents; more with clearing a minefield than with erecting a structure.

Precisely for this reason, the conceptual approach to learning is relatively less concerned with secondary questions than more textually or technically oriented approaches. Its thrust is overwhelmingly tilted toward fundamentals – above all, to the most basic of intellectual chores: definition. Armed with sets of categories, the conceptualist strives, first and foremost, to grasp the essential character of a particular element and, hence, to classify it. He seeks both to map a given subject and to probe it. The mapping is itself dual, both local and general. On one plane, he surveys the specifications of an object or an action, determining which are essential and which accidental. Is *nevelah* that becomes unfit for human consumption no longer denominated as *nevelah,* or does it retain its identity but is no longer prohibited? Can one distinguish between the two cardinal qualities of a mikveh, that it be stagnant and contain a minimum of forty *se'ah,* regarding the former as determining whether a body of water is a mikveh at all, while the latter only qualifies its certification for certain purposes? On a second plane, the conceptualist will place a datum within a broader ambience, thus fleshing out the general category and sharpening understanding of a specific element by precise comparison with related phenomena. In dealing with the inedible *nevelah,* for instance, he will explore its status as an *av ha-tum'ah* alongside its kashrut; and he will probably incorporate this discussion into a fuller treatment of the concept of food as it appears in diverse halakhic areas.

The process of definition entails recourse to a set of keys – some master, others individual. Among the former, probably the most familiar is the distinction between subject and object, person and datum; but a number of others recur and figure prominently. Of virtually every *d'rabbanan* innovation, one will ask whether and how it is subsumed under a *de-Oraitha.* With respect to positive and negative *mizvot* equally, one will often ask what is the prescribed or proscribed act and what the quintessential fulfillment or contravention of the divine will. The issue of essence and accident has already been cited; and closely akin is the determination of which specifications are mandated by which category. Is visiting one's rebbe on Yom Tov an aspect of *simhat ha-regel* or a dimension of *kvod ha-rav*?[8] Is the conjunction of the wearing of *tefillin* and the reciting of Keri'at Shema an enhancement of the former or of the latter?[9] Such points abound, inherently, in all areas of Halakhah, and they are grist for the mill of any aspiring *lamdan.*

Much of the foregoing is obvious if not rudimentary, but perhaps a brief example will, nevertheless, be instructive.

The opening mishnah in Massekhet Sukkah reads:

סוכה שהיא גבוהה למעלה מעשרים אמה פסולה ורבי יהודה מכשיר, ושאינה גבוהה עשרה טבחים ושאין לה שלש דפנות ושחמתה מרובה מצילתה פסולה.

A sukkah that is higher than twenty cubits is invalid; R. Yehudah declares it valid. And one that is not higher than ten handbreadths, and that does not have three walls, and whose sunlit portion is greater than its shaded portion is invalid.

Upon learning this mishnah, we shall obviously want to know the source and reason for these halakhot; and we shall duly find them in the gemara. But we shall not be content to do so. We shall compare the disqualifications cited and ask, with reference to each, what is its character and level. Does the preponderance of sun over shade negate the very definition of a sukkah, it being, quintessentially, a shady nook? Is it only rendered an invalid sukkah; or perhaps neither, with the *pesul* only precluding the resident's performance of the *mizvah*, even though the sukkah itself is kosher? And perhaps all of these are correct, but with regard to different levels of light? Analogously, how radical is the concern about excessive height? And might this be a function of the source?[10] If the Halakhah is derived from למען ידעו דורותיכם, the problem being that awareness of presence in a sukkah is obviated by the distance from *sekakh*, that is presumably a narrowly technical issue. If it is grounded in the fact that so high a structure constitutes a permanent edifice more than a temporary shelter – and if it is assumed that transitoriness is indeed essential[11] – the very definition of sukkah may hang in the balance, permanence being characteristic of a house, to which the sukkah is antithetical. At the other end, what is the requirement of ten *tefahim*? Is it an application of the general Halakhah that this is the minimal height for all *mehizot* or a local specification for livable space – and again, possibly both, but with respect to different situations?[12] And finally, what of the need for three walls? Is this conceived as a numerical quota or as a level of enclosure? And is the need for enclosure itself a technical requirement or critical to the definition of a residence?[13]

On the other side of the ledger, has this quartet exhausted the list of specifications requisite for a sukkah, or might there be others?[14] If so, why have they been deleted from the opening summary? The answers to these and similar questions are to be sought with sophistication and subtlety, through recourse to textual and logical proofs, with some of the latter – the determination that alternative A is correct because of its link to Halakhah B, which only makes good sense if A is assumed – hinging upon further proof of the sukkah's character. The point here, however, is simply to sketch the scope and character of the agenda, taking note of what is at center stage and what, possibly of critical importance for other purposes, is omitted.

The theoretical bias of the conceptual approach is reflected not only in the question it poses and emphasizes but in the interpretations it prefers. It has several pronounced, and interrelated, proclivities. First, wherever possible, its devotees prefer to explain detail, or controversy about detail, in terms of an ideational construct rather than with reference to factual or technical factors.[15] Typical is the reluctance to acknowledge the existence of a factual *mahloket*. Thus, if amoraim disagreed as to whether a debtor could be believed if he claimed that he had paid prior to the due date of his liability – Resh Lakish holding that he was not, inasmuch as חזקה לא עביד איניש דפרע גו זמניה, while Abbaye and Rava rejoin that his claim is valid, as עביד איניש דפרע גו זמניה[16] – the *lamdan* will abjure focusing the debate upon the evaluative description of debtor psychology and will direct it to the legal sphere. The issue is not what percentage of debtors might indeed prepay, but how high the number needs to be in order to establish the validity of a claim; and this, in turn, may depend upon halakhic considerations regarding the relation between debtors and creditors or the general level of probability needed to extract assets. Or again, upon encountering a *mahloket* as to whether the partial levy due if one's "innocent" animal has gored is to be viewed as a fine or as a discounted payment, this being grounded in the gemara on the question of whether סתם שוורים בחזקת שימור קיימי,[17] the *lamdan* will be inclined to view the discussion as related to the standard of responsibility and fault rather than to the normal mindset of oxen; and the standard may itself be a function of how one defines the basic source of liability for damage inflicted by one's property, whether the owner's negligence in failing to prevent the occurrence or the bare fact that it has been incurred.[18]

In some cases, the avoidance of a factual *mahloket* has a quasi-moral dimension. Given the esteem in which we hold Hazal, it seems inconceivable that, even in a pre-scientific age, they would have argued over what can be readily tested and determined. Thus, with reference to a *mahloket* concerning the edibility of certain vegetables, Rav Binyamin bar Levi asks:

דבר שאפשר לך לעמוד עליו חכמים חלוקים עליו?

Something that it is possible for you to determine yourself, the sages dispute over?[19]

Similarly, the Ramban prefaces his *hiddushim* to the perek in Hullin that deals with *terefot* – and that cites, *inter alia*, discussions as to whether an animal that has a *terefah* can survive more than a year – by asserting:

מה שנחלקו חכמי ישראל בטריפה אם היא חיה או אינה חיה תמוה הוא איך לא בדקו הדבר בנסיונות הרבה?

That which the sages of Israel disputed about regarding a *terefah,* as to whether it lives or does not live [with a year of its illness or injury] is puzzling; how could it be that they did not examine the matter with many experiments?[20]

However, as is made clear by the previous examples, with respect to which convincing empirical evidence is not so readily available, the recoil from a factual *mahloket* goes beyond absolving *gedolei Yisrael* from possible charges of indolence. It is part of an effort, both subliminal and conscious, to channel halakhic debate into the realm of ideas.

This tendency is equally manifest in the exposition of halakhic elements wholly removed from the factual sphere. Quantitative standards, for instance, are recurrently translated into qualitative categories.[21] If Rishonim disagreed as to whether the *kinyan* of *hagbahah* required raising the acquired object one *tefah* or three,[22] the disagreement is not viewed as a choice between two stations on the same continuum but as concerning the definition of the basic conception.[23] Does *hagbahah* entail an act that demonstrates, and hence creates, mastery, in which case the lesser sum may (but need not, of course) suffice; or does it constitute a change of venue, in which case the object must be uprooted from its prior location, for which purpose, in light of the status of the *shi'ur* of three *tefahim* encountered in numerous halakhic contexts, only that will do.

In this respect, the *mahloket* between Rashi and Rabbenu Tam concerning *hagbahah* may be strikingly similar to another, between Rav and Shmuel, regarding the sister *kinyan* of *meshikhah*. Here, too, the quantitative issue arises: How far must the object be pulled?

איתמר ספינה רב אמר כיון שמשך כל שהוא קנה ושמואל אמר לא קנה עד שימשוך
את כולה

As to a ship, Rav said: Once one has performed the act of pulling to the
minimal extent, he has acquired it; Shmuel said: He has not acquired it until
he has pulled all of it [i.e., its length].[24]

And here, too, with respect to the horizontal plane, the same interpretation suggests itself. On the assumption that a demonstrative process
requires less than an achieved result, one might assign the former view of
meshikhah to Rav and the latter to Shmuel.

There is nothing necessary about this line of reasoning. One could
contend, theoretically, that both amoraim worked within the same
framework, and that their *mahloket* was arbitrary, intuitional, the result
of psychic differences, or of varying commercial practices in Sura and
Neharda'a. No proof has here been suggested for either the interpretation herein developed of their disagreement, or for the premise that the
standard applicable to a demonstrative process is less demanding than
that requisite for effected change. The conceptualist is fully aware of this.
Moreover, he freely acknowledges that not all halakhic cruces lend themselves to this kind of analysis. Nevertheless, his own predilection is clear.
Of the aforementioned alternatives, he will regard some with ideological
revulsion. But even of those which equally pass muster on that score, he
has a clear preference. Recognizing that valid alternatives exist, he will opt,
wherever possible, for theoretically oriented *lomdut* over a practical *ba'al
batisher* approach.

Thus, to cite one further instance, the gemara in Bava Kamma ascribes
to Rav the position that כל המשנה ובא אחר ושינה בו פטור[25]; that is, that if one
deviates from normal behavior in a public setting and, as a result, suffers
damage inflicted upon himself or his property by a second deviator, the
latter is not liable. It then suggests that Rav Yohanan and Resh Lakish may
disagree as to whether this only refers to more extreme situations, such as
an animal lying down in the middle of a street, or may also include a more
moderate anomaly, such as setting down a pile of clothing or utensils. Obviously, one could simply contend that we are confronted here by a factual

issue over just how common such action might be; or, alternatively, by
a legal question regarding the definition of deviation and just how high
the bar should be set. Both are legitimate options. Terms like "normal"
and "deviant" cry out, *a priori*, for definition, and several alternatives
could be reasonably offered with regard to any particular context. The
lamdan will not be content with this, however. He will, at the very least,
explore the theoretical underpinnings of different definitions, and he will
tentatively advance the thesis that these spring from divergent views of
the substance of the exemption of *kol ha-meshanneh*. If it is, in essence, a
limitation of the responsibility of the *mazzik* – he cannot be expected to
forestall unanticipated strange eventualities – such a radical formulation
would require a more extreme deviation. If fundamental liability exists but
is, in practice, suspended by the fault of the victim, this more moderate
conclusion may be warranted by a lesser deviation. And in this, of course,
as in many parallel contexts where two grounds for a given Halakhah
may obtain, it is entirely conceivable that both may be tenable, so that we
envision a two-tiered structure, each with its respective specification and
ramifications.

I have spoken of sets of keys, master and individual, and I have briefly
described some of the former. The latter are local and plentiful. Each area
of Halakhah has its indigenous categories that serve to classify specific
data and by which they may be tested. Once certain distinctions, and the
respective constructs that flow from them, have been established, they
become part of the conceptual baggage to be applied in mapping and
analyzing a *sugya*, and its acquisition is one of the central aspects in the
development of a *lamdan*. The distinction between *kedushat Eretz Yisrael*
and *shem Eretz Yisrael* with respect to *mizvot ha-teluyot ba-aretz*; between a
get's specific character as a *sefer keritut* and its generic identity as a *shetar*;
between form and function with respect to implements; between a type of
tum'ah, abstractly conceived, and its physical manifestation; which details
of a proscribed *melakhah* relate to the concept of *melekhet mahshevet* and
which to the contours of, say, *keshirah* or *ketivah* – all these are questions
that recur in the course of mastering the relevant tractates.

The acquisition of keys and their proper use is the staple of the ordinary *lamdan*. At its highest plane, however, the conceptual approach finds expression in the cutting of new keys – some analogous to existing ones and extrapolated by transference, others perhaps wholly novel. These, in turn, enter the world of learning and enrich its vocabulary, providing fresh implements and fresh impetus for those engaged in the perpetual quest *lehavin u-lehaskil*.

The conceptual approach, as has been suggested, is inherently oriented to dealing with primary issues. Obviously, however, its practitioners can hardly be oblivious to secondary questions; and with regard to them, too, they are animated by a clear predilection. Contradictions between two authoritative texts can be resolved in several ways. One possibility is the emendation, where soundly based and legitimate, of either text. A second is the acknowledgement that the conflict is irreconcilable, but that both sources can be sustained by ascription to different persons or traditions. The third is the neutralization of one or the other text by confining it to a given case, either by recourse to previous knowledge or by the creative invention of a fresh limitation, suggested for the express purpose of resolving the difficulty at hand.

All of these methods are to be found in Hazal. *Eipukh* or *hassurei mehsera* alters the text; תרי תנאי ואליבא דרכי יהודה, תנא אתנא קא רמית and תרי אמוראי ואליבא דרכי יוחנן abandon resolution; הכא במאי עסקינן, whatever its variation, confines one of the conflicting poles. None, however, relates to the world of ideas. Hence, the conceptualist's initial and instinctive thrust is in yet another direction. He will strive, wherever possible, to disarm the contradiction by portraying it as illusory. Even when affirmative and negative statements are diametrically opposed, the propositions need not be contradictory. They may refer, respectively, to different halakhic areas, each of which has its own set of definitions. Even when the nomenclature is identical, the terms may vary, depending upon their contexts.

This mode is both grounded in simple logic and rooted in Hazal. When Rav Yosef was asked whether a needle whose eye had broken off could still be regarded as an implement, so that it could be moved on Shabbat, he responded affirmatively. Thereupon, he was rebutted on the basis of the mishnah in Kelim which states that such a needle is no longer subject to *tum'ah,* presumably because it is not a *keli,* a utensil; at which point Abbaye rejoined, טומאה מלבת קא רמית טומאה כלי מעשה בעינן שבת מידי דחזי והא נמי חזיא למשקלא בה קוץ "Have you, then, compared the laws governing purities to those governing Shabbat? As to purities, the requirement is that the vessel be one capable of accomplishing its work, [while] in regard to the laws of Shabbat [we require] something of some use, and this is useful for picking out up a thorn." Rava dismissed this answer, contending that the same standard should prevail in both spheres: אמר רבא מאן דמותיב שפיר קמותיב מדלענין טומאה לאו מנא הוא לענין שבת נמי לאו מנא הוא. "Said Rava: He who raises the objection does so correctly, since it is not a utensil in respect to purities, it is not a utensil in respect to Shabbat."[26] The interchange became the focus of a wide-ranging debate among the Rishonim, revolving around the question of whether Rava rejected the distinction between *tum'ah* and *muktzah* in general, or only opposed this particular application. Be that as it may, the discussion, equally relevant to additional areas in which the concept of *keli* figures, is an archetypal instance of the course upon which conceptual analysis thrives in resolving contradictions.

When resolution proceeds by simple application of known differences, it may be largely technical and mechanical in nature. When it engenders freshly conceived distinctions, however, it is the product of creative energy. As a scientist may be inspired by conflicting empirical evidence to suggest a novel theory that will take all the disparate phenomena into account,[27] so the *lamdan* will expound a distinction that will allow for harmonious coherence.

In this respect, primary and secondary questions are closely related. The quest for resolution serves as a powerful catalyst for renewed examination and deeper probing of halakhic material; and its upshot is frequently a revised and more precise understanding of basic categories. It would, of course, be naive to assume that the whole of *Hiddushei Rabbenu Hayyim HaLevi* was composed purely in order to defend the Rambam. Unquestionably, many of the seminal ideas had been developed independently, as part of the process of understanding the gemara, and here found application. But it is equally clear that much indeed was stimulated by the quest for reconciliation; and in this, as in many other respects, it typifies the conceptual approach and the benefit that its primary plane – always the prioritized focus of *lomdut* – derives from the secondary. This is reinforced by the fact that the resolving conceptualist, ideally, is not content with a distinction without a difference. He will seek to buttress his distinction with proof, much of it in the form of the correspondence and coherence of salient points with the proposed conception; and this, in turn, often requires a thorough scrutiny of an entire halakhic realm.

The interaction may be briefly exemplified by a discourse upon a difficult *psak* of the Rambam. The mishnah states that real property is exempted from oaths, even in the case of disputes in which chattels would be subject to them.[28] The Rambam extends this to include payments for land,[29] even though what is at present being demanded is money, as when the land had been damaged. The Rabad challenges this, and adduces a mishnah in support of his critique:[30]

א״א נראין דברים שתבעו למלאות החפירות ולהשוות החצירות אבל אם תבעו לשלם פחתו הרי היא כשאר תביעת ממון וכמי שאמר לו חבלת בי שתים והוא אומר לא חבלתי אלא אחת.

Abraham [i.e., Rabad] says: This would seem to be the case if [the owner of the land] demanded that he fill in the pits and make the fields level; but if [the owner] demanded that he pay the [field's] depreciation, this would be like any other monetary claim, similar to the case of one who said, "You injured me twice," while [the defendant] says, "I injured you but once."

The conclusion refers us to a mishnah which states that the category of *modeh be-mikzat*, imposing an oath for partial admission, applies if one has assaulted his fellow. Inasmuch as the Rabad assumes, as is likewise implied by the Rambam elsewhere,[31] that for such exemptions a person is equated to real property, the demand for payment due to assault is the equivalent of *demai karka*, and the mishnah therefore contravenes the Rambam's decision.

In response, after transferring the question, in effect, from the arena of one mishnah to another, Reb Hayyim offers two radical distinctions.[32] One is the differentiation between contexts and classes of oaths. *Shevu'at ha-dayyanim*, that which is administered by *bet din*, is a self-contained obligation, to be judged by the canons of oaths and of dispute as the source of the obligation. Hence, the root of the dispute is definitional. *Shevu'at ha-pikkadon,* on the other hand, administered by a party who claims he has been cheated, relates to the context of thievery, a false oath being regarded as a mode of embezzlement. In this case – and it is this situation that is discussed in the mishnah – what is denied and misappropriated is the just payment currently refused and withheld; and this, of course, is money rather than real property.

Alternatively, Reb Hayyim suggests a distinction between damage to property and assault on a person. With respect to the former, one's fundamental obligation is to repair or replace the damaged object; hence, it is the focus of the dispute. As regards the latter, repair is not usually feasible, as organs cannot be replaced, so that the obligation is fundamentally monetary, and its cause is of little moment. These distinctions clearly rest on a number of premises, some more firmly anchored than others. Each of these needs to be examined and, optimally, proven. And, of course, one needs to probe why and where the Rabad parted company with the explanations. Did he challenge the premises or only the inference from them? What is manifest is the impetus to cope with a secondary question by relating it to primary issues rather than by relatively incidental technical solutions. And what is equally manifest is the extent to which the understanding of entire areas is illuminated and fructified by the process of fundamental definition.

From the essentially ideational character of the conceptual approach there flow, almost as corollaries, several salient characteristics. The first concerns the timeless issue of the confrontation of text and reason – in part, a variant of the broader question of faith and reason; and in part, inasmuch as it arises in secular contexts as well, an independent concern. Instances in which the literal import of texts appear to contravene rational perception abound, and these invite a range of responses. In some, a consensus for reinterpretation may prevail. Few today would challenge the Rambam's view that the grossly anthropomorphic attribution of physical elements to the *Ribbono shel Olam* cannot be understood literally. Indeed, we would not regard this as philosophically motivated reinterpretation at all, but simply a manifestation of a form of symbolic expression. With respect to the attribution of emotion, by contrast, opinions will vary – reflecting theological differences, but also hermeneutic differences. With respect to aggadic material in Hazal, likewise, a spectrum of explication may obtain, and we recall the Rambam's classification of various tendencies in this connection, in his preface to Helek.

Much the same obtains with regard to the world of Halakhah, within which, at times, authoritative texts may seem to clash with one's understanding, inviting a range of responses. It should be clear that in the relevant spectrum, the conceptual approach leans, almost immanently, toward reliance upon rational principles and coping with the texts, rather than vice versa. This is not done eagerly – one would prefer that the confrontation did not exist – but within limits, it is done. Critics take understandable umbrage at the practice, but it is consonant with Hazal – admittedly, more in the Bavli than in the Yerushalmi. On one plane, it relates to the explication of *pesukim*. An amora, convinced that his halakhic position is correct, may acknowledge that it runs counter to the simplest understanding of a *parshah,* and yet hold his ground and seek to expound the texts accordingly, asserting, שבקיה לקרא דאיהו דחיק ומוקים אנפשיה, "Leave the verse, for it is required to establish its own [particular] case."[33] As one of the Rishonim explained, in analyzing whether *veha-met yihyeh lo* refers to the *mazzik* or the *nizzak*:

נראה לרבי דמשמעות דקרא משמע טפי דלמזיק קאמר דהכי משמע שלם ישלם שור תחת השור שור אחר תחת השור שהזיק והמת יהיה לו לעצמו למזיק ולא יחשב לו בתשלומיו אלא דסברא אינה נותנת לדורשו כפי המשמעות כמו שפירשתי שהדין נותן שהנבילה לניזק ודחיק קרא למידרשיה כפי סברת הדין.

> It appeared to my teacher that since the implication of the verse tends toward [the interpretation of the one who holds that the verse refers to the] *mazzik,* for this is what it means: "He shall surely pay for an ox in place of the ox" – a different ox in place of the ox that he damaged, "and the dead [ox] shall be his" – for himself, for the one who[se ox] did the damage, and it should not be considered as payment [for the ox]. However, his reason does not allow him to expound it according to its implication as I have explained, for logic argues that the *nevelah* [should belong] to the one whose property was dam-

aged, and so the verse is interpreted in a forced way [to make it conform] to
the logical argument.[34]

On another plane, the same tendency is reflected in some of the
shinuyei dehikki advanced in order to sustain a position as viable, in the
face of its apparent contravention by a baraita. When occasionally necessary, a similar inclination may be manifested by the conceptualist.

A related inclination concerns the attention – some might charge, the
inattention – to detail. The Rav addressed himself to this facet in listing
ancillary results of Reb Hayyim's innovations:

שיטה זו של יצירת קונסרוקציות צרופות אינה מבחינה בין עיקר לטפל, בין כלל
לפרט, הכל – מן המסד עד הטפחות – חשוב. גם אם הלמדן בטוח באמיתת תהליך
החשיבה, בתבניתה ובצלמה, וגם אם מרגיש הוא, שהוא נמצא בדרך הישר וגם רואה הוא
אורות מרחוק' לא ישקוט' ואם אפילו פרט קטנטן אינו מתיישב במערכת הקונצפציה
הכללית.

> This theory of the creation of pure constructs does not distinguish between
> an essential and an ancillary matter, between a rule and a detail, every-
> thing – from the foundation to the eaves – is important. Even if the *lamdan*
> is certain of the truth of his trend of thought in its shape and form, and even
> if he feels that he finds himself on the straight path, and even when he sees
> light emerging far off, he should not rest if even one tiny, minuscule detail
> does not conform with the array of his general concept.[35]

I find myself only in partial agreement with the passage. In one respect,
as I have already indicated and exemplified, even technical details receive
major attention in Reb Hayyim's world. However, this only applies to details
related to conceptual issues, and through which, whether as evidence or
as a possibly differential *nafke minah,* the issues can be refracted. Details
that are neither here nor there with respect to principles are likely to be
overlooked, for ultimately, as for Plato, it is the idea that is perceived as
ultimate reality and evokes true interest, rather than the detail.[36]

I likewise have some reservations about the second sentence; and
I am not certain that its substance always conforms to Brisker practice.
Unquestionably, for the *lamdan* as for the scientist, there are key con-
traindicating findings that may mandate discarding a much-cherished

theory. However, there are also peripheral minutiae for the sake of which a deeply held conviction will not be abandoned, in the hope that the difficulty will be resolved by someone, somewhere, subsequently. In this respect, a remark attributed to Reb Hayyim may be instructive. The story is told of a questioner who pressed Reb Hayyim about a certain difficulty. Reb Hayyim referred the questioner to a certain tosafot. Upon examining it, he was amazed to find that it was only a small section, opening with *teima* as an expression of difficulty, offering no subsequent resolution, and, what was worst, wholly unrelated to the topic about which he had asked. Puzzled, he returned to Reb Hayyim, who explained, "I just wanted you to see that one does not die of a *kashya*."

Third, pursuit of the conceptual approach has implications for canons of evidence. Pressed in the course of a *shi'ur* for the source of a point he had made, the Rav once responded, "A clear and logical mind." That was pithily and sharply stated, but it reflects a general tendency. As has already been suggested, definition is central to the approach, and it is a process frequently informed by various litmus tests. Their validity often rests, however, on the assumption of a link between a category and a characteristic, so that the presence or absence of the latter could help one determine whether a given phenomenon belonged to the former. The link is not always explicit, however, and its status is simply assigned by "a clear and logical mind." If, however, a differently minded opponent should challenge the link, the evidence falls and the point it was summoned to buttress remains unsupported.

We return, by way of example, to the first Mishnah in Sukkah. Arguing from Tosafot's view that if one sat under an opening of less than three *tefahim* in the sukkah, one could still fulfill the *mizvah*,[37] Reb Hayyim sought to prove that the preponderance of shade over sun related to the sukkah proper rather than to the *mizvah* of residing within it. The implicit premise is self-evident. Should one reject it and contend that, if the deficiency of sitting in a sukkah which has *hamatah merubbah mi-tzilatah* invalidates the act but not the sukkah, one could fulfill the *mizvah* under an empty sky, there would be no explicit text to refute this. Only the perception that this thinking was perverse would clinch the evidence. And so it is in numerous areas, within which different levels of coherence and reasonableness – tested by consistency with other data as well as with general rationality – are marshalled in order to establish propositions. The litmus test itself may need to have its status established by another litmus test, in an ascending order of certitude, until we have reached incontrovertible contentions. The result is a significant degree of networking as part of the process of weaving a halakhic fabric.

The conceptual approach is no recent innovation. Its primary features are clearly present in Hazal, recurrently manifest in Rishonim, and amply exemplified by many Aharonim who were precursors of the Brisker tradition, with which the approach is now most familiarly associated. Much of this is only perceived in retrospect, however, and unquestionably Reb Hayyim, for whom this approach was not merely one of the many arrows in his quiver, but the central mode of learning, gave conceptualism great impetus toward preeminence. In this respect, he certainly effected a major sea change – particularly noteworthy when his achievement is contrasted with the overall direction of most of his immediate forerunners and contemporaries.

Much of their work, *parshanut* and *pilpul* apart, was devoted to surveying a topic, mapping it adequately, ferreting out the major *shittot* and distinguishing between them, and examining their relation to basic sources, finding support in some and coping with seeming contravention in others. This was valuable, but it only went so far. Reb Hayyim did not content himself with surveying. He wanted to mine; and to that end he examined what he learned in the light of fundamental conceptual categories and finely honed distinctions. In the process, he brought to bear (in Coleridgean terms) not only fancy but imagination. In this undertaking, he surely had ample precedent and built upon predecessors. Just as surely, he was strikingly original.[38]

During the century-plus that has elapsed since his advent as a major luminary of the Torah firmament, his *derekh* has attained wide provenance, at first as state-of-the-art *talmud Torah,* and subsequently as the standard modus operandi in the most prominent yeshivot. This is truer of Ashkenazi centers of learning than of Sephardi, and, furthermore, more character-

istic of mitnagdim than of hasidim. On the whole, however, the gradual
ascendancy has been both broad and impressive. Although most richly
manifested in the sphere of Kodashim and Toharot, it has been successfully
applied in all areas of Halakhah; and while most immediately identified
with Brisk, its imprint is perceptible in many other pastures. For the Rav,
Telshe in general and Rav Shimon Shkop in particular were the epitome
of wrongheaded artifice. Yet the fact remains that the *Sha'arei Yosher* bears
a closer affinity to Reb Hayyim than either bore to the Radbaz. Perhaps
we should also note in this connection a remark apocryphally attributed
to Rav Eliezer Gordon to the effect that if Rav Simha Zelig (the *dayyan*
in Brisk and a close associate of Reb Hayyim) came to Telshe, he would
be granted the yeshiva, but that if Reb Hayyim came, he would be given
the whole town.

Nevertheless, the conceptual approach has not gone without opposition, and this from two divergent quarters, one firmly anchored in the
Torah world, the other perched on its periphery. Almost from the outset,
Reb Hayyim encountered resistance even in his own Lithuanian milieu,
Volozhin included, from *yoshvei bet ha-midrash*. Some was engendered by
sheer innovation. This is clearly implicit, even in the next generation, in a
passage from Rav Henoch Agus's preface to his *Marheshet*:

הקדמתי דברים אלה באשר ידוע הוא כי בזמננו נשתנו הרבה דרכי הלימוד בתלמוד
תורתנו הק', שסגנון סברתם ואופן הבנתם פלסו להם נתיב בבתי מדרש התורה והתלמוד,
וביחוד בבתי הישיבות בדורנו, ואני, כאשר כל ימי גדלתי בין חכמי ביה"מ הישן... בבואי
היום להפיץ מעייינותי החוצה... ואירא כי עירום אנכי מכתנות האור וההגיון בתלמוד
כאלה אשר חדשים מקרוב באו והביאו מסגנוני למודם, ואשר התלמידים הבאים אחריהם,
שתו ממי מעייינות אלו והיו בפיהם כדבש למתוק... והליכותי בחדושי הלכות הנן בדרך
הכבושה והסלולה מרבותינו קדמאי ובתראי ז"ל.

I have written this introduction in light of the well-known [development]
that in our time the ways of study in the learning of our sacred Torah have
changed considerably, and the style of their thought and manner of their
understanding have made a place [lit., "way"] for themselves in the *batei
midrash* of Torah and Talmud, and in particular, in the yeshivot of our
generation. As for myself, all my life I grew up among scholars of the old
bet midrash.... [And] when I come today to publish my novellae [lit., "my

wellsprings"]... I see that I am naked of the robes of light and logic in the Talmud like these which are newly come from near, bringing with them the style of their learning, and the disciples who come after them, who drank from the waters of these wellsprings, which tasted as sweet as honey in their mouths.... And my paths in *hiddushei halakhot* are [created in the manner] of the well-maintained, well-trodden paths of our teachers, early and later, may their memory be blessed.[39]

Some of the resistance, however, emanating from skeptics who somewhat condescendingly referred to Reb Hayyim as "the chemist," was strictly substantive. The criticism was two-pronged, denigrating conceptualism as both insufficient and erroneous, the two being perhaps related. The insufficiency was itself dual. One cannot labor on all fronts equally; and while all aspects of learning can conjoin in the harmonious quest for truth, psychological and practical exigencies mitigate the assignment of priorities. Hence, it was argued, the enormous emphasis placed upon analysis, and the palpable gratification deriving from its successful execution, inevitably came at the expense of other goals. The conclusion of the debate in Horayot[40] was being reversed, the *oker harim* now gaining preeminence over the Sinai, and both *beki'ut* and the ambition to attain it were being adversely affected. "The Brisker," Rav Eliyahu Feinstein once observed to his grandson, the Rav, "are very impressed with fine *sevarot*. But as far as I am concerned, if one has forgotten a mishnah in Ohalot, he cannot be regarded as a *lamdan*."

This objection, largely educational, is weighty per se. But the critique ran deeper, with a methodological cutting edge. Much of what Reb Hayyim superseded consisted of a literature of dexterous pyrotechnics of pilpul and ingeniously convoluted *hillukim*. However, knowingly or unwittingly, he likewise devalued works that elaborately or compendiously surveyed the various views regarding a given topic. And he also nudged aside the Maharsha and the Pnei Yehoshua, and even aspects of Rav Akiva Eiger's *Derush ve-Hiddush* – nudged aside, that is, works more consistently concerned with textual explication, with charting the ebb and flow of *shakla ve-tarya*, with reconstructing the movement from a Tosafot's opening to its conclusion.

Benign neglect of this material could be dangerous beyond the sheer constriction of range. For one thing, it might inherently be more prevalent. Perusal of much of this bookshelf is laborious, relatively mechanical, and often technical. For sheer beauty and excitement, tedious plodding through the Maharam Schiff cannot hold a candle to Reb Hayyim's soaring imagination and piercing insights. Radical conceptual analysis cracks open a *sugya* with illuminating force beyond the range of masters of combination and *heshbon*. But, second, such a gap was not only more likely but more deleterious. Ignorance of mishnayot in Ohalot is lamentable, but it will ordinarily have little impact upon one's understanding of Megillah or Menahot. However, rush to analysis or judgment on the part of some who seek to run before they have properly mastered walking, leaves more than gaping holes in one's overall knowledge. It may preclude mastery of the range of material, be it even in Hazal or in Rishonim, relevant to a topic. One cannot legitimately claim to present the full panoply of views regarding *hatikhah azmah na'asseit nevelah* if he has no knowledge of the Ravan's extensive but obscure disquisition on the topic.[41] Nor can one adequately discuss the issue of *hafrashat hallah* from dough owned by a Jew but kneaded by a Gentile if he is oblivious of the discussion of the problem by the Ravyah[42] and the *Or Zarua*.[43] Worse still, constricted knowledge and relative ignorance of the tradition of *parshanut,* in all its manifestations, may lead to erroneous conclusion within the ambience of a given *sugya,* as one has not examined its turf properly.

Concurrently, the conceptual approach has come under fire in the halls of academia; and there, too, the attack has been dual. The acolytes of *Wissenschaft,* like the traditionalist critics, charge conceptualism with insufficiency and error, although in a quite different sense. From their point of view, the conceptualists are indifferent to fundamentals. They put little effort into establishing the exact text, are blithely oblivious to realia, and often pay scant attention to the internal or external development of a *sugya.* In a sense, it is charged, they do not so much learn the gemara as use it.

Far more grievous is the second critique – that conceptualist conclusions are simply wrong. This contention rests upon two separate hypotheses. The first is that, sans scholarship, without an arsenal of philological, historical, and scientific tools, one just cannot arrive at sound conclusions even regarding ideational issues. The second is that the very rigor and illumination which is the pride of the conceptual approach attests to its falsity. Certain scholars simply refuse, *a priori,* to believe that Hazal could have attained or intended the degree of precision and sophistication achieved by nineteenth-century legists; and hence, as an article of faith, they decry *lomdut* as a gross misreading of the classical texts of *Torah she-be'al-peh.*

Other critics espouse a largely existentialist critique. The conceptual approach, they contend, is too rarefied, so that its votaries lose touch with visceral reality. One member of this group went so far as to suggest that the method may be all right for the Diaspora, where *lomdim* are insulated from the inner essence of their physical surroundings, but is wholly unsuitable for Israeli youth, to whom organic relatedness is crucial. This dilettante fusion of metaphysics and psychology borders on the preposterous, but the reservation can be advanced within more rational parameters. In his summary presentation of Reb Hayyim's methodological breakthrough, the Rav points out, *inter alia,* that he had elevated *Hilkhot Ta'aruvot* from the realm of pots and pans to that of conceptual categorization:

כיוצא בזה במקצוע איסור והיתר... מי ניחש, כי יבוא יום, ועניינים אלו ישתחררו מכבלי
העובדתיות, הסברי חוץ וסברות בעלי־בתיות וייעשו דברי הגות מופשטים ומושגים
מסודרים, המצטרפים לשיטה אחידה בעלת רציפות ועקיבות. פתאום נעלמו מהלכות
בשר וחלב הכפות והקדירות, הבצלים והצנון, מהלכות תערובת – המים הרותחים והשמן
שנפל לתוך היין והעכבר שנפל לתוך השמן, מהלכות מליחה – הדם והשמנונית, המלח
והשפוד. ענייני איסור והיתר הוסטו מן המשק הביתי ונעתקו לספירה אחרת של הלכה
אידיאלית שהכול בה מתגלגל בתכנים מחשבתיים. הכול נהפך ל"מציאות" הלכתית
והכול נקלט לתוך מערכת מושגית מופשטת. ההוראה מושתתת על יסודות מוצקים,
שכל הפורש מהם מורד בשכל ההלכתי ופורש מן החיים.

Similarly, in the area of *issur ve-heter*... who would have predicted that the day would come when these matters would be freed from the chains of facticity, explanations not intrinsic to the matter, and "ba'al*ebatische*" ideas, and become matters of abstract thought and orderly concepts, which combine [to produce] a unified, consistent theory. The spoons and pots, the onions and radishes, have disappeared from the halakhot of meat and milk; boiling water and oil that has fallen into wine, a mouse that has fallen into oil – all have disappeared from the halakhot of mixtures; blood and fat, salt and spit have disappeared from the halakhot of salting. Matters of *issur ve-heter* have been moved from the kitchen and into another sphere, that of ideal Halakhah, which is entirely concerned with conceptual structures. All has been converted to "halakhic reality," and all has been absorbed into its array of abstract concepts. *Psak* is based on solid foundations, so that whoever departs from them rebels against halakhic thought patterns and separates himself from life.[44]

However, what the Rav noted with evident pride, others simply deplore. Neither Lorenzos nor Jessicas, they are not attuned to the music of the spheres. They need to hear dishes rattling and utensils clattering in order to feel connected with what John Crowe Ransom called "the world's body." They postulate of Halakhah what Archibald Macleish wrote of a poem, that it "must not mean but be," and they sense, correctly, that Brisk points in a different direction. And still others, impelled by a holistic perception of metaphysical and spiritual reality, view analysis with a jaundiced eye, regarding it, with Wordsworth, as "that false secondary power by which we multiply distinctions."

Collectively, these objections pose a formidable challenge; and it behooves *Bnei Torah* who have encountered them as lomdim or as melamdim – albeit, in some cases, would that they had not! – to relate to them. Relation should be differential, however. The existentialist critique needs to be confronted on two planes. The first concerns fundamental personal orientation. How important, philosophically or religiously, is concreteness? On various levels, the question divides Platonists and Aristotelians, realists and nominalists, classicists and Romanticists; and while we all have our own inclination – one recalls Coleridge's dictum that "every man is born an Aristotelian or a Platonist"[45] – I would be reluctant to answer it with a normative "must." The second plane is factual. Conceptualization need not vitiate concreteness. The quest for abstraction certainly influences the direction and the character of intellectual endeavor during the process of learning. That having run its course, however, the emotional capacity to relate to a specific datum with a heightened sense of its immediacy is no more affected than the ability to listen to the *Eroica* intensely and appreciatively is eviscerated by having previously analyzed it. Whitehead's critique of Lockean epistemology was, in this connection, unquestionably sound, but it related to a metaphysics that championed the denudation of nature rather than to the analytic enterprise per se.

As for the more strictly methodological objections, some we ignore at our peril, others we entertain at our peril. The relative neglect (worse, at times even the disdain) of *beki'ut* is certainly of grave import – particularly insofar as it not only leaves whole tracts untouched but even dilutes or distorts the study of those that are. There is much to be said for the contention that an imbalance exists at present in much of the yeshiva world; and that, while the need to budget time will always exist, current priorities are somewhat skewed. Rav Yosef Baer Soloveitchik (of Jerusalem) once told me that Reb Hayyim, at one point, had two daily sedarim, each lasting six hours, and in each of which he covered eighteen blatt. When I remarked that this did not quite consort with the view I had entertained of him or his tradition, he responded, דאס איז אלץ געווען שפּעטער, "That all came later." Adopting the method without a shadow of the background can indeed be problematic; and this needs to be acknowledged and, to some extent, redressed.

At present, moreover, the issue is greatly complicated by unfortunate educational circumstances. The store of basic knowledge, even of raw information, that many yeshiva students possess today ranges from limited to abysmal, often through little fault of their own. In many segments of the modern Orthodox community, the lack of a social impetus to serious learning, and the related waste of time and energy during childhood and adolescence, produces *talmidim* who may be capable and well-intentioned but whose infrastructure is shallow and narrow. This situation confronts their *rabbeim* with a dilemma, and it induces diametrically opposed responses. Some feel it is ludicrous to dwell upon the niceties of a fine discussion of a Rambam when, just a bit to the right or a bit to the left, there lurks a precipitous chasm of ignorance. Others contend, contrarily, that meaningful scope being beyond reach in any event, it would be best to heighten at least the qualitative dimension and expose students to the power and the glory of *lomdut*. The quandary is sad; and, while technology is increasingly helpful in reducing the gap, the problem shall continue to plague us for some time. Quite independently of this factor, however, greater breadth, particularly within the confines of a topic, shall enable us to derive maximal benefit from the conceptual approach while avoiding the possible pitfalls.

As to the lacunae regarding textual accuracy, philological precision, and knowledge of realia, these admittedly exist, but they need to be placed in perspective. I trust that no one questions the significance of an accurate text of the gemara as the base of its study or the legitimacy of checking manuscripts in order to establish it. The Rishonim engaged in this sphere, and while they may have differed concerning the scope of emendation, they never regarded time and energy devoted to *girsaʾot* as wasted. Likewise, a number of major early Aharonim – the Bah, the Maharshal, not to mention the Gra – were active in this area. And with good reason. All of us can recall instances in which a single letter – *mishʾat ketivah* or *mishʾat ketubah, nishba* or *ve-nishba*[46] – turned a major *sugya* on its head, and innumerable cases in which nuances were substantively affected by variant readings.

Nevertheless, it is true that in an era dominated by conceptualism, the average *ben Torah* – probably the average *gadol ba-Torah* – devotes relatively scant attention to this field. There are, I believe, several factors at play here. One is the fact that *girsaʾot* are currently regarded as a specialty. The ability to gather and collate manuscripts, to choose between variants, and to delve into their nuances, is deemed to require linguistic and paleographic expertise not ordinarily found in the aspiring *lamdan*. A second factor is the advent of printing, and the enormous provenance of the Vilna Shas. This has imposed a degree of standardization unattainable in the days of manuscripts, and lent an aura of sanctity to the daf, whose possible revision might be regarded as undermining faith itself.

Thirdly, the fact that textual variants are so heavily emphasized by the *Wissenschaft* community, which much of the Torah world, for entirely different reasons, mistrusts, has served to alienate many from what ought to have been appreciated. When the *Dikdukei Sofrim* first appeared, it was warmly greeted and freely cited by a number of *gedolim*. A century later, that had changed.

I offer these conjectures by way of explanation but not of justification.

Indeed, the Torah world should pay more attention to this component. Even if few can or should acquire the specialized training needed for mastering the field, access to its findings can and should be more widespread than it is today. We need not exaggerate. The prevailing perception that the overwhelming majority of textual variants cited are of little or no substantive consequence is indeed correct. Nevertheless, greater awareness is in order; and in some instances, it can serve as a conceptual tool in the hands of a *lamdan* seeking to establish a given position. In my view, progress has been made in this direction – witness the editions of *mishnayot,* the Frankel Rambam (with, additionally, Bava Kamma the first *massekhet* of Shas to be published), the modicum of *apparatus criticus* woven into editions of many Rishonim during the last two decades – and more progress can be anticipated. In this textual area, as opposed to the gutting of Hazal's world through conjectural evisceration and stratification, the *bet midrash* can reap benefits from work now largely initiated on the outside.

Many of the points that have been raised with respect to textual accuracy apply equally to knowledge of realia. This, too, is the province of experts but accessible to a wider audience. This, too, can obviously be of critical halakhic import in some cases; and in making a plea for greater sensitivity to the subject, Professor Sperber had little difficulty in culling such instances.[47] Yet, here, too, most of the specialized knowledge is of little conceptual significance, except insofar as one simply wants to know, as fully as possible, what is being depicted in the gemara. I have recounted elsewhere Rav Saul Lieberman's shock upon discovering that an eminent *talmid hakham,* with whom he had discussed *redi'yat ha-pat,* did not know to which stage in the baking process the term corresponded. And I repeat here what I noted there. The shock is understandable, but the fact remains that one can discuss key issues regarding the phenomenon – such as the status of the category of *hokhmah she'ein immah melakhah,*[48] to which it belongs – without this information. Must one know the chemical composition of hametz in order to analyze the essence of the prohibition of *bal ye'ra'eh* and *bal yimazei*? Or the biology of menstruation in order to determine whether a *niddah* is defined as an *ervah* and the relation between the *tum'ah* and the *issur* related to her? Obviously, for certain purposes, especially as regards *psak,* knowledge of realia is often critical. While learning Bava Kamma, one can get by even if he thinks a *shor* is a donkey and a *hamor* an ox; but the same can hardly be said of learning Kil'ayim. For most of one's learning, however, approximation will suffice.

This is not to denigrate the importance of factual information or of those who labor to provide it. Anyone who engages in serious learning is indebted to them at some point, and the debt should be acknowledged. These remarks are intended to place this facet in proper perspective. To this end, we need to distinguish, without recourse to false antithesis, between central definitions and supplementary data. Finally, here too, one hopes that greater sensitivity to the value of factual knowledge can be integrated into the conceptual approach without significantly diluting it.

Admittedly, there are classes of information, especially literary and historical, that may bear more directly and substantively upon the structure and essence of a *sugya.* Full discussion of this element would, however, open up issues that lie beyond the scope of this paper. Here I shall content myself with stating again that this aspect likewise probably deserves more attention than the Torah world currently assigns it, but that it hardly deserves center court.

The second academic critique cuts much deeper – indeed, so deep that it challenges not Brisk alone but the whole tradition of the elucidation of *havayot de-Abbaye ve-Rava.* Bringing to bear its canons of interpretation and its historicistic orientation, it assigns limits to what can be reasonably denominated as the content and intent of primary texts and dismisses violators as out of bounds. Thus, Rabbenu Tam and the Rambam are rejected as expositors of the gemara; and, *a fortiori,* Reb Hayyim as an authentic rendering of all. These are grave issues, inhering at the interface of methodology and ideology. It should be frankly asserted that the "Brisker *derekh*" (like the yeshiva world in general) is grounded upon clearly conceived and richly experienced articles of faith – in the pliancy and depth of multifaceted Torah, in the sagacity and depth of *hakhmei ha-mesorah,* ויאמינו בה׳ ובמשה עבדו. This faith does not obviate the need to grapple with questions concerning the character of the gemara and the Mishnah as texts, and its relation to the intentions of authors and the perceptions of interpreters – issues that lie beyond the scope of this paper. However, it provides the context for that discussion, precluding, above all, a Procrustean bed for that which is ארכה מארץ מדה ורחבה מני ים.

The interaction of methodology and ideology impinges upon the conceptual approach in two ways. On one plane, considerations of *emunot ve-deʾot* effectively bar the acceptance of certain modes of interpretation; specifically, those that denigrate Hazal and challenge their preeminence, thereby running afoul of a definition of the Rambam's which the Rav was much wont to quote:

שלשה הן הכופרים בתורה... וכן הכופר בפרושה והוא תורה שבעל פה והמכחיש מגידיה כגון צדוק ובייתוס.

There are three who deny the Torah… also, one who denies its interpretation, namely, the Oral Torah, or denies its proponents, such as Zadok and Boethos [who rejected the oral teachings of the sages].[49]

A talmudic critic might sit in superior judgment upon the gemara because he can conjugate the aorist, while Ravina and Rav Ashi probably couldn't. Brisker scions harbor no such inclination.

This point, however, is not peculiar to Reb Mosheh Soloveitchik or Reb Isser Zalman Meltzer. It serves to divide traditionalists, of whatever ilk, from more venturesome academicians. A second factor, however, does influence the choice of a specific *derekh*, setting off Brisk from some other, equally traditional camps. As I have already intimated, conceptualists freely concede that other modes are dogmatically feasible, yet firmly and fervently champion their own. Much of pilpul is rejected as either far-fetched and fantastic or diversionary and trivial; it simply does not address the central and critical issues. But what is the basis of the no less emphatic rejection of a pedestrian *baʾal batisher* approach?

In part, admittedly, there may be a subjective element. The latter approach is far less gratifying. Both the questions it raises and the answers it suggest lack the excitement and the sparkle of conceptual analysis. Its votaries do not mine deeply and do not roam widely. The creative urge animating the conjunction of precision and sweep manifested in the best of Brisk simply does not characterize grappling and groping within the confines of a pragmatic mode. A measure of relative independence, derived, in part, from the direct link to the Gaon of Vilna, and, in part, from hashkafic inclination, was deeply rooted in Reb Hayyim personally, and it reverberates throughout his tradition. It found expression even in the relatively conservative area of *psak*. The Rav once quoted his father to the effect that "one should *pasken* on the basis of the gemara and the Rishonim, and control with the *Shulhan Arukh*" – a far cry from those for whom the *Peri Megadim* is categorically authoritative.[50] This quality has since been eroded somewhat, for Reb Hayyim's spiritual heirs have often found themselves constricted by him. Nevertheless, it remains a hallmark, and was celebrated as such in *Ish Ha-Halakhah*.[51] Moreover, it is not confined to Brisk, but is endemic and immanent in the conceptual approach. It surely is no accident that one of the most ringing affirmations of human engagement in the creative molding of Torah appears in the preface to *Kezot Ha-Hoshen*, one of the seminal texts of nineteenth-century conceptualism.

This element is complemented by a seemingly, but only seemingly, opposite consideration. Jewish tradition is suffused with the faith that *talmud Torah*, as immediate contact with the most direct vehicle of revelation, can enhance both personal spirituality and relation to the *Ribbono shel Olam*. Of course, in the process of study, one's attention is riveted upon a text or an idea, but the text or idea is experienced in context. It is as if one were observing a painting or attending a concert in a royal palace. One focuses upon the art or the music, but the sense of relating to it in the palace, rather than at an auction or in a subway station, is crucial. The sensitive soul is caught up by the association of royalty – its majesty, its history – and is drawn into a more intense relation (at times, perhaps, negative) to it. And the more keenly one peers, and the more intently one listens, the fuller and deeper the impact; the more one may be affected by the totality of the experience. The student of Torah enters the portals of Shekhinah, and within its confines, is caught up by its power – and its glory. The sharper, more vivid and precise his perception of what he encounters, the more powerful, potentially, his response; the fuller, as a *homo religiosus*, his submissiveness.

There is also, however, an objective factor, and I submit that it has strong ideological roots. While *lomdut* may indeed enhance the *lamdan* on one plane, it seems, first and foremost, to enhance Torah proper. We often speak, by analogy with a role ascribed in the *pasuk* to the *Ribbono shel Olam*, of seeking *lehagdil Torah ule-ha'adirah*; and this entails not merely absorbing and then disseminating, but literally elevating and enriching. Torah that is perceived as grounded upon rational principles and marked by consistency and coherence, that is developed and perceived as an organic unity, is nobler than one that is a potpourri of practical directives. As Einstein rejected Heisenberg's indeterminacy because he could not imagine God playing dice with the universe, so, I believe, Reb Hayyim espoused conceptualism because he could not imagine *devar Hashem* as a pedestrian amalgam of incommensurate detail. There is power, majesty, and grandeur in Torah, conceptually formulated, that a patchwork of minutiae, largely molded by ad hoc pragmatic considerations, simply cannot match.

Admittedly, from a certain point of view, precisely because of its relative paucity, the study of "dull, sublunary" Torah may entail and reflect a profounder religious commitment than more exciting conceptual *talmud Torah*. Inasmuch as one derives less intellectual benefit, one's learning is more purely selfless – more, if you will, *lishmah*. However, while this point may be correct, it is beside the mark. The Mishnah at the end of Bava Batra states, הרוצה שיחכים יעסוק בדיני ממונות "whoever wishes to become wise should occupy himself with the laws regarding monetary matters."[52] Ought we to suggest that the religious impulse should divert us from learning *dinei mamonot,* so that the self-willed desire for wisdom not be realized? At stake is the quality of Torah, not the merit of the learner. If, as is surely the case, the substance and the stature of Torah and the opus of *hakhmei ha-mesorah* can be enhanced and sharpened by a *lomdische* rendering, that rendering is optimal. If a simplistic reading reduces the Torah's stature, its status should be pegged accordingly. Torah may have seventy faces, but they need not be equally regarded. Unquestionably, this element needs to be weighed in the context of responsibility to truth. We must beware of golden error that may dazzle more than drab truth; and if ever we intuit that being wrongheaded is worse than being wrong, it is time to repent. The basic value judgment is, however, very much in order.

In the Rav's disquisition upon the Brisker method in "Mah Dodekh Midod,"[53] the section on the quality of *lomdische* Torah appears to blend with the discussion of another characteristic much emphasized by him: its autonomy. I am not certain, however, that the connection is necessary. Clearly, where a set of principles is dominant in a system, they can be regarded as governing the determination of detailed cases. However, this offers no intrinsic assurance that the principles themselves might not be externally derived or influenced. Contrarily, nothing prevents a conglomeration of practical directives from being, each and every one of them, indigenous. Perhaps *lomdut* increases the likelihood of autonomy, but no more. I do not wish to harp upon this point in this connection; but the overall theme of enhancing the quality of Torah is crucial.

Over and above these considerations, some may be sorely tempted to relate the conceptual approach to a specific theological infrastructure. I am certain that Reb Hayyim would have resisted the suggestion vigorously; and I, for one, would take him at his word. I do not believe that his basic assumptions in the area of *emunot ve-de'ot,* or the quality of spirituality that characterized him, were much different from the tradition in which he was reared, or that any presumed differences significantly affected his innovation. Of course, he was much opposed to rationalizing tendencies or apologetics with respect to *ta'amei ha-mizvot,* and unquestionably this fits in well with the focus upon definition. But the opposition was hardly peculiar to him. Certainly, his mode of interpreting Humash was very different from the Netziv's; but again, for reasons only marginally related to conceptualism. One can be a thoroughgoing conceptualist and still, as in the *Ha'amek Davar,* relate intensively to the human side of the Torah's narrative; and the Rav is a prime example. If contrasted with some aspects of Hasidut or with some formulations of Rav Kook, there are, of course, significant hashkafic differences. But viewed within its own ambience, the conceptual approach, in its modern manifestation, did not herald a theological transformation.

The last century has witnessed a triumphal ascendancy of the conceptual approach, in its Brisker visage. From its inchoate gestation in *shi'urim* at Volozhin, through semi-private learning with a devoted band of family members and *talmidim* in Brisk, the *derekh* has gone on to captivate the imagination of much of the Torah world and to capture many of its bastions. In the process, it has undergone certain changes. Inevitably, some of the qualities that marked Reb Hayyim personally, and his imprint generally, have been somewhat attenuated. A great creative wave recedes in time, and it is unrealistic to expect a pioneering spirit to sustain itself after it has become the establishment. The spirit of independence that guided his bold originality has gradually become more muted. Of first-class *gedolim*, this has been true by dint of the sheer fact that they were no longer establishing a tradition but were firmly ensconced within it, very much in the shadow of its founder. As to ordinary *Bnei Torah*, for many of them, independence has not been so much muted as consciously reversed, servile imitation and submissive acceptance of Reb Hayyim's *derekh* and of specific *hiddushim* adopted by many as the call of the hour. Reb Velvel is reputed to have sought a Shas without Rashi and a *Mishneh Torah* sans *nos'ei kelim*. Many presumed followers appear to seek editions with *Hiddushei Rabbenu Hayyim* and *Hiddushei Maran Ha-Griz* right on the page.

Concomitantly, the range of sefarim used has increased significantly. Reb Hayyim and his sons used relatively few; and in his *hesped* of Reb Velvel, the Rav noted this fact as a barometer of concentration and self-reliance. However, he himself ranged further afield than had Reb Mosheh, and his brother, *mori ve-rabbi*, Rav Ahron, יבל"א, half a generation younger, casts a far wider net than he did. The same is true, for instance, of Rav Mosheh Sternbuch's *Moadim U-Zemanim Ha-Shalem,* as compared with the sefer of his mentor, Reb Velvel. The change is partly due to the greater availability of material, but it also reflects a partial change of mindset. And the spate of monographs currently inundating the Torah world, some written in a Brisker context, reflects an Alexandrian aspect totally at variance with Reb Hayyim's emphasis. In the same vein, some purport to see a relaxation of the taut and relentless pursuit of *amittah shel Torah* and of the readiness to labor, mightily and intensively, in order to plumb its depths. Around fifteen years ago, Rav Abba Berman remarked to Rav Yosef Baer Soloveitchik here in Jerusalem that he thought "*yegi'at Ha-Torah* is going under." "You are wrong," was the pungent response, "it has already gone under." And indeed, the recent rise in the study of *Halakhah le-ma'aseh* at the expense of learning *be-iyyun* may reflect this decline.

No less significant are the changes in substantive content. The sharp thrust and clear lines characteristic of so much of pre-World War II conceptualism at its best are now less prominent, and frayed edges and convoluted arguments more in evidence. And there has been variety from the outset. While the modern conceptual approach is most directly identified with Reb Hayyim, it should by no means be confined to Brisk and its direct spiritual progeny. Rav Shimon Shkop, with a quasi-philosophic jurisprudential bent, has already been cited, and his disciple, Rav Gustman, might be mentioned in the same breath. Or again, while the imprint of the conceptual tradition is clearly perceptible in the comprehensive treasure trove of Rav Shlomo Zalman Auerbach זצ״ל – particularly in his remarkable sefarim on Zeraim – he was certainly no orthodox Brisker. And, of course, the Hazon Ish pointed in a different direction entirely.

Nevertheless, despite these changes, it remains a striking fact that over the past century, the approach and the content of conceptualism have remained remarkably stable. The key-rings have not become rusty. While vitality may have been sapped, the basic perspective and the fundamental ideas are very much with us. They have seeped into the learning and teaching of gemara at advanced levels, and thereby invigorated the yeshiva world; and it is even arguable that the method has had an impact upon the realms of *mahshavah* and Tanakh, as reflected in the writings of the Rav and *mori ve-rabbi*, Rav Hutner, or of Rav Mordechai Breuer. What the future holds – and I have been asked to relate to this – I am reluctant to predict. I have long since forsworn prognostication and admit to entertaining reservations about peers who have not. Nevertheless, I recognize the value, particularly for educational planning, of some kinds of projections. So I shall conclude with some qualified remarks about our subsequent methodological direction, in no small measure extrapolating from present portents for this purpose. I presume that the wish, to some extent, may be father to some thoughts; but I trust that my own admitted inclinations will not distort my perceptions.

I believe that the conceptual approach will continue, for the foreseeable future, to be a dominant force in the world of serious Torah learning. However, I also believe that its status will recede somewhat. And this, in several respects. First, the method itself is likely to be modified. Instead of pure distilled Brisk, we are likely to see more blended models – hopefully enriched rather than adulterated, but diluted nonetheless. Pure Brisker, who hang on to every scrap of the tradition, and perhaps on to little else, will continue to learn and possibly thrive, but their position will be less prominent. Trends previously cited will, in all likelihood, continue and possibly accelerate. We can anticipate greater awareness of factual points and recourse to a wider arc of sources. Moreover, the latter may be accompanied by thematic expansion. Classical Brisk tends to focus upon a narrow band of central *shittot* in any *sugya* – generally those that make the most logical sense or whose analysis poses the greatest challenge. In the spirit of *elu ve-elu*, however, the range can be extended to include not only extant peripheral views, but also those that inhere potentially, even if they have yet to be advanced. One might explore definitions or constellations that could be reasonably entertained on general grounds, analyze them, and examine whether and to what extent they conform with the textual and conceptual data relevant to a term or a topic.

Finally, the conceptual approach is likely to encounter greater competition than heretofore. Some of the initial momentum having been spent, and the *derekh* having become conventional, and in some cases even cliché-ridden, the danger of lapsing into what I.A. Richards called "stock responses" looms large; and these factors may erode the preeminence of the approach. This may be further affected by external developments. As we have seen, the focus of conceptualism is *lehavin ule-haskil.* It aims to engage the aspiring *lamdan* in the sacred task of probing and mastering *devar Hashem.* Per se, it relates to the content of Torah, its "what" and juridic "why," but not to a spiritual and philosophic "why." Major figures in the Brisker tradition may, of course, choose to undertake this task, and in doing so draw upon its central halakhic corpus. But this is not an indispensable component. Reb Mosheh eschewed this task, whereas his sons pursued it vigorously. Those who feel an existential need for learning that is not only ultimately relevant but immediately, and often shallowly, so, may find themselves disaffected by conceptualism and seek more appealing alternatives.

This factor verges upon the interface of methodology and education. Reb Hayyim did not need to "sell" Torah. He taught it to eager and overawed *talmidim*. The motivation of a captivated audience was taken for granted, and all his energies could be poured into learning. Educators today, by contrast, devote much, if not most, of their energy precisely to the area of motivation. In Israel especially, there has been much talk recently, within the *dati-leumi* community, of the flagging interest in gemara. Many young people, looking for instant spiritual gratification (sometimes with the encouragement of some of their elders), feel they must be "connected" to what they learn, and they may have difficulty in linking with *havayot de-Abbaye ve-Rava*. In this climate, the prospect that some educators will look toward a more existential *derekh*, less demanding in every sense than the Brisker, is a real possibility.

Educational considerations are important, and need to be viewed with an open mind and a sensitive heart. Certainly, חנוך לנער על פי דרכו, properly understood and implemented, must be our polestar. Nonetheless, we must beware the easy temptation of a modish search for easier options. Whatever our educational course, however, we must be certain that for ourselves – deeply committed to *talmud Torah* and searching for the best means of realizing it – we not lose sight of the significance of our methodological choice. I firmly believe that for most, the quest for quality learning, in depth, will continue to be best served by the conceptual approach. There may be complements, but for the time being, no substitute. Speaking not only out of loyal allegiance but out of considered judgment, I conclude with the conviction that the conceptual approach remains the optimal mode of attaining the twin goals of *lehavin ule-haskil* and *lehagdil Torah ule-ha'adirah*.

Notes

1. Yoma 4b.
2. Eruvin 54b.
3. Sanhedrin 26b.
4. See Sukkah 28b, Ta'anit 10b.
5. The largest single body of *sifrei Halakhah* is, of course, that of *she'elot u-teshuvot*. I have omitted reference to it here, however, because of its great variety.
6. Berakhot 11b.
7. Talmud Torah 1:11.
8. See Rosh Hashanah 16b and Rambam, Talmud Torah 5:7.
9. See Berakhot 15a and Rambam, Tefillin 4:26.
10. For various sources, see Sukkah 2a–3a.
11. A permanent residence is invalid as a sukkah, even if it meets all the technical specifications. See Rashi, Sukkah 8b, s.v. *penimit,* and 14a, s.v. *R. Meir.*
12. See Sukkah 4a and *Hiddushei Maran Riz HaLevi,* 9a.
13. See Sukkah 6b. This question may lie at the heart of the *mahloket* between R. Shimon and Rabbanan as to the number of walls required; or, alternatively, may depend upon the source from which R. Shimon derived his view that the minimum is three plus part of a fourth.
14. No mention is made, for instance, of a minimal area; see, in contrast, Rambam, Sukkah 4:1.
15. This inclination is often manifested even with respect to phenomena, such as minhagim, that presumably have some historical grass-roots origins and need not be attributed to a formal legal mold. For instance, the Rav consistently sought to refer the various levels of *avelut* obtaining during the period of *sefirat ha-omer* to halakhic categories. Although he recognized that they had developed over time and due to assorted national tragedies, he preferred to integrate them, as far as possible, into a coherent whole rather than regard them as an accumulation of random elements. This approach rests, apart from its general conceptualist proclivities, upon certain assumptions regarding communal religious development; and these are not always readily tenable.
16. See Bava Batra 5a–b.
17. See Bava Kamma 15a.
18. It is conceivable, however, that the status of *keren,* in this connection, differs from that of other *avot nizkei mamon.*
19. Yerushalmi, Terumot 3:1.
20. *Hiddushei Ha-Ramban,* Hullin 42a.
21. In *Ish Ha-Halakhah,* the Rav emphasizes, to the contrary, the halakhic tendency to quantify, which he views as being in line with modern scientific tendencies, as opposed to the qualitative character of Aristotelian physics. There is, however, no contradiction. The passage in

question deals with the nature of the system per se, whereas I am here concerned with the mode of its interpretation.

22. See Kiddushin 26a, Rashi, s.v. *ba-havilei,* and Tosafot, s.v. *i nami.*

23. The approach does very often cherish viewing two phenomena as different gradations along the same continuum, rather than as simply disjunct parallel tracks. This, however, obtains in situations in which the gradations are conceptual – being, in effect, two levels or two definitions of the same term – but not where the levels are purely practical.

24. Bava Batra 75b. On this view, one might conceivably differentiate between the *shi'ur* required for acquisition and that required for a *shomer* or a *gazlan.*

25. Bava Kamma 20a; cf. 24b and 32a.

26. Shabbat 123a. See Tosafot, s.v. *midi dele-inyan;* and cf. Shabbat 49b, Tosafot, s.v. *lo,* and Zevahim 93b, Tosafot, s.v. *minayin.*

   The precise substance of Abbaye's rejoinder (and, possibly, of Rava's response) is not clear from Abbaye's formulation. Is he distinguishing between two kinds of *kelim, keli ma'asseh* and an ordinary *keli;* or does he hold that *muktzah* does not depend upon designation as a *keli* at all, but simply upon being fit for any use, regardless of the label?

27. See Thomas S. Kuhn, *The Structure of Scientific Revolutions,* 2nd ed. (Chicago, 1970), chaps. 6–9.

28. See Shevuot 42b and Bava Mezia 56a.

29. To'en ve-Nit'an 5:2.

30. See Shevuot 44b.

31. See Mekhirah 13:15.

32. *Hiddushei Rabbenu Hayyim HaLevi,* To'en ve-Nit'an 5:2.

33. Pesahim 59b, Kiddushin 68a, Niddah 33a.

34. *Tosafot Talmid Rabbenu Tam ve-Rabbi Eliezer,* in *Shittat Ha-Kadmonim al Massekhet* Bava Kamma, ed. Y. Blau (New York, 1976), p. 55.

35. *Divrei Hagut ve-Ha'arakhah* (Jerusalem, 1981), p. 83. Strikingly, two pages later, the Rav writes: אין איש ההלכה משתדל לתרץ את כל הקושיות. הוא אינו שמח בתירוץ ואינו מצטער על הקושיא. תפקידו של האדם להבין. כשמביניהם את הקושי וההסתבכות שלא ניתן להסר – דיינו.

36. This has educational implications, particularly with respect to emphases, overt or subliminal, concerning retention. I presume that I am not the only one who repeatedly finds that he has forgotten much of the woof and warp of a particular *sugya,* but remembers the operative principles in light of which it was examined, and then uses them to reconstruct it.

37. See Sukkah 19a, s.v. *lo.* This is the prevalent view, as opposed to Rashi's, ad loc. Reb Hayyim's proof was cited in his name, orally, by the Rav.

38. Rav Yosef Baer Soloveitchik (of Jerusalem) told me that he once remarked to his father about the qualitative difference between the eye-opening character of Reb Hayyim's *hibbur* and the relatively conventional nature of the Bet Ha-Levi. Reb Velvel, eager to protect his grandfather's honor, responded heartily: "Listen, Berel, the *zayde* could have written a *sefer* just like father's; but he didn't want to." But the facts speak for themselves.

39. *Sefer Marheshet* (Vilna, 1931). While an element of critique is clearly perceptible (חדשים מקרוב

באו does not have favorable associations), it is fairly mild, as it appears as part of a hope and prayer that, despite its not being currently in mode, his work will be appreciated – and all this within a context of acknowledgment of methodological pluralism. Incidentally, during his sojourn in Vilna, the Rav established a personal relationship with R. Henoch Agus, and when the *Marheshet* appeared, sent him a list of comments to which he later responded.

40. See Horayot 14a. Some contend (I have heard the remark attributed to Rav Shlomo Kluger) that this conclusion only applied as long as *Torah she-be'al-peh* had not been recorded. Now, however, the order is indeed to be reversed; *a fortiori*, one might add, since the advent of a phalanx of reference works. This is matter for another discussion, however.

41. See *Sefer Ravan*, ed. Rav S.Z. Ehrenreich, II, 301b–305b.

42. See *Sefer Ravyah*, ed. A. Aptowitzer, I, 172–73, and the sources cited in the notes, as well as the discussion as to whether the Ravyah or his father had written the *teshuvah*.

43. See *Or Zarua* I:235, who also recounts how some Rishonim dealt with the issue in practice.

44. *Divrei Hagut ve-Ha'Arakhah*, p. 80.

45. *Table Talk of Samuel Taylor Coleridge*, ed. Henry Morley (London, 1884), p. 102; July 2, 1830.

46. See Bava Batra 176a and 128a, respectively.

47. See Daniel Sperber, "On the Legitimacy, or indeed, Necessity, of Scientific Disciplines for True 'Learning' of the Talmud," in *Modern Scholarship in the Study of Torah: Contributions and Limitations*, ed. Shalom Carmy (Northvale, N.J., 1996), pp. 197–226. Compare Rav Avraham Eliyahu Kaplan, "Al Arikhat Perush la-Talmud Bavli," *Be-Divrei Talmud* I (Jerusalem, 5708), pp. 10–17.

48. See Rosh Hashanah 29b; Rif, Shabbat 1b (in the Alfasi's pagination); and Ba'al Ha-Ma'or, Ramban, and Ran, ad loc.

49. *Teshuvah* 3:8.

50. I trust I need hardly add that this license was not suggested for every neophyte. The "one" in question is a halakhic master.

51. See *Ish Ha-Halakhah: Galuy ve-Nistar* (Jerusalem, 1979), esp. pp. 70–73 and 83 ff.

52. Bava Batra 175b. Interestingly, the opening qualification implies that there may be other legitimate ends for learning – perhaps each with its preferred texts.

53. See *Divrei Hagut ve-Ha'Arakhah*, pp. 75–82.

Chapter 3

Torat Hesed and *Torat Emet:* Methodological Reflections

In speaking of Torah, we commonly employ two principal terms[1] to define its essence. The first, *Torat emet*, was incorporated by Hazal in the concluding *birkat hatorah*, is familiar from the daily recitation of *u'va lezion*, and its use derives, ultimately, from a well-known *pasuk*. Speaking of the fountainhead of *kehunah* – variously interpreted as Aharon or Pinhas – Malakhi, as surrogate for the *Ribbono shel Olam*, expounds prophetically:

> תורת אמת היתה בפיהו ועולה לא נמצא בשפתיו בשלום ובמישור הלך אתי ורבים השיב מעון.

> The law of truth was in his mouth, and unrighteousness was not found in his lips; he walked with Me in peace and uprightness, and did turn many away from iniquity.[2]

The second term, *Torat hesed*, likewise derives from a familiar *pasuk*: פיה פתחה בחכמה ותורת חסד על לשונה "She openeth her mouth with wisdom, and the law of kindness is on her tongue."[3] However, while the meaning of the former is presumably quite clear[4] – except, of course, insofar as the concept of truth generally constitutes a philosophic and, particularly, epistemological, morass – the latter is richly ambiguous. At the plane of basic *peshat*, the phrase presumably does not refer to Torah at all, but rather denotes the tenets and practice of empathetic engagement and support. Thus, Ibn Ezra speaks of a willingness to perform kindness, שהיא מוכנה לעשות

חסד, while the Meiri explains, more expansively, that what is intended is inculcating the realization of *hesed*, הוראת עשיית החסד לכל הצריך לו, which he regards as encapsulating ideal morality, שלימות המדות, generally.

Beyond the literal, however, the term has traditionally been linked to Torah proper; and this, per se, can be understood in several respects. At the simplest, *Torat hesed* can describe Torah as pervaded and animated by *hesed*, whose substantive content constitutes so much of its corpus. "Thus you have learned," the Rambam observed with reference to the imperative to violate the Sabbath when mandated by *pikuah nefesh*, שאין משפטי התורה נקמה בעולם אלא רחמים וחסד ושלום בעולם, "that the Torah's laws are not as vengeance in the world but as mercy, lovingkindness, and peace in the world."[5] In a parallel, albeit different, vein, the appellation may suggest a Torah whose application and implementation is fraught with *hesed*, insofar as the process takes the human factor into consideration.

Alternatively, the referent may be the transmission of Torah, with *midrashim* speaking, variously, of divine *hesed* in its endowment and that of *Knesset Yisrael* in its acceptance. Or it may describe its study – especially, as regards *telos* and motivation. וכי יש תורה של חסד ויש תורה שאינה של חסד, "Is there, then, a Torah of *hesed* and a Torah devoid of *hesed*?" the gemara asks; and, in response, it offers two alternate interpretations:

אלא תורה לשמה זו היא תורה של חסד שלא לשמה זו היא תורה שאינה של חסד איכא דאמרי תורה ללמדה זו היא תורה של חסד שלא ללמדה זו היא תורה שאינה של חסד.

But Torah for its own sake is a Torah of *hesed*, whereas Torah which is not [engaged in] for its own sake is Torah which is not of *hesed*. Others say, Torah which is to be taught is a Torah of *hesed*; that which is not to be taught is Torah which is not of *hesed*.[6]

These elements, important, singly and collectively, in their own right, bear little relation to the subject of our present discourse: the contrast, implicit in my subtitle between *Torat hesed* and *Torat emet*, as reflected in the methodological realm. Quite apart from differences in source, *telos*, or content, we encounter marked difference with respect to the qualitative character of Torah, conceived as both an intrinsic phenomenon and as the object of study and development.[7]

The difference relates to texture. There is a Torah, firm and sharp, its outlines single-mindedly defined, hewn from the rock of truth and limned in granite, its message emblazoned as meridian sun and lucid as polar night. And there is a Torah, flexible and subtle, its frontiers boundless and shifting, supple as an infant's flesh and luxuriant as an equatorial forest. *Torat emet* bespeaks unitary truth. It denotes a definitive and static entity, an impenetrable and impregnable fortress, impervious to the vicissitudes of time and culture, ante-historical and meta-historical. It is, in the words of the *midrash*, identified with that which a person has received from his masters: רבי חונייא בשם רבי אמר תורת אמת היתה בפיהו אלו דברים ששמע מפי רבו.[8] *Hesed*, on the other hand, suggests dynamic centrifugal thrust. The term is associated with expansive *hitpashtut*, even excess; with the surmounting of barriers – at times, negatively, as in its application to incest.[9] *Torat hesed* is therefore marked by vitality and growth, by the opening of new chapters and the breaking of fresh ground.

The distinction may, in a sense, be ascribed to varied areas of Torah. In explaining the dual import of the core of the *berakhah* recited after each portion of Torah reading, אשר נתן לנו תורת אמת וחיי עולם נטע בתוכנו, "Who has given us Torah of truth and has implanted eternal life within us," the Ravya expounds:

דמקצת קאי אתורה מקצת קאי אישראל ושאר מצות כגון וחיי עולם נטע בתוכנו דקאי אשאר מצות וגמילות חסדים שישראל עוסקים בהם תדיר ואנו מודים להקב״ה על שניהם. וכן אשר בחר בנו דקאי אישראל ונתן לנו את תורתנו אתורה. ולהוציא מדברי האומר וחיי עולם נטעה בתוכנו דמשמע דקאי אתורה שאם כן לא היה צריך שתי ברכות.

In part, it refers to Torah, and, in part, to Israel. Thus, "And He has implanted eternal life within us" refers to other *mizvot* and to *gemilut hasadim* in which Israel engages constantly, and we thank God for both. Likewise, "Who has chosen us," refers to Israel, and "Who has given us His Torah" to Torah. This is to the exclusion of those who say, "And eternal life, He has implanted it within us," which suggests that this, too, refers to Torah; for, if that were the case, there would be no need for two blessings.[10]

The more prevalent interpretation is that which he cites only to reject[11] that the entire *berakhah* refers to Torah exclusively; and, as to the cavil against redundancy, it is presumably parried by the Tur:

פירוש תורת אמת היא תורה שבכתב וחיי עולם נטע בתוכנו היא תורה שבעל פה דכתיב
דברי חכמים כדרבונות וכמסמרות נטועים ולאפיקי מאותם האומרים ולחיי עולם נטעה
בתוכנו.

To wit, *"Torat emet"* refers to written Torah, and "And eternal life He implanted
within us" to oral Torah, as it is written, "The words of the wise are as goads,
and as nails well fastened." This is to the exclusion of those who say, "And to
eternal life He has implanted it within us."[12]

On this reading, *Torat emet* refers to the scriptural text – inviting
the presumption that *Torat hesed* is identified with the oral tradition; and
indeed, in a gemara alluded to by the Tur, Hazal invokes the imagery of
vibrant and luxuriant growth with respect to *Torah she-be'al-peh*, specifically:

נטועים מה נטיעה זו פרה ורבה אף דברי תורה פרין ורבין.

"Implanted" – just as a plant flourishes and increases, so Torah matters flourish
and increase.[13]

The point has unquestionable validity. Nevertheless, both epithets
can be applied to either Torah sphere. That, at any rate, was manifestly the
position of an arch-patron and master of *Torat hesed*, a giant most of us
admittedly rarely associate with philosophic discourse: Rav Aryeh Leib
HaKohen, generally better known as the *Ktzot*. In the course of the preface
to his magnum opus, *Ktzot Hahoshen*, he argues trenchantly for the validity
and veracity of *Torat hesed*; and I shall return to his comments presently.
For the moment, I simply note that they omit any differentiation between
the two component spheres of Torah. Evidently, the *Ktzot* assumed that
either could be viewed dually, and perhaps dialectically; and I am inclined
to agree. Rather than juxtaposing the scriptural and the oral, it behooves
us, therefore, at this juncture, inasmuch as the distinction between *Torat
emet* and *Torat hesed* revolves primarily around their respective monistic
and pluralistic characters, to scrutinize the nature and scope of halakhic
pluralism.

Its most familiar formulation is a well-known prooftext in a gemara
in Eruvin:

א״ר אבא אמר שמואל שלש שנים נחלקו בית שמאי ובית הלל הללו אומרים הלכה
כמותנו והללו אומרים הלכה כמותנו יצאה בת קול ואמרה אלו ואלו דברי א־לקים חיים
הן והלכה כבית הלל.

R. Abba stated in the name of Shmuel: "For three years Bet Shammai and Bet Hillel disputed. These say, 'The Halakhah is in agreement with us,' and those say, 'The Halakhah is in agreement with us.' Then, a heavenly voice issued, asserting, 'The statements of both are living words of God, but the Halakhah is in accordance with the views of Bet Hillel.'"[14]

This is sometimes understood, in a limited vein – that while surely only one view can be deemed as true, the adherents of both will be credited as having fulfilled the *mizvah* of *talmud Torah* for simply having engaged in the quest, be it abortive, for *amittah shel Torah*. On this reading, the statement parallels a similar assertion in a gemara in Kiddushin:

מחשבה טובה מצרפה למעשה שנאמר אז נדברו יראי ה׳ איש אל רעהו ויקשב ה׳ וישמע
ויכתב ספר זכרון לפניו ליראי ה׳ ולחושבי שמו מאי ולחושבי שמו אמר רב אסי אפילו
חשב אדם לעשות מצוה ולא עשאה מעלה עליו הכתוב כאילו עשאה.

Good thought is conjoined with deed, as it is said, "Then the God-fearing spoke one with the other; and the Lord hearkened and heard, and a book of remembrance was written before Him, for the God-fearing, and for those who thought His name." What is the import of "those who thought His name?" Rav Assi stated: "Even if a person intended to perform a *mizvah* and did not perform it Scripture credits him as if he had performed it."[15]

This quasi-Kantian principle of ascribing merit on the basis of effort and intention, irrespective of objective formal accomplishment, is not generally associated with halakhic thought. Its moral and popular appeal is, however, undeniable; and it does find expression in the world of Halakhah as well. To cite one example, it was enunciated, as a general principle, by the author of *Shibbolei Haleket*:

והדברים אלו כמה הם אדירים וחזקים ואין אדם יכול לצלול בהן ולהעמידן וכל איש
מקבל שכר על מה שרואה בדעתו אם דעתו מכוון לשים. הרי אתה רואה שתפלין שתפרן
בפשתן פסולות כדאמרינן בפרק אלו הן הלוקין ואמר רב חזינא לתפלין דבי חביבי

דתפירי בכיתנא ולית הלכתא כוותיה ובודאי ר׳ חייא הגדול היה לו שכר תפלין כשאר
החסידים ואע״פ שתפורות בפשתן.

And how mighty and powerful are these matters, so that one cannot plumb
them and establish them; and every person is rewarded [for acting] as he
understands, if his motivation is for the sake of Heaven. Take note: *Tefillin*
which are sewn with linen thread are defective, as is stated in Makkot 11a,
and yet Rav attested: 'I have seen the *tefillin* of the school of my cherished
[i.e. his uncle, Rabbi Hiyya], and they were sewn with linen. But his view
has been rejected? And assuredly, the great Rabbi Hiyya was rewarded, like
other pious persons, for [fulfilling the *mizvah* of] *tefillin*, even though they
were sewn with linen."[16]

However, as an interpretation of *elu v'elu*, this understanding is wholly
untenable. Shmuel is not concerned with reward or personal fulfillment, but
with defining the objective corpus of Torah. It is of this that he asserts, *elu
v'elu divrei E-lokim hayyim*, clearly stating that contradictory positions can
indeed be equally recognized as an element of Torah. That was, certainly,
the perception of the *ba'alei hatosafot*, as cited by the Ritva:

שאלו רבני צרפת ז״ל האיך אפשר שיהיו אלו ואלו דברי א׳-לקים חיים וזה אוסר וזה מתיר
ותרצו כי כשעלה משה למרום לקבל התורה הראו לו על כל דבר ודבר מ״ט פנים להיתר
ושאל להקב״ה על זה ואמר שיהא זה מסור לחכמי ישראל שבכל דור ודור ויהיה הכרעה
כמותם ונכון הוא לפי הדרש ובדרך האמת יש פנים לאיסור ומ״ט טעם סוד בדבר.

The French Rabbis asked: How is it possible that these and those should be
as living words of God, when one permits and the other prohibits? They
answered that when Mosheh ascended to Heaven in order to receive the
Torah, he was shown, with respect to each and every matter, forty-nine
facets for prohibition and forty-nine facets for license. He asked the Holy
One, Blessed Be He, about this and he was told that the matter would be
handed over to the sages of Israel in each and every generation, and it would
be resolved as they would determine. This is correct according to the *drash*
speculation; but at the mystical plane, there is an arcane explanation.[17]

The celebration of fecundity, albeit without reference to the problem of
contradiction or the terminology of *elu v'elu*, had previously been advanced
by an early *amora* in the Yerushalmi:

א"ר ינאי אילו ניתנה התורה חתוכה לא היתה לרגל עמידה מה טעם וידבר ה' אל משה
לאמר אמר לפניו רבונו של עולם הודיעני היאך היא ההלכה אמר לו אחרי רבים להטות
רבו המזכין זכו רבו המחייבין חייבו כדי שתהא התורה נדרשת מ"ט פנים טמא ומ"ט
פנים טהור מניין ודגל"ו.

Rabbi Yannai said: "If the Torah had been given cut [and dry] we would not
have a leg to stand on. How is 'And Hashem spoke to Mosheh,' to be understood? He [i.e. Mosheh] said to Him: '*Ribbono shel Olam*, tell me what is the
[definitive] Halakhah? He said to him: 'Follow the majority. If more assume
innocence, they acquit [i.e. the person being judged]; if more assume guilt,
they convict, so that Torah is interpreted in light of forty-nine facets to purify
and forty-nine facets to defile, in accordance with the number of *v'diglo*.'"[18]

The scenario envisioned here is that of the *bet din*, and not only of the
bet midrash. But the basic view of the halakhic process and, above all, the
recognition of multiple interpretation as immanent and inherent, *a priori*,
rather than as a lamentable accident,[19] is equally present.

One of the *ba'alei hatosafot* expanded the concept even further. Rabbenu Perez notes that *elu v'elu* could apply to prescriptive and normative
statements, for which conflicting interpretations, pro and con, could be
advanced. However, the concept could presumably not be entertained with
respect to descriptive statements, inasmuch as the reality they portray was,
in fact, clearly only one or the other. How could we, for instance, apply
the principle to the dispute over what had been the dimension of the
mizbeah? And yet, he responds, at the explicatory plane, it does nevertheless obtain:

דגס כולהו לא היה אלא בחד ענינא, אלא חד מוכח מקרא דבדין היה לו להיות הכי
וחד מוכח מקרא דבדין היה לו להיות הכי והא דקאמר אילו ואילו דברי ה' א-לוקים
חיים פירוש דמתוך הפסוקים יש משמעות למידרש כמר וכמר אבל ודאי לא היה אלא
בעינן אחד.

For all of them were also [only] in one vein, but one adduces from a verse
that it ought to have been thus and one adduces from a verse that it ought
to have been thus; and the statement, "*Elu v'elu* are the living words of God,"
means that, from the verses, one can elicit either meaning. Certainly, however,
in fact, the reality was only one.[20]

The language seems to suggest that the verses can be understood as prescribing guidelines which were presumably implemented, so that a normative element is present in this context after all. However, the governing logic is evidently relevant to purely factual description as well.

"The sages of Israel in each generation" do not simply grope amidst the welter of forty-nine pros and cons in the hope of fortunately hitting the right combination. Rather, confronted by texts or concepts which can be variously interpreted or defined and which can be reasonably and inherently understood in a number of ways – here represented by the symbolically exhaustive forty-nine – they seek, each according to his own lights, to create a Torah fabric by probing issues and arriving at conclusions. Every possibility with which a term is pregnant and which one of the *hakhmei hamesorah*, conscientiously and responsibly laboring with his best tools, adopts, is ipso facto a rendering of Torah.

This proposition is open to two distinct formulations. The narrower – insofar as the role assigned to *hakhmei hamesorah* is concerned, although broader, in other respects – would determine that any position which an acknowledged sage, working on the basis of the database of the raw material of Torah, written and oral, and, in accordance with philological, hermeneutic, and logical principles, could have plausibly adopted, even if none actually did, is part of the corpus of Torah, actual or inchoate. The more radical – again, as regards the place of *hakhamim* in defining the substance of Torah – would contend that only that which had been actually posited by a Torah sage qualifies as a component of Torah, over whose study the requisite *berakhot* may be recited, and which enjoys the deferential awe accorded to that lofty status. Torah sages are its custodians – but not only that. They do not just preserve or even discover, but, in a meaningful sense, create. Their imprimatur, variously perceived as restrictive or expansive, is critical as a sine qua non of entry into the canon.

Either formulation, but especially the latter, begs the obvious question of who is defined as a "sage of tradition," as well as of who effectively defines; and it may be justifiably argued that, to some extent, judgment is circular. It will be contended that some interpretations ordinarily regarded as heterodox, as they lack an acknowledged Torah sponsor, could, if redefined as within the pale, lend credentials to their sponsor, in view of what would then be regarded as his contribution to the Torah world; and his rehabilitated stature would, in turn, lend credence to his views as a legitimate rendering of the *mesorah*. On the other hand, if he is disbarred, or his novellae dismissed *ex cathedra* as erroneous or even heretical, the dialectic is reversed.

The question is legitimate. Moreover, we should expect, *a priori*, that there should be borderline cases in which the interplay could go either way. And yet – in an Orthodox context, surely – some mode of definition is inevitable. It may be formal, as during the epoch of technical *semikhah*, lineally derived from Mosheh Rabbenu; or, as in later times, the informal collective judgment, based upon personal and pietistic criteria no less than upon sheer intellectual prowess or erudition, of the historical Torah community. Saducees or Karaites – or, for that matter, Elisha ben Avuyah – shall not be ushered into that community by virtue of their scholarship, nor contrarily, shall their teachings be legitimized by dint of their authorship. Our reverence for Hazal, particularly, is such that even when one concedes that a given interpretation is consonant with a possible understanding of a primary element and could therefore, potentially, have qualified as a *hefza* of Torah, where it directly contravenes their consensual judgment, it does not assume its place within the tradition. Be that as it may, however, the conundrum of definition does not emasculate the centrality of the pluralistic aspect, albeit limited, of *Torah she-be'al-peh*.

This is the substantive gist of the gemara in Hagigah:

בעלי אסופות אלו תלמידי חכמים שיושבין אסופות אסופות ועוסקין בתורה. הללו מטמאין והללו מטהרין הללו אוסרין והללו מתירין הללו פוסלין והללו מכשירין שמא יאמר אדם היאך אני למד תורה מעתה תלמוד לומר נתנו מרעה אחד א"ל אחד נתנן פרנס אחד אמרן מפי אדון כל המעשים ברוך הוא דכתיב וידבר א־להים את כל הדברים האלה.

"Masters of assemblies": This refers to *talmidei hakhamim* who sit in varied assemblies and engage in Torah. These pronounce "pure," and those pronounce "impure"; these proscribe and those permit; these disqualify and others declare fit. Lest a person say, "How can I, henceforth, study Torah?" Therefore, the text states: "All have been given by one Shepherd." One God gave them, one leader uttered them, from the mouth of the Lord of all creation, Blessed Be He; as it is written, "And God spoke all these words."[21]

In this sense, too, we should understand a well-known comment found in the Yerushalmi:

אפילו מה שתלמיד ותיק עתיד להודות לפני רבו כבר נאמר למשה בסיני.

All that a seasoned disciple will declare before his master has already been transmitted to Mosheh, at Sinai.[22]

This, presumably, should not be taken to mean that the specific *hiddushim* were revealed at Sinai, but, rather, as the Rambam evidently understood in the introduction to his *Commentary on the Mishnah,* that, as latent possible developments and interpretations, they were, in *potentia,* present, only to be kinetically generated, subsequently. This is clearly intimated by the continuation of the passage:

מה טעם יש דבר שיאמר אדם ראה זה חדש הוא וגו' משיב חבירו ואומר לו כבר היה לעולמים.

What is the reason? "There is a matter whereof one says, 'Behold – it is new,' etc. To which his fellow responds and says to him, 'It has already been, for ages.'"[23]

On this view, obviously several different and even conflicting positions could be simultaneously entertained, even by the same person, as objective Torah; and, *a fortiori,* different *poskim* could each subscribe to one of several contradictory conclusions, each fully legitimate in its own right. At the level of definitive *psak,* confrontation is of course inevitable, as some practical resolution is necessary. Even at that plane, however, the need does not invalidate the inherent legitimacy of rejected *shittot,* all of which may retain their character as Torah. It is in this vein that one of the *ba'alei hatosafot* explains a Mishnah in *Eduyot,* which seeks to explain why rejected minority views are cited in Mishnayot, and thus presumably incorporated within the corpus of Halakhah. The reason cited is that they be available to later generations who might prefer to reverse their predecessors' decision, but lack the license or the stature to do so on their own. Rav Shimshon of Sens expands upon this theme:

"ולמה מזכירין דברי היחיד". כלומר כיון שבכל מקום יחיד ורבים הלכה כרבים, למה

הוזכרו דברי היחידים בין המרובים, שאם יראו בית דין דברי היחידי. כגון האמוראים
שפסקו הלכות וכשראוים טעם היחיד יכולין לפסוק כמותו. שאם נשתקעו דבריו לא
היו האמוראים יכולין לפסוק כדבריו שכבר אמרה תורה אחרי רבים להטות ואף על גב
שלא נתקבלו דברי היחיד בזמן ראשון ולא הסכימו רבים עמו כשיבוא דור אחד ויסכימו
רבים לטעמו יהי הלכה כמותו. שכל התורה נאמרה כן למשה פנים לטמא ופנים לטהר
ואמרו לו עד מתי נעמוד עד הבירור ואמר להם אחרי רבים להטות מיהו אלו ואלו דברי
א־להים חיים.

"And why do we cite the views of a lone dissenter?" To wit, inasmuch as
wherever a majority and a dissenter disagree, the view of the majority
prevails, why were dissenting views cited among those of the majority? "So
that if a *bet din* will encounter the dissenting views." For instance, amoraim
who decided halakhot – they shall be able to adopt the dissenting view, if
it seems reasonable to them. For if the dissenter's views had lapsed into
oblivion [later] amoraim could not have explicitly challenged the *tannaim*,
who were greater than them in wisdom and in number. Yet, on the basis of
the dissenter's words, they could adopt his view, for the Torah has already
stated, "To decide in accordance with the majority." And even though his
views had been rejected initially, as the majority had not agreed with him,
when a later generation comes and the majority then accepts his reasoning,
that shall be the Halakhah. For the whole of Torah was thus given to Mosheh,
with aspects to decide "pure" and aspects to decide "impure." And they said
to him, "How will we arrive at definitive conclusions?" And he said to them:
"To decide in accordance with the majority," but these and those are living
words of God.[24]

Prooftexts and methodological considerations aside, I find a pluralistic
view of Halakhah compelling from a moral standpoint. Given a purely
monistic perspective, one would have to assume – in light of, say, the controversy concerning the sequence of the *parshiyot* in *tefillin* – that either
Rashi or Rabbenu Tam had never fulfilled that *mizvah*. The failure was
admittedly unwitting, so that the imprecations heaped upon a *karkafta d'lo
monah tefillin*[25] are not in order; but, on this view, the harsh fact remains.
Is this assertion conceivable?[26] Or, can anyone imagine that, in the eyes of
Rabbi Yehudah, who proscribed unintended ancillary labor on Shabbat, his
adversary, Rabbi Shimon, was classified as an unwitting *mehallel Shabbat*?
Such judgments seem to me intolerable. Each and every of the *hakhmei
hamesorah* who seizes upon one facet of Torah in accordance with his

perception, *ipso facto* defines its content for him and his constituents.[27] Within the bounds of legitimate controversy, he therefore cannot err because his *psak* is, in effect, not only a judicial, but a quasi-legislative, act. The very process of reading Torah determines, for him, what is written within it.

This view has important practical implications, ranging from the possibility of relying, in extremis, upon rejected minority opinions to definition of the parameters of the *mizvah* of *talmud Torah*. At this juncture, however, I set these aside in order to deal with an underlying central and cardinal question: What, if anything, stands behind this phalanx of possibilities? Are all reasonable interpretations truly and genuinely equal, one of many rays emanating from a single splintered source of light? Do they each represent a band of the spectrum, the whole truth being fragmented and refracted through the prism of human engagement and only reintegrated through their fusion? Or is there one which, *primus inter pares*, is, in a sense, more truly valid than others, as an expression of the divine will?

Hazal's answer is unequivocally clear, and it is amply reflected in various gemarot, of which I shall be content to cite the two most famous. The first deals with a detail concerning laws of leprosy. A Mishnah stipulates that if a given symptom had preceded another, the plague is pure and innocuous, whereas if the sequence is reversed, it is impure and defiling; and it goes on to present two views as to a situation in which priority is uncertain.[28] Against this background, the gemara in Bava Mezia projects a remarkable scenario:

ספק הקדוש ברוך הוא אומר טהור וכולהו מתיבתא דרקיעא אמרי טמא ואמרי מאן מוכח
נוכח רבה בר נחמני דאמר רבה בר נחמני אני יחיד בנגעים אני יחיד באהלות.

In case of doubt, the Holy One, Blessed Be He, says "pure," and the entire heavenly assembly says "impure." And they said, "Who shall decide? Let Rabbah bar Nahmani decide. For Rabbah bar Nahmani said, I am singular in [matters of] *Nega'im*, I am singular in [matters of] *Ohalot*."[29]

The second, even better-known, text relates to a controversy concerning the so-called "serpentine oven." At issue was the question of whether an oven which had been dismembered is still susceptible of defilement or should rather be regarded as junk, having lost its functional capacity and instrumental character. Rabbi Eliezer, who assumed the latter, invokes divine support, and indeed a series of celestial omens appear to corroborate his contention. Nevertheless, this position is rejected, on the ground that *lo bashamayim he*, "It is not in Heaven."[30] Whatever prodigious signs may indicate, halakhic issues need to be adjudicated at the human plane, by those to whom Torah has been revealed, and who have been mandated to interpret its content and, hence, determine its canons.

Torah bears, then, both a monistic and a pluralistic aspect. In the case of doubtful priority, "pure" Torah, that which is stored in the divine treasure trove, unequivocally affirms, *tahor*; and yet, revealed historical Torah, entertaining many voices, leaves the decision to Rabbah b. Nahmani, "singular in the field of *Nega'im*, singular in the field of *Ohalot*." As it happens, his view coincides with that attributed to Hakadosh Barukh Hu, but that is not what renders it definitive. Or again, that same ideal Torah, written primevally, "in black fire upon white fire," determines that "the serpentine oven" is pure; and R. Eliezer marshals the evidence of a phalanx of marvelous signs to buttress his position. And yet, brandishing *lo bashamayim he*, Rabbi Yehoshua succeeds in steering a debate within *hakhmei hamesorah* to the conclusion that it can indeed be defiled. There is, if you will, *Torat emet*, the impregnable diamond of absolute halakhic and metaphysical truth, and there is *Torat hesed*, the subtle, supple, and luxuriant instrument of historical revelation.

And this brings us back to the *Ktzot*. Basing himself upon expositions of the Ran,[31] themselves rooted in Hazal, underscoring the decisive human role in defining the normative content of Torah – particularly, of its oral component – he anchors the discussion by reference to the familiar midrashic discourse over the debate between *hesed* and *emet* over the prospective creation of man. The concluding remark תעלה אמת מן הארץ, "Let truth ascend from the earth" – he regards as a ringing affirmation of his position; and he sharpens it by reference to our context:

והיינו פיה פתחה בחכמה ותורת חסד על לשונה משום דתורה שבעל פה ניתנה כפי הכרעת החכמים אף על שאינו אמת ונקרא תורת חסד וכדאיתא בש"ס אם חסד אינו אמת.

And this is the intent of "She openeth her mouth with wisdom, and the law of

kindness is on her tongue." For *Torah she-be'al peh* was handed down subject
to the decision of the sages, even though it does not correspond to the truth,
and it is called *Torat hesed*, as is stated in *Shas*, "If *hesed*, not *emet*."³²

As the preface goes on to emphasize, one obviously strives, with awe
and responsibility, for pristine truth. Even if it is not attained, however,
at the terrestrial plane, the mistaken correlative is not only sufficient but
hallowed.

This selfsame theme had indeed largely been struck several centuries
earlier in *Hut Hashani*, a fascinating, albeit now largely obscure, collection of *teshuvot*, penned by three generations of the Bachrach family.
The youngest, Rav Yair Haym, author of the *Havot Yair*, asked his father,
Rav Shimshon, to elucidate a discussion of Tosafot as to why more of
Torah she-be'al-peh had not been recorded or, at least, been transmitted
as *halakhah lemosheh misinai*, so that it could be better remembered.
He replies that, paradoxically, such transmission would exacerbate the
problem of forgetfulness rather than ameliorate it. Oral material is more
readily forgotten than scripture. Hence, if it is cast in a rigorous mold, any
distortion, however innocent, obliterates it. However, if it is more flexibly
formulated *ab initio*, it is safeguarded from oblivion as approximation will
suffice. Thus, the position of *Torah she-be'al-peh* is secured through the
pliancy which allows for numerous variants:

כי היא נדרשת במ"ט פנים טמא ובמ"ט פנים טהור ומחמת השכחה אי אפשר לעמוד על
האמת כמו שנגמסר למשה ומכל מקום אינה משתכחת לגמרי כי אלו ואלו דברי א־להים
חיים כדאיתא בחגינה זה מביא ראיה מן הכתוב וזה מביא ראיה מן הכתוב כי אחד דורש
לפי שכלו והקדוש ברוך הוא מסר הדבר לחכמי הדור אפילו אומר על טמא באמת שהוא
טהור או איפכא אין לך אלא שופט שבימיך ודעת הקב"ה מסכמת בכך לפסוק בכל דור
על פי הכרעת דעתם של חכמים המפרשים הפסוקים אם יכוונו לאמת או לא הכל יעלה
לפניו יתברך לרצון כי כך גזרה חכמתו להטות הדבר על פי הרוב דחכמי כל דור ודור
לפי מה שהוא שיקול דעתם.

For it is expounded in forty-nine aspects, "impure," and in forty-nine aspects,
"pure;" and, due to forgetfulness, it is impossible to ascertain the truth as it
had been transmitted to Mosheh. Nevertheless, it is not entirely forgotten,
as *elu v'elu* are God's living words, as it is stated in Hagigah. This [sage]
adduces proof from Scripture and that one adduces proof from Scripture,

each interpreting in accordance with his reason. And the Holy One, Blessed Be He, has handed the matter over to the sages of the age. Even if one states of that which, in truth, is impure, that it is pure, or the reverse, "You have but the judge who is in your generation," and the will of the Holy One, concurs with this, to determine in each generation in accordance with the decision of the sages who interpret the *pesukim*. Whether they attain truth or not, it will all be accepted by Him, Blessed Be He, with grace, for thus has His wisdom predicated, to decide the matter by the majority of the sages of each and every generation, in accordance with their considered judgment.[33]

I must confess that I find these formulations radical, if not strident. Torah devoid of *emet*? Torah divested of the divine imprimatur? Their very sweep, however, is consonant with the position I have suggested.

More moderately, however, I would prefer to speak in terms similar to those employed by medieval Averroists in dealing with the problem of faith and reason – to speak, that is, of a double truth. Torah is, preeminently, an expression of the divine will. That will has, however – as the Ramban emphasized in his introduction to his commentary on *humash*,[34] assumed two forms. It exists, first, from eternity, incorporated as a facet of absolute wisdom:

ה' קנני ראשית דרכו קדם מפעליו מאז. מעולם נסכתי מראש מקדמי ארץ... היה אצלו אמון ואהיה שעשעים יום יום משחקת לפניו בכל עת.

The Lord made me as the beginning of His way, the first of His works of old. I was set up from everlasting, from the beginning, ere ever the earth was.... Then I was by Him, as a nursling, daily all delight, playing always before Him.[35]

Integrated within the process of constriction and descent, it then accompanies the process of creation, and enters upon the natural and historical scene. Ultimately, it is revealed, as the culmination of immanent *vayered*, to a particular community in the form of a command, as a normative missive. Between these two modes, there is, *ab initio*, presumed identity. However, insofar as communication entails two participants the maintenance of that identity cannot be guaranteed. It is not just that דברה תורה בלשון בני אדם, "Torah has spoken in human language," but that, primarily, it registers in human ears. Hence, the normative message has a built-in limitation, on the one hand, and enormous capacity for growth and development, on the other.

In the event of a fissure between primal divine reason and optimal human perception of its normative expression, which takes precedence? I believe the answer is clear – and it can be introduced by an analogy. The Rambam,[36] it will be recalled, wrestled with the question of how the Egyptians could have been held culpable for oppressing the children of Israel inasmuch as that had been divinely foreordained in the covenantal revelation to Avraham. He answers, in sum, that while the overall course of events, ועבדום וענו אתם, "And they shall serve them, and they (i.e. the oppressors) shall afflict them," had been prophesied, the prophecy had only been predicated collectively, so that each individual Egyptian retained freedom of choice with respect to its implementation. The Ramban rejects this view, inasmuch as it implies that the decision to fulfill the divine plan, freely made, can be fraught with guilt; and he, for his part, suggests two alternative explanations: that the atrocities committed exceeded the bounds of the prophecy (a position previously suggested by the Rabad), or that while the Egyptians' actions were congruent with God's will, they had rather been motivated by their own malice and therefore deserved to be punished. In this vein, he goes on to contend that if a person had been designated on Rosh Hashanah to die in the course of the following year, his murderer is nevertheless liable; but that if that sentence had been communicated via a prophet, אם שמע אותה ורצה לעשות רצון בוראו כנגזר אין עליו חטא, "If he heard it (i.e. the prophetic decree) and wanted to fulfill his Creator's will, as decreed, he is guiltless."[37]

What the Rambam would have thought of these assertions, and whether or why he would have dismissed them, had he considered them, is a matter of speculation. Surely, however, it is more than conceivable that he would have countered that even if one were, theoretically, privy to providential master strategy and impelled by a genuine desire to realize it, he would still be punished for drowning infants or implanting their bodies in masonry. Unless their status is transmuted by divine fiat, these actions retain their character as murder. Their perpetrator is bound by normative categories, and so long as these have not been specifically countermanded, it is God's will that our primary fealty be to Him as commander rather than as the architect of history. Cryptographic access to a master code provides no release from obligation to statutes; and no Egyptian could have excused his actions on the basis of knowledge of *brit bein habetarim*.[38]

A similar approach can be adopted with respect to our perception and implementation of Halakhah. At the divine plane, it exists as quintessential *Torat emet*, whose contours and content, bereft of all uncertainty – ומי איכא ספיקא קמי שמיא, "Is there, then, doubt in Heaven" – down to the minutest detail and contingency is singularly and unequivocally postulated. What binds us, however, as commanded beings, is not this *lex absconditus* but revealed Torah, whose *mizvah* aspect imparts its normative message and imposes normative responsibility. The *Ribbono shel Olam*'s collective charge demands of us to hear and heed its call, as we integrate and interpret its substance. To that end, we need to study and assimilate that Torah, in accordance with traditional canons of explication and exposition; and it is to the result of that process, the Word of God as heard by man, that we owe ultimate fealty and obedience.

What guides and binds us is not the rational divine will in its totality but that facet of it which has been constricted within the revealed command. The revelation proper one must of course seek to apprehend and appreciate with the best tools at his disposal. Having done that, however, he is responsible to the halakhic norm rather than to the metaphysical design. That is precisely the point of Rabbi Yehoshua's rejoinder, *lo bashamayim he*, which, properly understood, means not only that the decisive juridic authority is not supramundane but that the definitive codex proper includes a human variable. The kind of conflict envisioned by Hazal as being decided by the Rabbahs of this world does not constitute an antithesis between a "true" and an "erroneous" Torah but between two kinds of truth: that of Torah as an absolute metaphysical system and that of Torah as a revealed normative order.

The inclusion of a human variable necessarily introduces a dimension of pluralism – a dimension, that is, of *Torat hesed*.

כשם שאין פרצופיהם שוין זה לזה אלא כל אחד ואחד יש לו דעת בפני עצמו.

As their visages are not identical, so their thought is not identical, but each has his own mind.[39]

And if their views and perceptions define, in some measure, the substance of Torah, that substance is, invariably, multifaceted. Moreover, it prescribes a certain character to *talmud Torah*. The study of Torah is not to be regarded as a semi-mystical attempt to grasp the *Ribbono shel Olam*'s ultimate absolute will. It is rather an endeavor to grasp, through human instruments, that which has been expressed through human language – to master the terms and the categories as they inhere and can be reasonably read within the divine message; and to master not just one but all possible legitimate renderings of that message, all מ״ט פנים לטמא ומ״ט פנים לטהר, even if one is finally to be preferred. The focus is upon observed content more than upon presumed intent – or, upon the latter, insofar as it illuminates the former; upon fecund *Torat hesed* rather than austere *Torat emet*.

What has been presented heretofore, relates to *matan Torah*, and its receiving, in the narrowest sense, when bestowed by the *Ribbono shel Olam* to *Knesset Yisrael*. However, the underlying principle obtains at other levels of Torah transmission as well. At this juncture, we encounter an issue which currently exercises much of the scholarly community; and to a related charge often leveled by the academic votaries of *Torat emet* against the teeming *Torat hesed* of the yeshiva world in general and of the Brisker tradition, in particular. Included in a list of topics posed by students for discussion, I once received the query: "In the course of our learning, do we apprehend the mind of Rishonim or do we merely study ourselves?" I responded then and I submit now that there is a third alternative: we learn the Torah of Rishonim. This *katuv hashelishi* asserts that the focus of our legacy from these luminary spirits is not just themselves but their corpus. It may indeed perhaps be doubtful whether in codifying his positions regarding, say, the status of *ohel zaruk* or the exemption of *hefker* from the obligation to set apart *hallah*, the Rambam personally sought to communicate everything Reb Haym expounded by way of explication. And yet that ought not deter the exposition. The potential for the whole of *Hiddushei Rabbenu Haym Halevi* is surely latent within the raw material of the *Mishneh Torah* – within its individual components and the sum total of their interrelation – although it may have taken a genius of Reb Haym's stature to extract and elucidate its content. And that is what primarily concerns us. To paraphrase a celebrated and previously cited passage from the Yerushalmi:

אפילו מה שתלמיד ותיק עתיד לחדש בפירוש דבריו נאמר על ידי רבנו משה בן מיימון לדורות.

Everything which a seasoned disciple will innovate in explaining his words was stated by Rabbenu Mosheh ben Maimon for posterity.

Would the Rambam have recognized his own recast handiwork? Let us assume that the point is moot. But have we forgotten the gemara's wondrous imaginative portrayal of Mosheh Rabbenu's experience in an analogous situation. Having been transported in a vision to Rabbi Akiva's *bet midrash*, he is at first astounded and yet, subsequently, becalmed:

הלך וישב בסוף שמנה שורות ולא היה יודע מה הן אומרים תשש כחו כיון שהגיע לדבר אחד אמרו לו תלמידיו רבי מנין לך אמר להן הלכה למשה מסיני נתיישבה דעתו.

He went and sat behind eight rows, and he could not comprehend what was being said. In consequence, his strength was sapped [i.e. his spirits sagged.] When he [i.e. Rabbi Akiva] reached a certain point, his students asked him: "Our rebbi, whence [do you know this]?" He replied: "It is a Halakhah transmitted to Mosheh from Sinai." At that point, he [i.e. Mosheh] was assuaged.[40]

With respect to the Rambam or Rabbenu Tam, too, then, there is a narrow *Torat emet* and an expansive *Torat hesed*, the latter no less true than the former, although, possibly, in a different sense and with a different focus.

But, it will be objected, the comparison does not hold. Primal Torah can be dichotomized into the absolute and the revealed because in the process of *matan Torah*, its Source has chosen to create and transmit an entity of open-ended "Torah which has been handed to *hakhmei Yisrael*." *Hakhmei Yisrael*, themselves, however, had neither the authority nor the desire to license such development. Hence, their dicta can only be perceived as their personal interpretive elucidation, whether as gloss or elaboration, of the basic corpus rather than as laying the foundations for subsequent discussion; and they must therefore be read purely in terms of subjective intent.

I grant that the critique is not without merit. Inasmuch as *hakhmei hamesorah* engage in explication of a canon to which they are responsible, and insofar as their role is judicial rather than legislative, the creative aspect of their labors, and the concomitant gestation of fresh texts for consideration by their successors, cannot compare with the process ascribed by Rishonim to original *ex cathedra matan Torah*. And yet, the fundamental analogy is valid. In a very real sense, *hakhmei Israel* throughout the ages are both receivers and donors of Torah. This is the essence of the course of *mesorah*. When the Mishnah states, משה קיבל תורה מסיני ומסרה ליהושע, "Mosheh received Torah from Sinai and handed it to Yehoshua,"[41] it did not merely state that he passed it along, as if it were a baton in a relay race. It rather meant to convey that, having been given Torah, Mosheh mastered it, thus acquiring it, so that he then transmitted it as a legacy. The *pasuk* in Malakhi speaks of תורת משה עבדי, "the Torah of Mosheh, my servant;" and Rabbi Yossi ben Rabbi Hanina boldly asserts:

לא ניתנה תורה אלא למשה ולזרעו שנאמר כתב לך פסל לך מה פסולתן שלך אף כתבן שלך ומשה נהג בה טובת עין ונתנה לישראל ועליו הכתוב אומר טוב עין הוא יבורך.

Torah was but given to Mosheh and to his progeny, as is stated, "Write thee [these words]," "Hew thee." As the chips [of the tablets] are to be yours, so likewise the text. Yet Mosheh, acting out of generosity, gave it to Israel; and of him, the verse says, "He that has a bountiful eye, shall be blessed."[42]

Mosheh's spiritual progeny have, likewise a dual corpus: their *Torat emet* – that which, as best as can be perceived, constitutes, an accurate statement of their consciously willed position; and their *Torat hesed* – the possible multiple readings of their dicta which, in a sense, lead their own lives, regarded both as independent entities and in relation to the halakhic order as a whole. Indirectly, they thus enrich the world of Halakhah progressively, the increment being in no way at variance with the core, but innovative nonetheless.

The analogy to *matan Torah* serves to differentiate our problem from parallel discussions. The question of whether a work should be primarily defined, studied, and appreciated with reference to intent or content is of course not peculiar to Halakhah. Readers of *The Personal Heresy*, a series of debates – a model of urbane, civilized, and incisive discourse – between E.M.W. Tillyard and C.S. Lewis, will recall that, at mid-century, the issue served as a focus of controversy within the world of esthetic, and especially literary, criticism; and it reverberated then through much of the dispute, often acrimonious, between historical and so-called "New" critics.

That controversy centered, however, upon defining and striking an optimal balance between artist and reader. It dealt with the reliability of criticism torn loose from historical moorings; with the dangers of arbitrariness and the implications of constant shifts in the presumed meaning of a poem or a painting; with the extent to which an author can be assumed to have been fully aware of the impact of his work and its concomitant associations; with the prerogative of a reader to explicate with reference to his own ambient culture rather than the artist's. These factors are relevant with respect to Torah as well – although the analogy of Halakhah and art is open to question. Does one assess the "intentional fallacy" with regard to physics? Beyond them, however, we must consider a countervailing element: the process of renewed *matan Torah*. Its import is clear and relevant. A *talmid hakham* who, in interpreting a *rishon*, possibly goes beyond the latter's presumed intention is not just engaged in subjective learning. He is rather exercising the right and the duty with which that *rishon* has invested him: to examine objective content of his *Torat hesed*.

The analogy with law in general is more to the point; but here, again, we should be mindful of difference as well as similarity. To believe, as a Jew must, in the uniqueness of *Knesset Yisrael* and *torat Israel*, is to believe also in the uniqueness of their historical development; to assert, אין מזל לישראל, "Israel is not subject to Fortune" – nor, wholly, to the causal nexus. In our case, this means that we should understand that the legitimacy and desirability of *Torat hesed* does not derive from its being sufficiently flexible to adapt to societal stresses and changed historical circumstances, but from its own internal character, from the fact that it was given through a process of *vayered*, "and He descended," as, avowedly, *lo bashamayim he*, "It is not in Heaven." And if not in Heaven, then surely not ensconced within the confines of subjective intent.

The readiest comparison relates to critical and intellectual trends which have obtained currency and prominence during the last two decades: deconstruction and postmodernism. And indeed, attention has periodically been called to possible links between these movements and Jewish, and even Talmudic, modes of thought and language. These attempts are not without foundation; but, if I understand their arcane formulation roughly, my own views, developed independently of these theories, are far from coinciding with much of their content. The primary difference, and it is crucial, relates, again to scope. On both moral and literary grounds, I neither espouse nor cherish a general subjectivism in relation to texts, with the denudation and chaos this sometimes invites. The course I have charted is preeminently the prerogative of acknowledged masters – specifically, of *talmidei hakhamim*, and of students who ride their coattails. And it is theirs because of the unique character of Torah as multifaceted revelation.

Given this general approach, several caveats are nonetheless in order. First, what has been suggested pertains primarily to interpretation and exposition. The situation may alter somewhat with reference to *psak*. Insofar as texts stimulate and illuminate, on a particular reading, and are integrated into a *posek*'s train of thought, there is of course no difference. However, to the extent that earlier decisors are cited as sources, by way of reliance upon precedent and authority, *Torat hesed* may be significantly modified. In that case, it is presumably the personal voice of the Rosh or the Rivash that is being invoked, with all that their stature and prestige entail. Full weight can only be properly assigned, however, when fidelity to the substance and tone of their dicta obtains; and to that end, we need attend not only to what Rishonim could or might have thought but to what they presumably intended.

Second, *Torat hesed* entails the expansion of a base, of a core which was given, *ab initio*, at Sinai, and, subsequently, by *hakhmei hamesorah*. It operates primarily at the level of analytic interpretation. We must ascertain, however, that the data being interpreted has, indeed, been, literally, given. To this end, philology and the determination of accurate textual *girsa'ot* is significant, in helping us determine what, at the primary level – in which language and with which lexicographic meaning – has been said. Inevitably, we will encounter gray areas, with respect to which we may entertain different views as to what is literal and what is interpretive. The basic distinction is, however, clear.

Third, while, as the Ramban noted, *hesed* connotes expansive *hitpashtut* and the bursting of limits, it is not boundless. Virtually *a priori*, parameters of legitimate interpretation need to be determined to assure that *Torat hesed* be consonant with canons of reason, on the one hand, and with norms of tradition on the other. In this respect, the guidance of *mesorah* is critical – the practice *of gedolei Yisrael* no less than their precept. גדולה שימושה של תורה יותר מלימודה. "The apprenticed service of Torah is greater than its study."[43] That practice is most keenly manifested with respect to the attitude to Hazal – not only deferential but reverential. Its votaries are not content with grudging acceptance of the dicta of Amoraim, to whose halakhic authority they submit. They, rather, gladly acknowledge Hazal's superiority. They seek to probe the gemara's interpretations and to plumb the depths of its formulations – but all in a spirit of humility and awe before the creative genius and personal stature of its masters.[44]

In conclusion, I believe it may be fairly stated that the facet of Torah study which has been our focus is particularly characteristic of the yeshiva world. Quite apart from spiritual and ideological differences between the halls of academia and the *bet midrash*, they generally differ, methodologically, as well. The world of *Wissenschaft* envisions itself as primarily devoted to *Torat emet*. It focuses upon facts, is committed to the hegemony of authorial intent, and is marked by a measure of austerity – critics would say, of aridity. It bears, in sum, a monistic cast. It of course stresses, often contentiously, the element of change and development within Halakhah. Given a historicist orientation, however, this is frequently ascribed to external factors, and is thus perceived as a corrosive process, reflecting presumed relativism.

The yeshiva community, by contrast, is largely engaged in *Torat hesed* – although, admittedly, not all of its members would accept the account herein suggested. It is primarily – at times, excessively – oriented to ideas rather than facts. It luxuriates in efflorescence, its universe of discourse teeming with burgeoning thought; and it thrives upon examining possibility and conjecture. It, too, acknowledges development, but regards it as a preeminently internal dynamic, the realization of אפילו מה שתלמיד ותיק עתיד להודות נאמר למשה בסיני, of that innovation by seasoned disciples which, in a sense, had already been transmitted to Mosheh at Sinai, which in no way undermines the inherent integrity of Halakhah.

    Ultimately, the *ben Torah* strives for the interrelated apprehension of both facets of *devar Hashem* – "As my two eyes," in Robert Frost's phrase, "are one in sight." He seeks the seminal kernal of *emet*, even as he traces its diverse course within the ambient world of *Torat hesed*. Full coincidence is possibly reserved, if at all, for meta-history – when, as some Kabbalists would have it, the provenance of the views of Bet Hillel will be superseded by *psak* in accordance with those of Bet Shammai. Meanwhile, we glory in the enterprise, both prerogative and responsibility, of creative understanding. Perhaps both aspects are suggested by a single *pasuk*: פיה פתחה בחכמה, "She opened her mouth with wisdom," possibly that of *Torat emet*, ותורת חסד על לשונה, "And *Torat hesed* is on her tongue."

Notes

1. In *nusah Ashkenaz* of the concluding *berakhah* of *shemoneh essrei*, a third term appears: *Torat haym*, "the Torah of life."
2. *Malakhi* 2:6. The possible referents I cited are suggested by Radak. Rashi cites Elazar as well. Both agree that a specific historical referent is intended. One could, however, conceivably interpret the passage as referring, typologically, to an ideal *kohen*; cf. Hagigah 15b.
3. *Mishlei* 31:26. See commentaries of Rishonim, *ad locum*.
4. Clear, that is, in liturgical and common usage. In *Malakhi*, however, Radak assumes that the focus is upon consistency and personal integrity: כמו שהיתה תורת ה' בפיו שהיה מורה אותה מורה לרבים כן היתה בלבו זהו תורת אמת שלא היה בפה אחד ואחד בלב זהו ועולה לא נמצא בשפתיו.
5. Shabbat 2:3. The Rambam goes on to ascribe the view that *pikuah nefesh* does not override Shabbat to heretics who misrepresent the substance of Halakhah and its sensitivity to human needs.

6. Sukkah 49b. It is noteworthy that, on the second view, the term applies to Torah which is learned with the intention of teaching it, even if one has yet to realize that goal.

7. I trust it is self-evident that the distinction herein suggested in no way contravenes the thrust of the question posed by the gemara in Sukkah or the responses cited. The questioner is puzzled by the possibility that one could conceive of Torah divorced from *hesed*. The respondents accept the premise of linkage with regard to content, but point out respects in which the prospect of Torah with or without *hesed* can nevertheless be entertained, at the objective plane. This does not foreclose the possibility of alternative distinctions concerning the phrase, for terminological purposes.

8. *Bereshit Rabbah* 1:14.

9. See *Vayikra* 20:17, and Ibn Ezra, *ad locum*.

10. *Sefer Ravya*, sec. 168; 1:181.

11. The criticism may be variously understood. Aptowitzer takes it to refer to the opening and closing sections of the *berakhah*. I am more inclined to assume that the need for both the *berakhah* which precedes the reading and that which follows is questioned, if both refer solely to Torah. The question of the extent of the thematic gap between the *berakhot* may be of halakhic relevance in determining whether one needs to repeat; *b'diavad*, if he has erroneously reversed the sequence. See *Orah Haym* 139:4 and aharonim thereon.

12. *Tur Orah Haym*, 139.

13. Hagigah 3b. The JPS rendering of *netu'im*, in line with the Vulgate's *defixi*, obviously has mechanical, rather than organic, associations.

14. Eruvin 13b; cf. Yevamot 14a. The adjective, *hayyim*, could refer either to God, i.e., "the words of the living God," or to the words proper. The former would be analogous to *Devarim* 5:23, where *kol E-lohim hayyim*, clearly refers to E-lohim, as *kol* is in the singular. However, in our context, I intuit that the referent is *divrei*, and I have translated accordingly.

15. Kiddushin 40a. It should be noted that the credit cited does not pertain to thought as such but, rather, to thought which is, virtually, regarded as action.

16. Sec. 80. In the citation from the gemara, it is not clear whether it is Rav or the anonymous redactor who notes that Rabbi Hiyya's view has been rejected.

    See *Hiddushei Haritva*, Makkot 11a, who contends that it is unthinkable that Rabbi Hiyya would have worn invalid *tefillin*, and therefore prefers a reading which relates the discussion to *sifrei Torah*, with respect to which the use of linen thread is more of an open question. Cf. *Sh'eylot Uteshuvot Rav Po'olim*, 4:2.

17. *Hiddushei Haritva*, Eruvin 13b, s.v. *elu*. The term *drash* may either refer to imaginative and speculative interpretation, or to a specific midrashic text. The editor of the Ritva, in the Mossad Harav Kook edition, assumes the latter and cites *Midrash Shohar Tov, Teh.* 12:4.

18. Sanhedrin 4:2.

19. The view of controversy as a mishap, and the concomitant desire to limit it, is of course, found in Hazal. See *Tosefta*, Sanhedrin 7:1 and Hagigah 2:4; and Sanhedrin 88b. I believe, however, that these statements refer to a continual *mahloket*, with possibly attendant acrimony, which

festers without being resolved in accordance with the relevant halakhic procedure. For a succinct and stimulating discussion of attitudes towards controversy, see Shalom Rosenberg, *Lo Bashamayim He* (Alon Shevut, 1997), pp. 57ff.

20. *Tosafot Rabbenu Perez Hashalem*, ed. R. Haym Dickman, Eruvin 13b, s.v. *elu v'elu*. Cf. Rashi, Ketubot 57a, s.v. *ha;* and see Rosenberg, *LBH*, pp. 50ff.

    Hagigah 3b. Cf. Sanhedrin 34a: דבי ר' ישמעאל תנא וכפטיש יפוצץ סלע מה פטיש זה מתחלק לכמת ניצוצות אף מקרא אחד יוצא לכמה טעמים. However, there the focus is upon variegated readings, which are not, necessarily, contradictory.

22. Yerushalmi, Pe'ah 2:4.

23. *Loc. cit.* The verse cited (but with the omission of the word אדם) is from *Koh.* 1:10.

24. *Tosafot Sens*, on *Eduyot* 1:5. It is not clear whether, towards the end of the passage, the question regarding conclusive decision is posed to Mosheh or to the Ribbono Shel Olam.

    As to the total thrust of the passage, the Tosefta, 1:2, clearly understood that the Mishnah refers to the prospect of reliance upon the minority *in extremis*, בשעה גוסס, and not to a total reversal of the original *psak*. This is the view cited and adapted in the commentary of the Rabad, *ad locum*.

25. "A head which does not wear *tefillin*." See Rosh Hashanah 17a, and *Tosafot*, s.v. *karkafta*.

26. The Sheloh was scandalized by this possibility and he invokes mystical categories in order to reject it. He suggests that each *hakham*, in accordance with his level and his personality links up with a layer of the multiplanar roots of a given *mizvah* or Halakhah, and thus arrives at his own conception of it and its content. See *Bet Hakhmah*, in *Shnei Luhot Haberit* (Jerusalem, 5723), p. 19b. However, as I suggest, the issue can be resolved in purely rational terms.

27. See Shabbat 130a. The right – and, possibly, the duty – of an individual *talmid hakham* to act in accordance with his private judgment, even against collective authority, is of course a central issue, but lies beyond the pale of this discussion. Briefly stated, the prevalent view is that where, as in the period of the Sanhedrin, an issue had been discussed within a designated milieu, and a majority decision formally adopted, it is binding upon dissenters as well. However, where no such formal event had occurred, and the question is only the relevance of the general guideline יחיד ורבים הלכה כרבים, "If an individual is pitted against many, the Halakha is in accordance with the many," the principle is not binding upon the minority, or upon its constituents.

28. See *Nega'im* 4:11 and Niddah 19a.

29. Bava Mezia 86a.

30. Bava Mezia 59b.

31. See *Derashot Ha-Ran*, ed. Aryeh L. Feldman (Jerusalem, 1977), pp. 83–6, 111–114.

32. *Ktzot Hahoshen*, "Preface." For the midrash cited, see *Bereshit Rabbah*, 8:8.

33. Resp. 53. The recurrent reference to contemporary decisors, found in other discussions of *elu v'elu* as well, relates to the standing accorded to sages of each generation, at the primary level. In practice, it is of course qualified and, at times, even counterbalanced, by the acknowledged authority of earlier links in the tradition, to whom, of course, Rav Shimshon deferred.

34. Specifically, the Ramban states that Torah has dual content. At the mystical plane, it is an unbroken concatenation of divine names. At the rational, it consists of ordinary language and its elements are components of common speech, to be read as such: והיה אפשר קריאתה שתקרא על דרך השמות ותקרא על דרך קריאתנו בענין התורה והמצות (במהד' הרב ח.ד.שעוועל, עמ' ז').

35. *Mishlei* 8:22–3, 30. The use of the term *hokhmah* in *Mishlei*, as elsewhere, is multifaceted and has been the subject of much discussion. Its correlation with Torah here is derived from *Avot* 6:11 and Nedarim 39b.

36. See MT, *Teshuvah* 6:5 and the critique of the Rabad thereon.

37. *Ber.* 15:14.

38. Conceivably, the Ramban might have agreed with the basic position here set forth, but he does not apply it as he regards knowledge derived through a prophet as the equivalent of an explicit normative dispensation.

    The discussion of this theme is obviously bound up with the broader issue of antinomianism and *averah lishmah*; cf. Nahum Rakover, *Matarah Hamekadeshet et Ha-Emza'im* (Jerusalem, 2000), esp. ch. 2.

39. *Midrash Tanhuma, Pinhas*, 10; cf. Sanhedrin 38a and Berakhot 55a.

40. Menahot 29b.

41. *Avot* 1:1.

42. Nedarim 38a.

43. Berakhot 7b.

44. The issues raised in this paper require special treatment, both conceptual and empirical, insofar as they relate to the internal world of Hazal. That would take us far afield, however, and deserves independent consideration.

Chapter 4

A Consideration of Synthesis
from a Torah Point of View

Few matters concern us – both disturb and affect us – more than the relationship between our religious and secular studies. As students committed to Torah and the study of Torah, and yet deeply engaged in the pursuit of a general education, we feel – and should feel – a strong need to understand the respective positions of the two areas in our lives. The need is related to both our outlook and our experience. Philosophically, we recognize the necessity to determine how these varied aspects of our pluralistic culture coalesce within our overall *Weltanschauung*. Practically, we are often confronted with the need to reconcile the demands that these aspects make upon our loyalties and our energies. The formulation of a Torah attitude toward this question thus takes on paramount importance.

Torah as a Way of Life

How is such an attitude to be formulated? I think that it must rest upon three fundamental premises. The first must be a clear and unwavering recognition of the primacy of Torah as a way of life. This we posit as the supreme value – in a sense, as the *only* value. Fulfilling our spiritual destinies, furthering in ourselves and others the development of Torah, strengthening and deepening our consciousness and experience of God, stimulating our love, fear, and knowledge of Him – this is the alpha and the omega, our first, last, ever-present goal. Religion demands an axiological monopoly; *yihud Hashem* means simply that religion alone has absolute and comprehensive value. Everything else, no matter how socially or intellectually desirable, has only relative and secondary importance. Its worth is derived solely from the extent to which it contributes, however remotely, to the fulfillment of the divine will. On this point there can be no compromise and should be no misunderstanding. A man's religion means everything or it means nothing.

Torah Study

Our second premise is that the achievement of *hayyei Torah,* a Torah life, is dependent on *talmud Torah,* Torah study. *Yahadut* has always held that the highest development of the Jew's spiritual personality is impossible without the fullest exertion of his intellectual faculties – *lo am ha-aretz hasid.*

This is true for many reasons. Most obviously, study is a necessary prerequisite to proper religious observance. The fulfillment of moral and ritual norms is hardly possible without clear and accurate knowledge of both their general nature and their particular details. But, as was pointed out by the Bet HaLevi, *talmud Torah* is not merely a preliminary to observance. It is itself a *mizvah* – indeed, one of the most basic. Torah study, ideally conceived as both an intellectual exercise and a religious experience, is imposed by the Halakhah as a universal daily obligation. Insisting that God must be served with the head as well as with the hands and the heart, *yahadut* sees intellection as an integral aspect of the religious life of every individual. It has never seen religious study as the private preserve of an ecclesiastical hierarchy or of a privileged intellectual elite. On the contrary, it posits *talmud Torah* as the duty and destiny of all. It realizes that great success in the exercise of reason as part of man's search for God cannot come to all, or even to many, but it considers this no reason for abandoning the attempt. It is precisely for the effort, the *process* of the *recherche,* that the Halakhah presses most insistently. Of *yedi'at Ha-Torah,* the knowledge of Torah, Hazal has relatively little to say; but of *talmud Torah,* they can never say enough.

The significance of Torah study is twofold. First, it gives the Jew an insight, as direct and profound as man is privileged to attain, into the revealed will of his Creator. It affords us an opportunity to get (*salve reverentia*) a first-hand knowledge of the divine will, to deepen and broaden our minute understanding of God's infinite reason. In its essence, the Torah – particularly the Halakhah – constitutes an immanent expression of God's transcendent rational will. By studying its texts, analyzing its principles, and developing its ideas, we are able to approach, however haltingly, that unattainable goal toward which Mosheh Rabbenu strove so desperately – *hodi'eni na et derakhekha,* "Let me know Thy ways."

Insight into Divine Wisdom

Second, Torah study, when properly pursued, affects our total spiritual personality. Partly because it does afford us a better insight into inscrutable divine wisdom, and partly because it engages the mind – and with it the whole man – in pursuit of religious knowledge, it transmutes our innermost being. The knowledge we can acquire of God's will increases our conscious, and subconscious, awareness of Him; the very act of weighing His words or of analyzing His laws draws us imperceptibly nearer to Him and to them. *She-ma'or she-bah mahziran le-mutav* – the light of Torah returns us to Him. It matters not what segment of Torah we study. Provided that we approach it with an awareness of its true character, Bava Mezia will do as well as Berakhot, and Hallah will affect us no less than Avot. As was agreed by both the Ba'al Ha-Tanya and Rav Hayyim Volozhiner, respective pillars of Hasidut and Mitnaggedut, an analysis of the most technical minutiae of *mego lehotzi* or *hometz nukshah* in the proper context is, at bottom, spiritually uplifting. Torah study leaves an indelible imprint upon our total personality and, in the process, transforms it. Of course, it can only effect this spiritual renovation if we approach it with the proper attitude. If a fundamental awareness of the divine character of Torah is lacking, study can have little force. Indeed, if negatively approached, it may even have a pernicious effect: *lo zakhah (le-lomedah li-shmah ule-kayyemah* – Rashi), *na'aset lo sam mitah.* But given this basic acknowledgment, Torah study becomes the prime agent in effecting a gradual spiritual regeneration. Paradoxically, through a constant reciprocal process, it both sustains piety and is sustained by it. Keener study leads to greater piety, and more fervent devotion leads to profounder knowledge. The dialectical interplay of *talmud Torah* and *yir'at shammayim* is the heart of Torah life.

General Studies

If our first two premises are an insistence upon the primacy of Torah and an awareness of the overriding importance of Torah study, our third is the recognition of the great, albeit ancillary, value of a broad spectrum of general studies. The practical value of general studies is obvious. They provide both professional or vocational training and a general orientation toward the innumerable pragmatic exigencies of human life. These are, in themselves, matters of no little moment; but I am at present concerned with the directly spiritual significance of general studies. To begin on a negative note, secular knowledge is invaluable for an understanding of the environment in which we all, willy-nilly, find ourselves. No matter where we live, we are in the midst of a society that is generally indifferent, if not hostile, to religious values, one in which advancing the development of Torah entails an almost perpetual struggle. "Paganism," said Eliot, "has all the best advertising space." "And paganism" (to adapt a remark once made about the so-called genteel tradition) is best defeated "in the classical way, by understanding it." We cannot combat worldliness until we know what it stands for; we cannot refute the secularist unless we have mastered his arguments. Furthermore, if we wish not merely to react to our environment, but to act upon it, we must be thoroughly familiar with its mores and its values. If *Bnei Torah* are to exert some positive religious influence upon modern society, they must maintain some contact with it. To this end, secular study is virtually indispensable.

We may go even further. In our circumstances certainly, general knowledge is necessary not only for influencing others; it also helps us to preserve our faith. The Mishnah tells us that we should be able to answer the apikoros. The person it has in mind need not be a freethinker or an idolater.

There is an apikoros within, a serpent potentially lurking in the finest of Edens, and we must be ready to reply to his proffer of the bittersweet apple. But we must first read a treatise on serpentine psychology.

Aids to Torah Study

Secular knowledge is not merely a tactical weapon, however. It possesses considerable intrinsic merit. We may consider it under two headings. First, secular studies are often invaluable as a direct accessory to *talmud Torah* proper. Consider simply the aid we derive, by elucidation or comparison, from linguistics in Amos, history in Melakhim, agronomy in Zera'im, physiology in Niddah, chemistry in Hometz u-Matzah, philosophy in Yesodei Ha-Torah, psychology in Avodah Zarah, political theory in Sanhedrin, torts in Bava Batra – one could continue almost indefinitely. As the Gaon insisted, there is hardly a province of Halakhah for whose mastery scientific, historical, and linguistic knowledge is not only helpful but indispensable. If pursuing such knowledge is not *talmud Torah,* it is, at the very least, *hekhsher talmud Torah.* And contrary to the general assumption, it is precisely the weaker student who stands most in need of auxiliary aid of this kind. While learning Sanhedrin, R. Hayyim Brisker evolved his own political theory. Most of *us* merely fumble.

Develop Spiritual Personality

While the importance of general knowledge as a direct auxiliary in the study of Torah is great, it is perhaps even more significant in a third capacity. Secular studies possess immense intrinsic value insofar as they generally help to develop our spiritual personality. Time and again, they intensify our insight into basic problems of moral and religious thought. History and the sciences show us the divine revelation manifested in human affairs and the cosmic order. The humanities deepen our understanding of man: his nature, functions, and duties. In one area after another, a whole range of general studies sustains religion, supplementing and complementing it, in a sense deeper and broader than we have hitherto perceived. Of course, we cannot always see how a specific isolated detail can have such an effect. One could easily seize upon a minor point – say, L'Hospital's rule or the dates of Louis-Philippe's reign – and ask how that will improve us in any way. We should remember, however, that knowledge is attained only by degrees – nay, by minutes and seconds. Whether a specific fact is sufficiently relevant to merit study is a question that must be decided with reference to a particular context. No doubt one may lose wisdom in the search for knowledge, and knowledge in the search for information, but we shall continue to pursue all three. No one would contend that metrics or grammar has any intrinsic merit. Yet their value as instrumental knowledge led the Ramban and the Ba'al Ha-Maor to master the one, and all *gedolei Yisrael* to learn the other.

Nor should we be deterred by the illusion that we can find everything we need within our own tradition. As Arnold insisted, one must seek "the best that has been thought and said in the world," and if, in many areas, much of that best is of foreign origin, we should expand our horizons rather than exclude it. "Accept the truth," the Rambam urged, "from whomever states it." Following the precept and practice of Rabbenu Bahye, he adhered to that course himself; and we would be wise to emulate him.

The explicitly systematic discussions of Gentile thinkers often reveal to us the hidden wealth implicit in our writings. The Gentiles, furthermore, have their own wisdom, even of a moral and philosophic nature. Who can fail to be inspired by the ethical idealism of Plato, the passionate fervor of Augustine, or the visionary grandeur of Milton? Who can remain unenlightened by the lucidity of Aristotle, the profundity of Shakespeare, or the incisiveness of Newman? There is *hokhmah ba-goyim,* and we ignore it at our loss. Many of the issues that concern us have concerned Gentile writers as well. The very problem we are considering has a long Christian history, going back to Tertullian and beyond. To deny that many fields have been better cultivated by non-Jewish than by Jewish writers is to be stubbornly, and unnecessarily, chauvinistic. There is nothing in our medieval poetry to rival Dante, and nothing in our modern literature to compare with Kant, and we would do well to admit it. We have our own genius, and we have bent it to the noblest of pursuits, the development of Torah. But we cannot be expected to do everything.

Realistic Problems

I have so far been dealing with our question on a more or less ideal, abstract plane, on which the respective positions of Torah and *madda* can be neatly charted, and can be seen as existing in easy, perfect harmony. We are all well aware, however, that no such easy concord exists. We are only too familiar with complex problems and recurrent conflicts. Certainly, these problems neither can nor should be ignored; we slight them at our own peril. Indeed, they are so formidable that they have led many to question whether religious and secular studies can enjoy any fruitful relationship; whether, in the life of a *ben Torah,* there is any room at all for serious general education.

At Yeshiva University, of course, we take this for granted. Historically, however, the question has been persistently and fervidly debated – and at the very highest levels. *Hakhmei Yisrael* have clearly been divided. As the Rama put it, *zu makhloket yeshanah bein ha-hakhamim.* In Hazal proper, references to the problem are relatively few and, taken as a whole, rather inconclusive; they can be, and have been, interpreted in either direction. Subsequently, however, two conflicting views developed, and they have persisted, with alternating ascendancy, through the centuries.

If the Sephardic Rishonim were mostly in favor, the Ashkenazic were generally opposed. If the Maharal extolled philosophy, the Maharshal condemned it. R. Yisroel Salanter might send his prime students to the finest universities in Europe; but Volozhin, easily the greatest yeshiva of modern times, shut its doors rather than introduce the most limited of secular programs. We are dealing here with *gedolei Yisrael,* not mere obscurants. The problems arising from the integration of Torah and secular studies must have been pressing indeed if they produced such controversy – and they are still pressing. We would be committing the gravest folly were we to regard this controversy (as I am afraid many of us do) as a remotely irrelevant issue, almost as a historical curiosity. I have referred to it briefly to underscore its seriousness and, at the same time, to remind us of its pertinence. A question *gedolei Yisrael* could discuss with such fervent interest cannot be lightly dismissed.

Even if we feel justified in rejecting the verdict of some – we cannot, after all, agree with everyone – the very awareness that so many of our greatest men, before whom the best of us can only stand with bowed heads, steadfastly opposed secular studies, should in itself prove a sobering influence. By giving us the proper perspective, it may, above all, enable us to grasp the basic problems. For in the course of the controversy, virtually all the major questions concerning the relationship of religious and secular studies have been raised. These questions are so fundamental that any formulation of a Torah view on this issue must not merely answer them but consider them as part of its basic frame of reference.

The Danger of Secular Studies

What are the problems? The principal objections against secular studies will bring them into clear focus. To begin, it has been asserted that secular culture, especially of a freethinking nature, may exert a dangerously powerful influence over students, luring them from the fold of Jewish tradition. Hence, the discussion has tended to center around the question of studying philosophy.

It has also been argued that the study of even innocuous subjects constitutes a waste of precious time, time which might – nay, must – be spent more profitably in deepening and expanding one's knowledge and understanding of the Torah. Vocational training, so runs the argument, might be necessary, but every moment available for spiritual or intellectual concerns must be devoted solely to Torah study. Finally, many have objected that, quite apart from the time which they consume, secular studies weaken the individual's religious position simply by diverting his interest, thus sapping his personal resources. By focusing his attention elsewhere, often by riveting it upon trifling vanities, they drain him of intellectual and emotional energy. Diversification leads to both diversion and distraction; it leaves the student involved with irrelevant matters but unmindful of his vital religious concerns, "weeping the death of Dido for love of Aeneas, but weeping not his own death for want of love to Thee – as Augustine recalled of his early self in the *Confession.*"

Influence

First, the problem of influence. A consideration of influence leads us back to our initial premise. We have been concerned so far with the primacy of Torah on the axiological plane, in the realm of values. The primacy of Torah is also logical, however. We recognize it as the basis upon which all human culture, all arts and sciences, must stand. This recognition is two-fold. First, on the objective level, we see the Torah as the logical groundwork of all truth. Its principles constitute the premises to which everything else is related; and they provide a philosophic framework within which all knowledge attains meaning. Of course, the details of thermodynamics or of the declension of *pes* can hardly be referred back to a specific pasuk or Halakhah. In its totality, however, Torah constitutes the objective foundation of all truth: *istakkal be-oraita, bara alma.*

The Torah: The Basis

Second, Torah must be the subjective basis from which, as students, we judge all else. From a religious point of view, secular studies, especially the social sciences and the humanities, should derive not only their value but their meaning from a religious source. For us, Torah is at once the criterion of truth and the touchstone of value. Whatever the *ben Torah* reads, he will read through its eyes; whatever he studies, he must judge by its standards. Its *Weltanschauung* becomes the prism through which everything is seen. The importance of viewing all subjects with a critical appraisal of their relation to Torah can hardly be exaggerated. Failure to do so can only lead, at best, to intellectual schizophrenia. Whatever the Hegelians may say about history, in education, the successive independent study of thesis and antithesis hardly produces synthesis. "Literary criticism," Eliot wrote, "should be completed by criticism from a definite ethical and theological viewpoint." This may be applied to virtually every field of study. Of course, it does not apply with equal force to all areas. Some subjects – the humanities, for instance – are closer to our religious life than others. Even within the same subject, some aspects are more significant – potentially more enlightening and more dangerous – than others. In all areas, however, Torah furnishes at least a perspective. In some, its relation is much more direct, as it may give us specific guidance.

In a larger sense, the need for a religious approach to secular culture is universal. At one point or another, everyone is in contact with secularism. And critical appraisal in the light of Torah is particularly necessary precisely at those points at which we tend to lower our guard.

I doubt that any yeshiva student has ever been much corrupted by Augustine's *Confessions* or Aquinas's *Summa*. But can the same be said of Ibsen's drama and Whitman's poetry? Berlioz's music and Titian's art? Do we recognize the determinism latent in the writings of so many social scientists – often so pervasive as to be assumed rather than stated? Are we taken in by the quasi-religion of an Emerson or a Carlyle? Do we judge political events by religious standards? Our scrutiny must perhaps be keenest when we are furthest from the library or lecture hall. To return to Eliot, "Explicit ethical and theological standards" must be especially applied to "works of imagination." All of us may be influenced by these.

The Primacy of Torah

The position I have been advancing suggests a practical corollary. If secular culture is to be judged from a religious perspective, religious knowledge is an obvious prerequisite to its study. Ideally, the primacy of Torah should therefore also be chronological. This is, indeed, what the Rambam held – *venimmuko imo*. The student's understanding of his own religious outlook should always be more perceptive and more advanced than his appreciation of corresponding secular viewpoints.

There is, however, a practical difficulty. How is one to know when he is ready? There is no simple answer. Every student's situation is different, and each case must be decided on its individual merits. With regard to the study of idolatry, Hazal established the principle of *lo tilmad la'asot, aval attah lomed lehavin u'le-horot* – "You shall not study (if it may lead) to practice, but you may study in order to understand and pass judgment." When may one venture, confident of his purpose? The question must be decided on the basis of individual circumstances. A second difficulty is that, in some cases, the lack of early religious training makes the priority of Torah knowledge almost impossible. Under these circumstances, the gap may be partially filled by guidance from friends and teachers (to some extent, such guidance is needed by all of us). But in any event, it is important that the principle be kept intact.

Some may find my position illiberal. Perhaps it is. But are we to sacrifice eternal salvation on the altar of untrammeled objective inquiry? The danger of having our faith undermined by our studies is one which we dare not underestimate. Ideas are potent. They are powerful agents, directly affecting the growth of our spiritual personality.

"It must never be forgotten," Whitehead declared, "that education is not a process of packing articles in a trunk.... Its nearest analogue is the assimilation of food by a living organism, and we all know how necessary to health palatable food under suitable conditions is. When you have put your boots in a trunk, they will stay there until you take them out again; but this is not at all the case if you feed a child with the wrong food." Of course, we prefer to think we have passed out of our nonage. But adults also watch their diets.

If nothing else, the success of modern propaganda has taught us how naive was Mill's notion that the free clash of ideas must result in the triumph of truth. Falsehood does not always stick to the rules. We must be on our guard, and we must not venture out of our depth. Objectivity is fine, but one should beware of indifference. If knowledge is to be meaningful, it must be approached with a point of view. In engrossing ourselves in the "objective" study of a subject, there is danger that we may forget why we wanted to study it in the first place; hence the need for seeing it in a Torah perspective. Absolute *perishut* is the wrong solution, but *zehirut* must be unrelenting.

Our second major problem, no less pressing than the first, is of a more practical nature: simply a matter of budget. Working within the bounds of limited time and energy, we are constantly confronted by the need to balance the conflicting demands imposed by various studies. We return once again to our fundamental premises. Thus, translating the primacy of Torah into pragmatic terms, we must make the study of Torah our principal intellectual endeavor. Especially during our formative educational period, the high school and college years, it is imperative that we devote the major portion of our time and effort to *talmud Torah.* First and foremost, above and beyond all personal and professional ambitions, every student at Yeshiva College should have one overriding aim: to become a *talmid hakham.*

If *talmud Torah* gets the lion's share of our attention, general studies nevertheless are left with a sizable portion. The purists, of course, see them as a waste of time. One must point out, however, that we are dealing with a quantitative rather than a qualitative problem – not a question of whether to study, but how much. If the principle of *bittul Torah* were to be carried out consistently to its logical conclusion, then in applying it to, say, mathematics, we should stop teaching children how to count. The suggestion has yet to be entertained. Where, then, are we to stop? With multiplication? Fractions? Square roots? Logarithms? Determinants? Complex numbers? Clearly, budgeting is a process of weighing *sakhar ke-neged sakhar,* advantage against advantage; and again it should be obvious that no single answer can be offered.

It would be ridiculous to insist upon a uniform standard of so much or so little secular education for all students at all times. Conditions vary, and vary widely. The point of diminishing returns – that at which the loss due to time spent on secular studies exceeds their contribution to the cause of Torah – differs in every case. For some, no doubt, a double program at the college level is too much. For many if not most, stretching the college program over the summers, adding a fifth year, or both, would be highly advisable. The principle to be kept in mind, however, is that the student's development as a *talmid* must come first. As to everything else, a proper sense of proportion must be preserved.

I have hitherto been concerned with the liberal phase of education, that which merely concerns our development as human beings. As Hazal recognized, however, education also has a professional aspect – *le-lammedo ummanut.* This aspect presents a new problem. Hopefully, many students, especially the better ones, will go on to find careers in working for Torah, either in the rabbinate or in education. For these, professional study (one hates to call it that) will happily coincide with further intensive *talmud Torah.* Such a course cannot be followed by all, however; and for those hoping to enter other fields, the problem of budgeting time acquires a new dimension. Particularly in a period so dominated by specialization, placing the primary emphasis upon the study of Torah would seem to block the path to professional success. Our fundamental thesis remains unshaken, however. As liberal educators from Newman to Hutchins have argued, full professional preparation should come in graduate school rather than in college. The graduate student, like the practitioner, may have to shift his emphasis, but the critical college years should focus upon personal development, and this means upon growth as a *ben Torah.*

Of course, college also has a strong bearing upon a student's future. Some will never attend graduate school, and even for those who do, previous college preparation is important. But no matter – first things first. Students who find that their general education interferes unduly with their religious studies could, as I have suggested, stretch out their college program. However, many should be able to combine the two areas. An undergraduate program is not quite that rigorous. Good students putting in what most schools consider a full day on the study of Torah should still be able to pursue a serious college program. Of course, this would require diligence. Full concentration, no frills, no flimflam. But it can be done.

Commitment

The final problem, that of diversion, must be met by a single word: commitment. Realizing the danger of possible distraction, we can avert it by sincere dedication. We must recognize that, deeply involved as we are in other fields, we are committed to only one thing: Torah. This commitment should be both profound and comprehensive. It cannot merely involve an occasional resolution. Commitment is the permanent recognition, both emotional and intellectual, that Torah is our principal concern. Whatever else we may be doing, we know that Torah and its study, the conscious development of our spiritual personality, is the main thing. Compelling reasons may temporarily force us to lay it aside; but we can hardly wait to return. As Rabbenu Tam said, there can be no *heseh ha-da'at,* no distraction, with regard to *talmud Torah.* Any other activity, whether auxiliary to Torah or independently necessary, we regard as incidental. We have only one spiritual destiny: *Lalekhet ba-hem,* says the Sifre, *ve-lo lippater mitokham.* We can never be done with the study of Torah.

Hence, even in later life, when many will find it necessary to devote the bulk of their energies to earning a livelihood, *talmud Torah* can never cease. Indeed, one should always recognize that *torato ummanuto,* one's main occupation is *talmud Torah,* all else is secondary. As the Rosh pointed out, primacy is not measured by the crude yardstick of time. Most likely, the financier and the grocer spend more time working than studying. What is important is, first, the value-judgment, and second, the determination to devote one's spare time to the study of Torah. A person's avocation – that to which he turns with joy when the fetters of obligation have been cast off – reveals more of his character than does his vocation. As *Bnei Torah,* committed to a life of Torah, we shall know where to turn.

Lifelong study, quite apart from its intrinsic importance, is what gives this commitment a focus. It provides us with an activity that indeed renders everything incidental. Only through study, furthermore, can our total religious life become meaningful.

As Coleridge so keenly perceived, faith can be neither profound nor enduring where the intellect is not fully and actively engaged in the quest for God: "The energies of the intellect, increase of insight, and enlarging views, are necessary to keep alive the substantial faith in the heart. They are the appointed fuel to the sacred fire." Where the mind is dormant, the whole man becomes torpid.

Conclusion

In conclusion, I should like to place our whole problem in a somewhat broader perspective. Ultimately, one's view of the relation of secular and religious studies depends upon a corresponding attitude toward the relation of religious and secular life. On the one hand, there may be a dualistic conception that would set up a rigid barrier between the two, a conception that conceives of man's purely natural life as intrinsically corrupt, that sees the religious as established not upon the secular but despite it; that, in short, considers *kodesh* and *hol* not simply distinct but disjunct. On the other hand, we have a unified conception that stems from a deep-seated belief that life is basically one, that the secular and religious aspects of human experience are in fundamental harmony, the latter perfecting rather than destroying the former; and finally, that while *kodesh* and *hol* are neither identical nor coextensive, they are contiguous and continuous. I think that the attitude of Torah is clearly aligned with the latter view, with what a Canadian scholar has called "the principle of integration." Our whole *Weltanschauung,* from eschatology to ethics, is firmly grounded upon the profound conviction that the physical, the natural, the secular, is not to be destroyed but to be sanctified. The Halakhah stresses not rejection but inclusion, not segregation but transmutation. It has never sought to mutilate life in some Procrustean bed. Rather, with its vitality, flexibility, and breadth, the Halakhah has repeatedly proved to be as expansive and as inclusive as life itself. Its catholicity, its magnificent sweep, and its extraordinary scope – these are of its essence. The Torah is neither world-accepting nor world-rejecting. It is world-redeeming. In the education of a *ben Torah,* therefore, there is room for both secular and religious studies. Not equal room, to be sure; the obverse of integration is the hierarchy of value, and within that hierarchy, Torah reigns supreme. At bottom, however, the comprehension of Torah's outlook establishes a rich education as the basis of a rich life. The final word is with integration and harmony.

Chapter 5

The End of Learning

I would like to preface this evening's lecture with two preliminary and admittedly personal remarks.

First, I cannot but acknowledge the presence of *mori ve-rabbi*, my master and mentor, Rav Aaron Soloveichik. Ever since I first entered his *shi'ur* forty years ago, he has been to me a polestar of integrity and a font of inspiration, a role model whose image and message have influenced me in so many critical respects. My debt to him is beyond words; and I am deeply moved by the honor he has accorded me by his presence.

Second, a word about my slightly anomalous position with respect to the ongoing discussion of the issue of *Torah u-madda*. Something funny happened to me on the way to this forum. During the decade that I spent on the faculty of the Rabbi Isaac Elhanan Theological Seminary, I poured much energy into *talmud Torah* and pressed, vigorously and continually, for enhancing its quality and stature at Yeshiva University. Apart from my regular *shi'ur*, I was privileged to be instrumental in rejuvenating the *kollel* and, *inter alia,* had a hand, albeit a secondary one, in the molding of many who went on to become YU Roshei Yeshiva. Seventeen years after our aliyah, having gone on to engage in the study and dissemination of Torah in Eretz Yisrael, I find myself cast in the eyes of some, including former *talmidim,* as an apostle of culture. An explanatory comment may therefore be in order, so that my own view of the matter will be clear.

I do not believe that my principled position concerning the value of culture has changed drastically over the last twenty years – although, at the level of educational implementation, contextual circumstances must obviously be taken into account. I held then, and hold ever more firmly now, that Torah is the heart of our personal and collective spiritual existence – *ki heim hayyenu ve-orekh yameinu* ("For they [i.e., the elements of Torah] are our life and length of days" and I held then, and hold now, that this existence can be enhanced by the enriching and energizing force of general culture. What has changed is the social and intellectual milieu within which such views are conceived and articulated.

I trust it is self-evident that if I speak, as I shall tonight, of the Jewish value of humanistic culture, I do so with an eye to maintaining a certain balance, Torah being primary and central, and all else, ancillary. If that balance is upset, its redress may require different counterpoises, depending on the source and direction of the disequilibrium. In the 1960s, there was no doubt but that the cause of Torah had to be pressed, massively and constantly. Today, we have, thank God, witnessed a resurgence of *talmud Torah* in all segments of the Orthodox world. Unfortunately, albeit understandably, however, that has often been accompanied by what I would regard as an excessive decline of the cultural component. Hence, the need to emphasize its importance in order to strive to restore an optimal balance. Needless to say, emphasis upon the centrality of Torah is perennially necessary, and doubly so when the Jewish world is enveloped by an ambient secular society. However, at a time when even many Yeshiva University students attend college for vocational rather than intellectual reasons, there exists a concomitant need to elucidate the spiritual value of a general education.

My remarks this evening are, in one sense, narrowly focused; but at the same time, they are presented in the context of a broader current debate over the humanities, their place in society and in the educational system that presumably prepares the young for life in society. Probably few in this audience are familiar with the Summer 1983 issue of *Daedalus,* wholly devoted to the subject of "The Arts and Humanities in America's Schools." Its first half celebrates the impressive achievements of certain select schools, while the second laments the bleak picture prevalent in the broader educational establishment. This picture, and the questions it raises, is starkly delineated in the preface. "Our failure," wrote Stephen R. Graubard,

> is not partial. It is not that we know how to teach English, but that French eludes us; not that we know how to teach economics, but that eighteenth-century diplomacy is boring; it is simply that the relevance of all – or any of these subjects – is obscure. This is another way of saying that we do not know what competencies we wish to instill in the young, that we no longer understand why writing well or speaking correctly matters.[1]

Presumably, many more of you are familiar with some recent books – Allan Bloom's *The Closing of the American Mind*, E.D. Hirsch Jr.'s *Cultural Literacy*, or *What Do Our 17-Year-Olds Know? A Report on the First National Assessment of History and Literature* by Diane Ravitch and Chester E. Finn Jr. – all bemoaning the sad state of humanistic education in this country and pregnant with apprehension about the implications of ignorance for the future of the American polity.

As previously indicated, my own presentation this evening is both independent of, and yet related to, the broader debate. It is independent in the sense that I speak out of concern for the Jewish – and particularly, the Torah – world, rather than the local venue; and the priorities and problems of that world with respect to the humanities differ markedly from those of Newark or Scarsdale, of inner-city cauldrons or exurban oases. And yet it is related, because the central issue is not one of means but of ends; not of how best to study or teach history or literature, but, if at all, why. "It is simply that the real relevance of all – or any of these subjects – is obscure." It is to this crucial question – I might almost add, to this question alone – that I address myself tonight. I shall not deal extensively with either the demand, normative and/or axiological, for total preoccupation with *talmud Torah*, narrowly defined, or with the possible conflict between humanistic sources and values and a true Torah worldview. These issues are crucial to any discussion of *Torah u-madda*; and I have, in part, dealt with them elsewhere,[2] and hope to return to them in the future.[3] However, the question frequently raised today is far more radical. It is simply: What is the use? Who really needs Plato or Pico? Quite apart from the potential conflicts, of what value are humanistic studies per se?

The query is multipronged. Some acknowledge the intrinsic value of humanistic studies as a civilizing influence, but regard them as superfluous for a *ben Torah,* who imbibes such influences, more purely and more richly, from our own sources. Others, even among those who do not reject secular studies categorically, go further and question whether any benefit whatsoever is in prospect. Drawing a clear distinction between the sciences and the humanities, they contend that the former deal with objective truth, and do so with rigorous precision, while the latter concern themselves with subjective constructs and perceptions. The study of nature, perhaps even normatively mandated, relates to the divine order, the humanities to cultural artifacts. Moreover, chemistry and mathematics are universal, history and literature merely local. Finally, there is, of course, the pragmatic consideration, collective and personal. Many who have never heard of Francis Bacon's *The Advancement of Learning* have nevertheless imbibed the essence of his equation of knowledge with power or of his contention that anyone who wishes to be Nature's master must first be apprenticed as her slave. No matter how arcane scientific research, it can generate the faith that inspired Faraday's response to Queen Victoria's query about the usefulness of electricity: "Of what use is a little baby?" On a personal level, concomitantly, the sciences are perceived as providing the technology that ameliorates and possibly enriches life, and as the key to a prestigious and remunerative livelihood.

The humanities, by contrast, are bereft of both profit and glamour. They unlock no secrets and create no marvels. Their progress is dubious; Aristotle's *Poetics* or *Nicomachean Ethics* still being avidly discussed long after his *Physics* had been deemed beneath notice of all but historians or antiquaries. As for personal gain, they make one a livelier dinner companion, but tangible pragmatic rewards are barely perceptible. Small wonder, then, that for many contemporary Roshei Yeshiva, as for seventeenth-century Puritan divines, if secular studies are to be seriously pursued at all, let it be the sciences rather than the humanities. They are both safer and more rewarding.

What, then, do I offer you as an alternative? Some of you may be puzzled by the title of this lecture. It does not, of course, denote "the termination of Torah study," although I gather that some critics have half-jokingly taken it as such, and I will admit to having anticipated this reading and puckishly selected the caption nonetheless. Seriously, however, it refers to the *telos* of study, and is drawn from an essay, "Of Education," by one of the greatest of religious poets. "The end, then, of learning," wrote Milton,

> is, to repair the ruins of our first parents by regaining to know God aright, and out of that knowledge to love him, to imitate him, to be like him, as we may the nearest by possessing our souls of true virtue, which being united to the heavenly grace of faith makes up the highest perfection. But because our understanding cannot in this body found itself but on sensible things, nor arrive so clearly to the knowledge of God and things invisible as by orderly conning over the visible and inferior creature, the same method is necessarily to be followed in all discreet teaching.[4]

Milton here posits both an end and a means. To the former, we can surely assent wholeheartedly, unless we take exception to the possibly Christian emphasis upon original sin and heavenly grace; or, perhaps, unless we interject, in the spirit of R. Hayyim Volozhiner, that some learning may be for its own sake, pure and simple. As to the means, as committed *Bnei Torah,* we can hardly assert that "orderly conning over the visible and inferior nature" is the sole avenue to "true virtue." Neither can we question, however, that it is *an* avenue to both the possession and the exercise of virtue. Knowledge of the *Ribbono shel Olam*'s work is indeed both illuminating and ennobling.

But what is the apex of that world? We need only open a Humash for the unequivocal answer:

> And God said: "Let us make man in our image, after our likeness; and let them have dominion over the fish of the sea, and over the fowl of the air, and over the cattle, and over all the earth, and over every creeping thing that creepeth over the earth." And God created man in His own image, in the image of God created He him; male and female created He them.

> (Bereshit 1:26–27).

Regardless of whether we adopt the anthropocentric position of classical religious humanism, so frequently enunciated by Rishonim and, *prima facie,* already pervasive in Hazal, that the world was created for the sake of man; or subscribe, alternatively, to the Rambam's view that every species is the *raison d'être* of its own existence,[5] surely Judaism has persistently postulated the view that man is, at once, the pinnacle and center of terrestrial creation:

> Yet Thou hast made him but little lower than the angels,
> And hast crowned him with glory and honor.
> Thou hast made him to have dominion over the works of Thy hands;
> Thou hast put all things under his feet:
> Sheep and oxen, all of them,
> Yea, and the beasts of the field;
> The fowl of the air, and the fish of the sea;
> Whatsoever passeth through the paths of the sea.

> (Tehillim 8:6–9)

Is it conceivable, then, that anyone could consider contemplation of God's handiwork as adequate, while omitting study of its fullest manifestation? That the great chain of being could be comprehended without its upper rungs? That knowledge of the photoelectric effect or analysis of sulphur dioxide should take precedence over the understanding of human nature?

Such skewed priorities dominated the dawn of Western philosophy, as reflected in the pre-Socratics' preoccupation with cosmology and the elemental structure of matter. But in his quest to perceive God's handiwork, can any serious *ben Torah* reject Socrates' and Plato's shift to a preeminently humanistic emphasis? The Delphic counsel, *gnoti seauton,* "Know thyself," which animated their cardinal tenet that the unexamined life is not worth living, not only posited a demand but reflected an attitude. That attitude entailed an overriding concern with the study of man as the primary component in an understanding of the world. It is an attitude the Torah world should surely share. In this respect, at any rate, we would all do well to emulate the masters of the mussar movement.

But what about man do we primarily seek to know? The physiologist, cell structure; the geneticist, recombinant DNA; the behaviorist, Pavlovian responses – but the committed Jew, *tzelem E-lohim.* However this elusive concept is defined, it certainly relates to man's spiritual being. Is it possible that of all people, *Bnei Torah*, who vigorously challenge Darwinism because it defines metaphysical man in purely animal terms, should commend biology but disdain literature, confront man as body but not as spirit?

The study of man as spirit is, however, what the humanities are all about. In essence, they deal with man, qua individual and in society; with the record and re-creation of his habitat and activity; with speculation about himself, his context, and their interaction; with his spiritual needs and religious aspirations; with the expressions of his creative self. The importance of such knowledge can be readily gauged from the Ramban's preface to his commentary on the Torah. Elaborating upon the principle that all knowledge of the world is, in some form, embedded in the Torah, he writes:

> In the creation of the world there are fifty gates of understanding; it is as if it is said that there is one gate of understanding pertaining to the creation of the minerals, their force and their effects, one gate of understanding pertaining to the creation of the vegetation in the earth, and similarly, as regards the creation of trees, beasts, fowl, creeping things, and fish, that there pertains to each of these one gate of understanding. This series culminates in the creation of the rational soul [, for the gate pertaining to this latter creation] enables man to contemplate the secret of the soul, to know its essence and its power in "its palace" and to attain [the degree of understanding] that is alluded to in the saying of the sages: "If a person stole, he [who has the aforesaid understanding] knows and recognizes it on him; if a person committed adultery, he knows and recognizes it on him; if one is suspected of having intercourse with a woman in her state of uncleanness, he knows and recognizes that on him."

Knowledge of man is here properly placed at the apex of the "orderly conning over the visible and inferior creature"; and the implications for us are clear. As committed Jews, we must categorically reject Alexander Pope's dictum that "The proper study of mankind is man."[6] *The* proper study is the *Ribbono shel Olam*. But *a* proper study, as an aspect of our effort to understand the created world within which He has placed us and with respect to which He has charged us, that man surely is.

This knowledge, however, is not only important but elusive. "The heart is tortuous above all things, and it is exceeding weak – who can know it?" (Yirmeyahu 17:10). Understanding of the human psyche, psychology in its deeper sense – not the technical province of experimenters and clinicians, not therapeutic concern with pathology or aberration, but genuine insight into the human soul, in all its grandeur and complexity – is one of the most challenging of enterprises. And it is one to which the humanities address themselves directly, in various contexts and on many levels.

Let us begin with the area which, both in the classical tradition and in our own world, is often taken as the distinctive characteristic of elemental humanity: the capacity for speech. *Vayehi ha-adam le-nefesh hayyah* (Bereshit 2:7), more literally translated, "And man became a living soul," is rendered by Onkelos, *le-ru'ah memallela*, "a speaking spirit." Language – or, following Cassirer, Langer, and many others, symbolic representation generally – defines creative human existence, the term *medabber* being synonymous in medieval philosophical terminology with man; and one need not be a philosophic votary of modern linguistic analysis, which I certainly am not, to recognize that an understanding of its nature, structure, and development provides invaluable insight into the human character.

Moreover, humanistic culture does not merely elucidate language but inculcates its proper use. Narrow education often entails paucity of expression, and, correspondingly, of thought. This is an area insufficiently appreciated in the yeshiva world – despite Rav Hayyim's oft-quoted comment that poor *hasbarah* generally reflects deficient *havanah* – but of considerable importance nonetheless. The issue is not florid rhetoric or belletristic virtuosity, but simply lucid, structured verbalization. The humanities, through direct linguistic instruction as well as by the teaching of literature, instill sensitivity and precision with respect to what we have to say, and what we hear and read. "Writing well or speaking correctly matters," to return to Graubard's phrase, not merely as a means of conforming to social convention but as a vehicle of exact and effective expression.

To be sure, the Romantic in us, and not just the *ben Torah,* reacts against excessive formalism. We are wary of exaggerating the importance of artificial molds. Subliminally, we often regard form and substance as competing for concern, so that the issue becomes not only linguistic but educational and even moral. My father zt"l was fond of telling the story of the ill-lettered *Ostjüde* who conceded that he confused *mir* and *mich* but contended that his cultured hosts interchanged *mein* and *dein*. We have all encountered stultifying pedantry, and probably none of us understands, much less shares, the preoccupation of sixteenth-century humanists with imitating Ciceronian orations or their confident expectation that this would contribute much to producing the perfect gentleman. For that matter, we lack their abiding faith in education all together – a faith sustained, as Douglas Bush once suggested half in jest, because they did not attend alumni reunions. We do not, and should not, assign to rhetoric anywhere near the importance attached to it by, say, Quintilian, whose remarkable treatise, *Institutio Oratoria,* is, in effect, a prescription for producing the ideal man and citizen.[7] On the other hand, we should not underestimate, as we unfortunately often do, the role of language and its understanding as a vehicle of thought, expression, and communication. Who could be oblivious to Yeshayahu's declaration, ה' א' נתן לי לשון למודים לדעת לעות את יעף דבר, יעיר בבקר בבקר יעיר לי אזן לשמע כלמודים. "The Lord God hath given me the tongue of them that are taught, that I should know how to sustain with words him that is weary; He wakeneth morning by morning, He wakeneth mine ear to hear as they that are taught" (Yeshayahu 50:4)?

But the humanities do not simply teach us language in general. They initiate us into the world of *ruah memalela* at its finest, introducing us, in Arnold's celebrated phrase, to "the best which has been thought and said in the world."[8] Great literature presents either a rendering, factual or imaginative, of aspects of the human condition, or a record of the artist's grappling with the ultimate questions of human existence: man's relation to himself, to others, to the cosmos, and, above all, to the *Ribbono shel Olam*. Study of great drama exposes us, profoundly and powerfully, to two levels of being: Clytemnestra or Hamlet in the play, Aeschylus or Shakespeare as their creators. Our perceptions of the interaction between the levels depend, in part, upon aesthetic theory (the classical and Romantic perceptions of the artist's subjective relation to his work differ radically), and, in part, upon the accessibility of the material. We know far more about Goethe than about Shakespeare. But some dual exposure generally obtains. Even such classically oriented giants as Dante and Milton have indelibly imprinted themselves, as persons, upon our imagination.

Great literature, I have stated, provides profound insight into "the most tortuous of all" – whether the contorted convolutions of Alyosha Karamazov, the pathetic intensity of Lear, or the sublime acceptance of Samson Agonistes; and these, not as singular individuals but as archetypal and universal. However, in its totality, it does not just illuminate. Quite apart from precision, economy, suggestiveness, and force, great poetry may be imaginative and passionate – and, as such, inspiring, exhilarating, and ennobling. How impressive is the sense of self-realization through self-transcendence in the majestically sublime conclusion to one of Keats's sonnets:

> Then on the shore
> Of the wide world I stand alone, and think
> Till love and fame to nothingness do sink.[9]

Or the imperative thrust encapsulated in the serene final stanza of Robert Frost's "Stopping by Woods on a Snowy Evening:"

> The woods are lovely, dark and deep
> But I have promises to keep,
> And miles to go before I sleep,
> And miles to go before I sleep.

On another plane, literature deals with the collective as well as the personal. In this respect, it frequently conjoins with the most humanistic of the social sciences: history. As a record of human existence, of man's achievements and failures, of his aspirations and shortcomings, history deals with both individual and society – and often with their interaction. It helps us to study *sefer toledot Adam* ("the book of the generations of Adam"), and, as well, to contemplate the ways of Providence, in fulfillment of the mandate, זְכֹר יְמוֹת עוֹלָם בִּינוּ שְׁנוֹת דּוֹר וָדוֹר שְׁאַל אָבִיךָ וְיַגֵּדְךָ זְקֵנֶיךָ וְיֹאמְרוּ לָךְ "Remember the days of old, consider the years of many generations; ask thy father, and he will declare unto thee, thine elders and they will tell thee" (Devarim 32:7).

Obviously, however, history presents us with much more than a record. Covertly or overtly, depending upon the historiographic orientation, it conveys clear moral import. Who can read Thucydides without being responsive to the implications of his narrative for the use and abuse of power? Moreover, there are clear practical ramifications. As we learn to perceive pattern and structure, we deepen our understanding of the dynamics of human existence, so that study of the past helps us not only to relate to the present, but, in the spirit of the challenge implicit in the *pasuk,* וְהָיָה כִּי יִשְׁאָלְךָ בִנְךָ מָחָר לֵאמֹר מַה זֹּאת וְאָמַרְתָּ אֵלָיו בְּחֹזֶק יָד הוֹצִיאָנוּ ה' מִמִּצְרָיִם "And it shall be when thy son asketh thee in time to come" (Shemot 13:14), to anticipate the future.

The humanities, in sum, enable us to expand our horizons with reference to man and society beyond the bounds of narrow personal experience that ordinarily circumscribe us, wherein we are confronted by what Bacon called the idols of the cave and of the market-place. In doing so, they significantly enhance our ability to cope with the two primary challenges of the moral and spiritual life: *tikkun* of self within this antechamber to the world-to-come; and *tikkun* of the antechamber proper. "I call, therefore, a complete and generous education," Milton added later in his essay, "that which fits a man to perform justly, skillfully, and magnanimously all the offices, both private and public, of peace and war."[10] Within such an education, the humanities can surely find their place.

I am not oblivious to the difficulties attendant upon assigning that place. Quite apart from the issue of *bittul Torah* involved in diverting time from Torah study to other pursuits – a problem that exists with respect to the sciences as well – we are confronted by several objections specifically related to the humanities. Focus upon man and his creation may, in effect, entail the assertion of man at the expense of God (to invert a phrase once used to describe Jonathan Edwards's thought), the cardinal sin with which Toynbee charged Greek culture. Moreover, history and literature, in particular, include much that is objectionable from a Torah standpoint, philosophically or even morally.

Wordsworth once explained that he wrote no love poetry because he did not want to arouse passions he could not gratify; and, of course, Plato had reservations about poetry as arousing any passion at all. Surely, we need to examine where our hashkafah stands on such issues. The issue is exacerbated if we deal with modern, largely secular, literature, worlds apart from Milton or even Shakespeare, but is not confined to it. From another perspective, humanistic studies may be desiccated by an overlay of scholarship – "Grant I have mastered learning's crabbed text," lamented Browning's grammarian, "Still, there's the comment"[11] – so that their votary at times wonders, with T.S. Eliot, "Where is the wisdom we have lost in knowledge? Where is the knowledge we have lost in information?"[12]

These are, I repeat, crucial questions that must be confronted, fundamentally and candidly. For the moment, however, we simply need to reject Philistinism and transcend pragmatism; to open ourselves to recognize and assert the value of humanistic learning as a means toward a fuller manifestation of the spirituality of man.

Notes

1. *Daedalus* 112, no. 3, p. xii.
2. See "A Consideration of Synthesis from a Torah Point of View," *Commentator*, April 27, 1961, pp. 5–6; reprinted in *Gesher* 1 (1963): 7–17, and in this volume.
3. These issues are dealt with extensively in a chapter I have, subsequent to this essay, contributed to *Judaism's Encounter with Other Cultures: Rejection or Integration*, ed. J.J. Scheacter (Northvale, N.J., 1997), pp. 217–292.
4. "On Education," in *Areopagitica and Other Prose Worke* (London, 1949: Everyman), p. 42.
5. See *Guide* III:13. Earlier, in the introduction to his *Perush Ha-Mishnayot*, the Rambam had adopted, as a matter of course, the more prevalent view that he subsequently rejected and, to an extent, almost ridiculed:

   אך כלל הדברים כל הנמצאים תחת גלגל הירח לא נמצא אלא בשביל האדם בלבד. (תרגום הרב יוסף קאפח במהדורתו [ירושלים, תכש"ד], עמ' כא–בא)

6. *An Essay on Man*, II, 2. To the opening line, "Know then thyself, presume not God to scan," we would have a mixed response, depending on how "scan" is understood.
7. Some of the more salient passages have been published as a volume entitled *Quintilian on Education*, trans. William M. Smail (Oxford, 1938). The first book of Cicero's dialogue *De Oratore*, in marked contrast to the pervasive spirit of Aristotle's *Rhetoric*, is animated by the same faith as Quintilian's and served as one of his sources. Traces of the politician in Cicero are very much in evidence, however, and his treatise has a more pragmatic bent.
8. "Literature and Science," in *The Portable Matthew Arnold*, ed. L. Trilling (New York, 1949), p. 409.

9. "When I Have Fears."
10. Ibid., p. 46.
11. "A Grammarian's Funeral."
12. Choruses from "The Rock," in *The Complete Poems and Plays, 1909–1950* (New York, 1950), p. 96.

Chapter 6

Get You Wise Men:
Marshalling the Rabbinic Alumni to
Meet Contemporary Halakhic Problems

I.

The subject assigned to me dictates a decidedly practical focus, so that this discussion constitutes a pragmatic island in an otherwise intellectually oriented conference. This is somewhat of a change for one who, relatively speaking, is cloistered in a yeshiva ivory tower – albeit not the *tour d'ivoire* within which Sainte-Beuve complained that Alfred de Vigny confined himself, but the *migdal ha-shen* which, according to the midrash, signifies the *lishkat ha-gazit*; yet an ivory tower nonetheless. Moreover, it may seem slightly presumptuous for me to present some armchair strategy to battle-scarred veterans of *milhamot Hashem* gathered here for a brief respite before they plunge once again into the maelstrom of communal life. Nevertheless, there are valid reasons for making the attempt. For one thing, the practical area involved is that of Halakhah and *hora'ah* proper. For another, the notion of a radical distinction between town and gown has never struck deep Jewish roots. On the contrary, we have always emphasized the interaction of *talmud* and *ma'asseh,* and we have traditionally sought both social and intellectual leadership from the same inspired source. Finally, within the last few years, even in the general American community, the gap between the academic and "pragmatic" sectors has been narrowed considerably. I hope, therefore, that I shall be able to make a modest practical contribution, at least by way of suggestion. If this scholarly excursus becomes nothing more than a prelude to further discussion, it will be well worth the effort.

Having presented this prologue, I shall permit myself the liberty of opening the body of my discussion with some "academic" remarks after all. I do so, however, not by way of abandoning a pragmatic orientation but rather as the first step toward realizing it. We can "meet" halakhic problems in two senses: either by proposing solutions or by implementing them. I shall be concerned with the first – with the scientific rather than the technological aspect, so to speak – and to this extent we shall find ourselves moving on a theoretical plane. However, inasmuch as our focus will not be the intellectual means of coping with halakhic questions but rather the practical and logistical methods of organizing the personnel and machinery to deal with them, our thrust will be pragmatic. We shall not deal with modes of learning and scholarly approaches, but with the problem of marshalling present and potential rabbinic alumni to cope with issues of Halakhah and *hora'ah*.

II.

In virtually every area of Jewish life, the critical problem is personnel. *Hora'ah* is no exception, and therefore we might best begin by asking what type of person, generally and ideally speaking, the *moreh hora'ah* should be. With which qualities should he be endowed?

I presume that you are all familiar with the qualities or character and intellect which the Rambam, drawing upon the Yerushalmi, the Sifre, and other sources, posited for a *dayyan*. Every member of a *bet din*, even the smallest three-man tribunal, "must be endowed," he tells us, "with seven qualities, and they are the following: *hokhmah, anavah, yir'ah, sin'at mamon, ahavat ha-emet, ahavat ha-beriyot lahen,* and *ba'alei shem tov.*"[1] While the Rambam deals directly with a *dayyan* acting formally and officially as a member of a *bet din*, it should be obvious that the same qualities are equally requisite for the *moreh hora'ah*. Indeed, we might recall that the Rambam held that *semikhah*, in the original and technical sense of the term, applied not only to civil or criminal judgment but to decisions of *issur ve-heter.*[2]

Nevertheless, for our immediate purposes, I should like, by expanding upon some of the Rambam's criteria and by introducing others, to present, in slightly different terms, another list, drawn up with an eye upon our current situation. Of course, one could simplify matters greatly by just saying that a *moreh hora'ah* should be a *lamdan* and a *zaddik*. But apart from the fact that I am not sure I could define what a *zaddik* is, I suspect that the very breadth of such a definition would preclude any real insight into our problem. Perhaps a more specific, if more prosaic, catalogue should therefore be set forth after all. To be sure, the *moreh hora'ah* is much more – qualitatively more – than the sum total of his attributes. Nevertheless, it might be useful to see what these are.

To begin with the intellectual qualities, while the Rambam requires only one all-embracing endowment, *hokhmah* (the Sifre, incidentally, also lists *binah*), we might best analyze it into at least five components. First, the *posek* must of course know Halakhah; and not only Halakhah but halakhot. He should have mastered basic texts, he must be able to thread his way through major collections of *teshuvot*, and he must have a clear idea of the historical development of certain institutions. It is not necessary that he have everything in his head simultaneously; nor, generally speaking, would this be feasible. As has been suggested with respect to the Rambam's view that a *samukh* for even a limited area must be *ra'uy le-khal ha-devarim,*[3] the crucial point is that he must have ready access to all areas, that he have the key with which, upon reasonable notice, he can master a given problem.

Second, the *posek* must not only know but understand. He must be able to analyze texts and concepts in depth, to distinguish between controlling ideas and incidental details, to dismiss superficial resemblances, on the one hand, and to detect hidden similarities, on the other. And no less important, third, is the quality of imagination. Whether or not, as

Napoleon contended, it rules the world, imagination (I use the term more in Whitehead's sense than in Wordsworth's) is certainly the motive force in the process of *hora'ah*. The capacity to grasp a problem vividly, to energize knowledge, to probe boldly and to think creatively – this is the very heart of the process, although by no means the whole of it.

Fourth, the *posek* must not only know and understand Halakhah and be able to handle it imaginatively, he must also be familiar with the methods and modes of *hora'ah*. This involves far more than hermeneutics or logic. It entails the knowledge – in a sense, it is more than knowledge – of how much weight to assign to conflicting claims, of how various opinions may be balanced or combined, of the scope and the limits of halakhic flexibility. It entails, in short, a knowledge not only of Halakhah but of how one applies Halakhah.

In this connection, finally, another element is crucial. It is not enough to know ideal principles; one must also know the reality to which these must be applied. I need hardly point out that, in modern times, this has become increasingly difficult. I am not thinking so much, as perhaps most of you are, of technological questions. These, while often complex, are generally well defined in scope, and in dealing with them, one can usually obtain authoritative guidance from a competent consultant. I am thinking primarily of social issues (which, to be sure, may often be the result of technological change). In a highly mobile and interdependent society, the origins and ramifications of a problem are not easily defined, and the *posek* who would grapple with it must have a clear sociological and historical perspective.

So much for *hokhmah*. With what other, nonintellectual, attributes must the *posek* be endowed? I think we can agree upon five basic qualities. He must, first of all, be a man of unflinching honesty, both personal and intellectual. Second, he must be totally committed to Torah and its values. Hence, he is painstakingly careful to avoid both outright error and any compromise with either the letter or the spirit of Halakhah. Third, the ideal *posek* is endowed with profound humaneness. Proper application of Halakhah requires genuine sympathy for people and their needs. To be sure, the ideal *moreh hora'ah* will be at neither pole of the facile dichotomy between those who would destroy every Jew for a *din* and those who would destroy every *din* for a Jew. But he will be sensitive to the human dimensions of a situation, to the manner in which Halakhah can enrich it, in one sense, and take account of it in another.

As a person, the *posek* is, fourthly, firm – at times, even aggressive. He is aware of his awesome responsibility as a custodian and transmitter of *mesorah*, and he resists vigorously the pressures of those who would debase or destroy it. He is not shaken by mere clamor, nor is he overwhelmed by the latest popular fad. He has a sense of his own authority. He knows (to paraphrase Jackson's celebrated dictum) that if, in one sense, he is right because he is final, in another sense, as the vehicle of the masorah, he is final because he is right. Finally, if the *posek* is staunch, he is also genuinely humble. While he can be vigorous in opposing the debunkers of Torah, he is ever ready to listen to those who speak out of commitment to it. Eventually, of course, he will arrive at his own decision, but never with a trace of arrogance. His awareness of the importance of his function precludes it. He works, in Milton's phrase, "as ever in my great Taskmaster's eye."

III.

Such, in brief, is the typological portrait of an ideal *moreh hora'ah*. Needless to say, even under the best of circumstances, we can expect no abundance of men who can significantly satisfy every criterion. It is not only that, statistically speaking, the fortuitous union of so many sterling qualities is highly unlikely. Worse than this, some of the attributes themselves are, to a certain extent, mutually exclusive. Not in theory, of course, but very much so in practice. The imaginative daring and the penetrating insight that are the hallmark of the genuine *lamdan* are precisely the characteristics likely to deter him from the laborious and labyrinthine plodding often necessary for *hora'ah*. Conversely, the balanced and judicious temperament that is so admirably suited for rendering routine decisions tends to preclude the sweep and scope so desperately needed in confronting basic halakhic issues.

Or, to take an example that has special contemporary relevance, the very devotion to Torah that enables the *posek* to develop authoritative knowledge of Halakhah militates against his attaining the broad awareness of his social and natural milieu that alone can enable him to apply it meaningfully in all areas of life. This conflict derives, in part, from the real difficulty of insufficient time and in part, albeit unfortunately so, from a lack of initiative and inclination. *Talmidei hakhamim* are disinclined to involve themselves too deeply in mundane affairs. How many would emulate Rav and spend eighteen months on a farm in order to study animal physiology? Rav's was perhaps a radical example, but even far more modest tasks – say, some basic reading in economics or chemistry – frequently go untended. Conversely, those who are securely grounded in worldly knowledge – I speak even of those who have received a basic halakhic training – often lack the commitment requisite for true mastery of Halakhah.

One could cite a number of other factors, but I think I have said enough to indicate the nature of the difficulty of developing outstanding *morei hora'ah*. Its inherent and perennial character is aggravated, however, by a number of specifically current factors. One – of which I shall have more to say later – is the problem of attracting qualified young *talmidei hakhamim* to careers that will enable them to become first-rate *poskim*. At a time when secular professions attract many of the ablest yeshiva-trained college graduates, and when the tragic polarization of our religious life has mutually alienated some of our leading yeshivot and much of the overall Orthodox community, this is no mean task.

Secondly, halakhic problems have become intrinsically more difficult. For one thing, the case of the typical modern *she'eylah,* conceived even as an isolated phenomenon, tends to be more complicated than were *she'eylot* even as recently as the turn of the century. Technology, urbanization, and a host of other factors have rendered the basic elements of our social and physical life far more complex than would have been imagined by the Hatam Sofer or the Netziv. Moreover, due to both the passage of time and, especially, the acceleration of change in the modern world, it is increasingly unlikely that the specific question at hand, or even a clear-cut equivalent, will have been already treated in standard *poskim*. Most crucial, finally, is the fact that the modern *she'eylah* very often does not deal with an isolated phenomenon. The hallmark of a modern industrialized society is inter-dependence, in almost every sphere and at virtually every level. Whether the subject is birth control, labor relations, free trade, or air pollution, the complex or interacting social, economic, and political elements sweep an increasingly wider arc. Dislocation in one sector of life has a significant impact – not simply the tenuous influence of which the *ba'alei ha-mussar* spoke, but a directly traceable and palpable impact – upon innumerable other sectors. Correspondingly, the task of providing halakhic guidance, in both the narrower and the broader sense of the term, becomes ever more difficult, even as, ironically enough, the need for it constantly increases.

The growing complexity of contemporary *hora'ah* may be indicated by yet another factor. Modern halakhic problems are not only more complex but frequently also more elusive, even in a crude physical sense. The issue at hand may not concern the familiar tangible realities of the *Shulhan Arukh* but more subtle, more sophisticated, and, halakhically speaking, more murky phenomena. And this is true not only of the moral order, whose contemporary chiaroscuro character has often been noted, but of the physical order. Consider, for instance, the concept of *ko'ah*, literally "force," but perhaps better translated as "cause." It is clearly a basic concept, concerned with defining one facet of human action and responsibility for it, and we encounter it in numerous halakhic contexts: *shehitah, mazik, shabbat, heset, yayin nesekh, rotze'ah,* and others. In its familiar form, it deals with some rather concrete realities: a stone is hurled and shatters a window, or some wine is poured from a bottle. What of less palpable instances, however? Does affecting a change in an electromagnetic field that may, in turn, produce a chain of significant consequences constitute *melakhah* on Shabbat? To what extent should a laser beam be considered *koho*? To take another example, we ordinarily think of theft as the surreptitious removal of a physical object from its owner's premises. But what of photocopying a document rather than absconding with it? Or the theft of an idea, copyrighted or not, as exemplified by industrial espionage? Should we assume that pilfering a toothbrush constitutes *gezelah* but the imitation of multimillion-dollar drawings does not? Perhaps, but it is a sensitive and awkward question. Likewise, how are we to judge – legally, and not just morally – numerous forms of imperceptible invasions of privacy? And, in an age of subliminal advertising, how much latitude should be given the concept of *mekah ta'ut*?

I do not mention these difficulties as being either unprecedented or insuperable. I am neither so ignorant nor so presumptuous as to suppose that problems of this type have never arisen before, and I do not have so little faith in Halakhah as to imagine that they are insoluble. However, I do feel that their scope is different from anything we have experienced recently, and I think that an awareness of the nature and magnitude of our present problems is an essential first step toward solving them. In developing or designating *morei hora'ah*, the one direction in which we ought not to move is that of underestimating the difficulties. What we can least afford is to compromise our standards and relax our efforts. Even attributes that are, to an extent, mutually exclusive must be preserved. Genuine *lomdut*, in the fullest sense of the term, must be the *sine qua non* of *hora'ah*. This has always been important, but at a time when fewer and fewer *she'eylot* can be "looked up" in an explicit reference, the need for sound theoretical underpinnings and a basic insight into central issues is absolutely crucial. And to take our second example, at the highest level, certainly, we must have *poskim* who, without accepting its mores, are fully attuned to the realities of modern life.

IV.

I have stated that the problem is primarily one of personnel; I have broadly depicted the ideal *posek*, and I have briefly indicated why, at any time but especially at present, he is not easily found. Where, practically speaking, do we, the rabbinic alumni, go from here?

We are addressed by this question in two capacities: qua *Bnei Torah* generally, and qua *musmakhei ha-yeshivah* specifically; and our responses may be correspondingly different, although of course the general thrust is the same. As students and devotees of Torah, we have a responsibility to lighten the unconscionable burden currently being borne by our *gedolim*. Theirs is an almost unbearable load, and, to the extent that the situation can be remedied, it is nothing short of criminal. When we read the Rambam's graphic account of his daily schedule and the fatigue resulting from ministering to the medical needs of Saladin's court, harem and all, we are shocked and grieved that such precious energy was wasted upon so relatively unimportant a task, one which, moreover, could just as easily have been performed by a far lesser person. Yet do we husband our own spiritual riches any more carefully? Don't we impose substantial drudgery, from fund-raising to administration to organizational politics, upon our greatest? What opportunity do we allow them simply to think – or, for that matter, to learn? How much of their time is truly theirs – to reflect upon both immediate and ultimate realities, to observe the present and relate it to a transcendent past and future?

The ramifications of this question extend far beyond our immediate subject. But one has to start somewhere, and in the area of *hora'ah*, the call for relief has, at any rate, an unimpeachable precedent. I refer, of course to Yithro's ominous warning, as relevant in our day as in his. From personal observation I am familiar with the incessant jangle of the telephone in the Rav's home, and I gather from Rebbitzen Feinstein – as if one couldn't have envisioned it – that the situation in her home is generally worse. I know that both the Rav and Rav Mosheh Feinstein are extremely conscientious about accepting *she'eylot,* answering them even when they might be inclined to decline other calls; and I have heard neither complain about this particular onus. Yet I cannot help but ask myself two related questions: How often have they had a train of thought interrupted by a call? How many times has peace of mind been shattered by a ring? How many fleeting insights have gone the way of the latter part of "Kubla Khan"? And what has been the toll in frayed nerves and personal attrition? What the cost in unwritten essays and unedited *hiddushim*? Second, is their burden, indeed, inevitable? Could not many, if not most, of the *she'eylot* have been easily answered by men of lesser stature? Must every *be'atha be-cutha* be referred to *gedolei ha-dor*? And if not, isn't the overwhelming burden we impose upon them a shameful testimony to our collective inefficiency and insufficiency, our selfishness and our sloth?

These questions are all, of course, rhetorical, and they point to a single solution. It is, again, Yithro's. We should relieve our *gedolim* by setting up local or regional centers for *hora'ah* to which *she'eylot* from a given area would be referred. These centers would be staffed by men who are competent and knowledgeable, although not necessarily first-rate *poskim* of the type I have depicted. Before assuming their posts, they would be briefed on *pesakim* concerning a number of key issues and standard *she'eylot* in a given sphere, and these they could then proceed to apply. *Veha-davar ha-kasheh* – the more difficult questions, and these alone, would be referred to a gadol for decision. Of course, the participating individuals would have to master the basic material – to this end, some preliminary seminar-type groups might be organized – and, above all, they should know now to diagnose a *she'eylah* even when they cannot solve it. They must have the capacity, the honesty, and the courage to distinguish between what does and does not lie within their competence. They need not be giants, however; and I am confident that men – or rather, groups of men, for it might be advisable to assign different halakhic areas to individuals who could specialize in them – who are able and willing to serve in such a capacity, can be found in sufficient numbers.

The resultant benefit would be threefold. First, of course, some of the pressure would be taken off our *gedolim*. They would deal with fewer *she'eylot*, and even those that were referred to them would often be presented at a single session rather than as a series of interruptions. Our foremost figures would thus be able to channel their energies to more creative work, to tasks that truly demand men of their stature. Second, such a program would provide fresh élan for the participating rabbis. It would challenge them intellectually and engage them communally. It would overcome the helplessness that many feel in attempting to bridge the gap between Halakhah and *ma'asseh*. And, of course, as an aspect of *shimmush*, it would constitute an invaluable apprenticeship for future first-rank *poskim*. Finally, the creation of such regional centers would reinvigorate the communities in which they were located. Not that this would necessarily affect the average layman; we ought not to be excessively sanguine. However, it could have a definite impact upon anyone who has had, at one point or another, significant contact with the study of *Torah she-be'al-peh*. This is no mean attainment.

A second program might aid not only in applying *hora'ah* but in formulating it. We could assign an individual or a group to research a given subject – to posit its practical and theoretical problems, work up and organize its material, and present it in a tentative position paper upon which *gedolim* could then draw. This would be roughly analogous to the service performed by a clerk to a justice of the Supreme Court, and the results would be equally beneficial. The older member and the younger member would both profit greatly from their mutually fructifying relationship. Of course, the prerequisites for participating in this program would necessarily be more rigorous than for the first. However, here again, given the right conditions, I think that men of the proper caliber can be found.

A third program, of no less help to the tyro than to the mature *posek*, would develop basic tools rather than provide auxiliary personnel. As compared with secular fields – and indeed, by any other standard – we are woefully short of research equipment that can lend ready access to works of both past and present *poskim*, not to mention the most fundamental halakhic texts. Mining the rich lodes of the past, retaining the findings in one's personal storehouse, and, as well, keeping *au courant* with rapidly changing contemporary problems are tasks that stagger the imagination. Both could be considerably eased by the availability of serviceable and reliable research tools. Current digests, abstracts, indices, bibliographies – all are in short supply and (or at least they should be) in great demand. We have very few reference works dealing with Rishonim; and the later periods, which have been more generously treated, could also benefit from fresher and fuller treatment. The *Pithei Teshuvah* is not exactly recent. Some work in this direction is currently being done in Eretz Yisrael, of course, but it is only a start – and, in a number of instances, a rather unpromising start at that.[4]

I am by no means unmindful of the dangers inherent in moving in this direction. Alexandrianism and academicism; the incarceration, if not interment, of a living tradition in scholarly sarcophagi; the leveling attendant upon including the brilliant and the insipid in the same comprehensive compilation; the loss of vitality and sweep resulting from a pseudo-scientific quest for "scholarly" precision – these are all dangers of which I am acutely, I might almost say obsessively, aware. I have seen something of their corrosive impact upon humanistic studies, and I think it crucial that we avoid such corrosion. *Talmud Torah* must remain a vital pursuit, experiential as well as intellectual. We can never be content with the tone-color of a *Wissenschaft des Judentums,* even though we may appreciate some of its contributions. Nevertheless, I do not believe that we must throw out the baby with the bath water. If we approach our task with sufficient religious commitment, we should be able to integrate a measure of scholarship without stultifying imagination or inspiration. Moreover, this problem impinges upon education in far greater measure than upon *hora'ah.* On the one hand, the potential dangers are less ominous. To the *posek,* heavy reliance upon the whole corpus of critical apparatus comes after a profound emotional nexus to *talmud Torah* has already been established. It does not substitute for the evocative atmosphere of the *bet ha-midrash* but rather is subordinated to it. The clear, cold light of the research facility does not supplant the *kumi roni ba-laylah,* but rather supplements it. On the other hand, the need for instant access to knowledge as well as for comprehensiveness and precision is greater for the *posek* than for the melammed. Gilbert Highet once wrote that scholarship must be accurate, whereas teaching must be interesting even if not wholly accurate. The teaching – and the study – of Torah must be not only interesting but inspiring. Yet its creative character lends it a provisional dimension. We do not definitively decide a *she'eylah* on the basis of an idea tentatively advanced in a *shi'ur.* In *hora'ah* there is no such leeway, however; hence, the far greater need for maximal certainty.

V.

So much for what we, the rabbinic alumni, can do as members of the general community of *Bnei Torah.* Is there anything further we can do in our specific capacity as alumni, as *musmakhim* of our yeshiva who are particularly concerned for its welfare and who are in a position to have some impact upon its action? I believe there is, and here I come to a genuinely practical question – the current economic status of Roshei Yeshiva. Let me, however, preface my remarks with one emphatic disclaimer. I have not come here to lament my own situation. While I would not claim to be genuinely wealthy according to the Mishnah's definition, a complete *sameah be-helko,* I am definitely not in the habit of complaining about my financial condition, nor, personally, have I much cause for lament. I discuss this matter only insofar as it has a direct bearing on our immediate topic, although the implications of what I shall say obviously extend a good deal further.

Does any such bearing exist? Well, I am far – very far – from being a Marxist, but I think the answer is indisputably yes. Consider the situation. I have stated that the critical problem is that of personnel. Let us now imagine that an excellent prospect is at hand, a talmid of our yeshiva with the proper personal and intellectual, moral, and religious qualifications. I discuss with him the possibility of devoting his life to the study and dissemination of Torah. I stress the urgency of our collective need for spiritual guidance, and I point out to him his responsibility to meet this need. We discuss ways and means, and I suggest that, while the rabbinate can be very rewarding, given his own bent, he could fulfill himself and serve the community best by becoming a Rosh Yeshiva. To this end, I encourage him to devote a few years to intensive learning – preferably to enter the Kollel – so that he could truly grow as a *talmid hakham.* The idea takes root. Our prospect realizes, of course, that there are drawbacks, nor do I attempt to distract him from them. He knows that the relative leisure and acclaim that could be his as a professor or a physicist are beyond the Rosh Yeshiva's ken. He recognizes the burdens of communal leadership. He has no doubt but that it would be far easier to undertake a secular career and simply become an honored member of someone else's shul. But he loves learning, he has a deep sense of commitment, and he perceives that, while the Rosh Yeshiva's heartaches are incomparably greater than the chemist's, so are his personal joys. So the idea takes root. If at some point he should ask me, however, what he might expect to earn at, say, our yeshiva, I must hang my head in shame and tell him that the prospective remuneration is far below that of peers entering the field of medicine or law.

I shall not dwell upon the injustice of the situation. It is, in any event, far too obvious to require discussion. Consider, rather, the implications for our particular problem. For a position which, by any responsible educational criterion is full-time in every sense of the word, our prospect will earn a salary barely sufficient to designate him as middle-class. Remember that, almost by definition, our prospect is no cloistered *batlan*. If he is indeed to be a potential future mentor, he must be aware of the world around him. It is virtually certain, for instance, that he knows that at the City University or at Fordham, not to mention in an even more lucrative scientific career, he could start at double his initial salary as a Rosh Yeshiva. With equivalent preparation – the years spent learning for *semikhah* or in the Kollel would be about enough to earn a doctorate – and for fewer hours, he could earn many additional thousand dollars a year. To put it differently, in asking him to become a Rosh Yeshiva, I am asking him to contribute almost half his future potential annual income to the yeshiva. How many of us have contributed this much lately?

For some of our older Roshei Yeshiva, the higher salaries available elsewhere are simply so much grass on the other side of the fence. The positions or careers that command those salaries no longer constitute – if indeed they ever did – real alternatives. To our young prospect, however, they are a fork in the road. If, again, he is genuinely our man, that chair at Stony Brook or a post at IBM is a live option. His question about salary is not a reflection of idle curiosity. It concerns a matter that will affect a vital decision.

What are we prepared to do, haverim, to formulate a better answer? It will not do to rejoin that the question should never have been posed. Of course, anyone entering upon a spiritual vocation – certainly, any potential leader – should be idealistically motivated, and it may strike you as a bit crass that so ungenteel an item as money should be mentioned. I am fully aware, moreover, of the Rambam's strictures concerning those who use spiritual positions to attain material gain. Before we give vent to pious horror, however, let us keep a few things in mind. First, it is one thing to say that wealth should be no motive; it is quite another to say that hardship should be no deterrent. There is no question here of amassing riches, just of rising above subsistence levels. However one answers the Rambam[5] – after all, our universal practice has been contravening him for centuries – monastic vows of poverty are not part of our tradition.

Furthermore, the question of salary is not purely material; it is spiritual as well. For the simple fact is that the Rosh Yeshiva will probably not be able to maintain a reasonable standard of living on his yeshiva salary alone. So he will moonlight. *Rabbanut,* other teaching positions, *hekhsherim* – anything that will help meet his bills, but alas, that may also stunt his growth. The opportunity to learn, to think, to create, to publish – all may be partly frustrated by both the additional workload and the anxiety generated by economic insecurity. I am not unmindful of the "uses of adversity"; and I am sufficiently under the spell of Robert Frost to recognize that, at a certain level, one kind of genius thrives most under stress. Nevertheless, as the gemara in Kiddushin might remind us, one normally learns and grows best when not weighed down by a financial albatross. Sustained creative effort ordinarily requires a degree of leisure of which our Roshei Yeshiva currently enjoy far too little. This lack is reflected, incidentally, in another way: the fact that Roshei Yeshiva are not, as are all other faculty members at our university, granted sabbaticals. The chance to refresh and recreate one's mind to expand horizons or to exhaust an area, to reflect or to concentrate – this chance is not afforded them.

For both selfish and altruistic reasons, we dare not content ourselves with lecturing budding *talmidei hakhamim* on the need for idealistic motivation. If we can agree that a measure of justified apprehension over financial future does not automatically disqualify someone from becoming a *moreh horaʾah,* then we should stop asking why he is not willing to make even greater sacrifices than he must make, even with a decent salary. Let us instead recognize that we have no right to demand them, or rather that we have a duty to obviate the need for them. Let us exert our efforts to assure, first, that both in our own institution and in the broader Jewish community to which it relates and upon which it draws, proper Torah priorities are sustained; and second, that the means requisite to redressing the current situation become available.[6] To be sure, money alone will hardly suffice. Leadership is not a commodity. But in a competitive world, it can be a highly significant factor.

I began by indicating that I would speak in a practical vein, and it is on this note, having possibly exceeded my bounds, that I conclude. I trust that these remarks will be practical not only in their content but also in their consequences. Some could be of immediate relevance, others are of a long-range nature. The crucial thing is to begin moving in the right direction. Let us just start marshalling.

Notes

1. *Mishneh Torah,* Sanhedrin 2:7; see *Lehem Mishneh* ad loc. Cf. Sifre on Devarim 1:15, and the comment of *Emek Ha-Netziv* thereon.
2. See Sanhedrin 4:8, based upon Yerushalmi, Hagigah 1:8.
3. See ibid. The source for this position, too, is in the same passage in the Yerushalmi. The interpretation to which I here allude was cited by the Rav zt"l in the name of his father, Rav Mosheh Soloveichik zt"l.
4. This is, obviously, a very dated paragraph, perhaps better omitted. I have retained it nonetheless, in part to convey a sense of how our situation was perceived, barely a generation ago, in part because, *mutatis mutandis,* some of the lacunae, especially as regards current work in progress, still exist; and in part because some of the broader concerns raised in the next paragraph are still very much an issue.
5. See *Perush Ha-Mishnayot,* Avot 4:5, and *Mishneh Torah,* Talmud Torah 3:11–12. For an opposing view, see *Tashbez* 1:42–47.
6. To an extent, this last section, too, is somewhat dated, as the situation has certainly improved during the last thirty years; but only to an extent.

Chapter 7

The Ideology of *Hesder*

Half a dozen years ago, advocacy of the cause of *yeshivot hesder* before the American Jewish public would have seemed largely superfluous. The impact of the Yom Kippur War was then still strong, the memory of the role of hesdernikim in it still vivid, the halo of the heroic student-soldier yet fresh. The religious community, in particular, took great pride in a clearly perceived *Kiddush Hashem*. Almost everyone had seen some striking picture or heard some moving story: of boys (they really were not much more) who had gone into battle wearing *tefillin*; of a group that had stunned its brigadier by inquiring, during a nocturnal lull in the Sinai campaign, whether and when they would be provided with a lulav and etrog; of another which, after a disheartening day on the battlefield, improvised Simhat Torah dancing and *hakafot* by the banks of the Suez Canal. Almost everyone had read comments by officers of Zahal, the Israel Defense Forces, praising the courage and commitment of *bnei yeshivot*, noting both the inspirational qualities that had done so much to boost collective morale and their vital role in the forefront of the actual fighting. And there was, of course, the litany of suffering, the grim statistics of the highly disproportionate casualties of the yeshiva students, to attest to that role. In the context of the pervasive sadness and pride, the ideological presentation of hesder seemed largely unnecessary. The reality spoke for itself.

Today, thank God, such a presentation is in order. Time has healed many wounds and dimmed many memories. Above all, it has opened fresh vistas and posed new challenges, these hopefully unrelated to the battlefront. We have seen the first glimmers of peace; and, for the moment at least, the country appears relatively secure. And as our sense of danger dulls, as our roseate hopes lull us into a sense of imagined security, as the perception of just how close Syrian armored columns once came to swooping down upon the Galil and beyond becomes blurred, hesder and its cause evidently needs, if not an advocate, at least an expositor. This brief essay is therefore presented as a modest exposition of the essence of hesder and its significance, at least as viewed from the perspective of Yeshivat Har Etzion.

The typical graduate of an Israeli yeshiva high school is confronted by one of three options. He can, like most of his peers, enter the army for a three-year stint. Alternatively, he can exempt himself from military service on the grounds that *torato umnuto,* "Torah is his vocation," while he attends a yeshiva whose students receive the Israeli equivalent of an American 4-D exemption. Finally, he can enroll in a yeshivat hesder, in which case, over roughly the next five years, he will pursue a combined program of traditional Torah study with service in the army. While at the yeshiva he will learn full-time (hesder is *not* an Israeli ROTC), but there will be two protracted absences from it, one of nine months and the other of six months, for training and duty.

Of these three courses, hesder is, in one sense, perhaps the easiest. Properly speaking, however, it is also the most arduous. The advantages, judged from a student's perspective, are fairly clear. Most obviously, the tour of actual army service is shorter. While a student is tied down by hesder for almost five years, he only spends, unless he becomes an officer, about sixteen months in uniform. Most important, however, hesder provides a convenient framework for discharging two different and to some extent conflicting obligations. It enables the student, morally and psychologically, to salve both his religious and his national conscience by sharing in the collective defense burden without cutting himself off from the matrix of Torah. Socially – and this, of course, has religious implications as well – hesder offers him a desirable context, for while in the army, he will often be stationed with fellow hesdernikim. And hesder enables him, pragmatically, to keep his future academic and vocational options open. Unlike his peers at non-hesder yeshivot, he can, upon completing the hesder program, legally pursue any course of study or employment or both in the mainstream of Israeli society.

These are legitimate and even important considerations. But they are not what hesder, ideally considered, is all about. Properly understood, hesder poses more of a challenge than an opportunity; and in order to perceive it at its best we need to focus upon difficulty and even tension rather than upon convenience. Optimally, hesder does not merely provide a religious cocoon for young men fearful of being contaminated by the potentially secularizing influences of general army life, although it incidentally serves this need as well. Hesder at its finest seeks to attract and develop *bnei torah* who are profoundly motivated by the desire to become serious *talmidei hakhamim* but who concurrently feel morally and religiously bound to help defend their people and their country; who, given the historical exigencies of their time and place, regard this dual commitment as both a privilege and a duty; who, in comparison with their non-hesder confreres, love not, to paraphrase Shakespeare, Torah less but Israel more. It provides a context in which students can focus upon enhancing their personal spiritual and intellectual growth while heeding the call to public service, and thus it enables them to maintain an integrated Jewish existence.

To be sure, the two aspects of hesder, the spiritual and the military, are hardly on a par. The disparity is reflected, in part, in the unequal division of time. Primarily, however, it concerns the realm of value, within which two elements, each indispensable, may yet be variously regarded. When the Mishnah states, אם אין קמח אין תורה אם אין תורה אין קמח, "If there is no flour, there is no Torah; if there is no Torah, there is no flour,"[1] it hardly means that both are equally important. What it does mean is that both are, in fact, equally necessary, although, axiologically and teleologically, flour exists for the sake of Torah, and not vice versa. *Il faut manger pour vivre, il ne faut pas vivre pour manger* ("One must eat to live, and not live to eat"), declaims one of Molière's characters; and so it is with hesder. The yeshiva prescribes military service as a means to an end. That end is the enrichment of personal and communal spiritual life, the realization of that great moral and religious vision whose fulfillment is our national destiny; and everything else is wholly subservient. No one responsibly connected with any yeshivat hesder advocates military service for its own sake. We avoid even the slightest tinge of militarism, and we are poles removed from Plato's notion that the discipline of army life is a necessary ingredient of an ideal education. No less than every Jew, the typical hesdernik yearns for peace, longs for the day on which he can divest himself of uniform and Uzi, and devote his energies to Torah. In the interim, however, he harbors no illusions, and he keeps his powder dry and his musket ready.

In one sense, therefore, insofar as army service is alien to the ideal Jewish vision, hesder is grounded in necessity rather than choice. It is, if you will, *b'diavad,* a post-facto response to a political reality imposed upon us by our enemies. In another sense, however, it is very much *l'hathillah,* a freely willed option grounded in moral and halakhic decision. We at Yeshivat Har Etzion, at any rate, do not advocate hesder as a second-best alternative for those unable or unwilling to accept the rigors of single-minded Torah study. We advocate it because we are convinced that, given our circumstances – would that they were better – military service is a *mizvah,* and a most important one at that. Without impugning the patriotism or ethical posture of those who think otherwise, we feel that for the overwhelming majority of *bnei torah,* defense of Israel is a moral imperative.

Hence, to the extent that the term *hesder,* "arrangement," connotes an accommodation arrived at between conflicting sides, it is somewhat of a misnomer. Hesder is not the result of a compromise between the respective positions of Roshei Yeshiva, and the Ministry of Defense. It is a compromise with reality. We do occasionally argue with the generals over details, and they do not always sufficiently appreciate the preeminence of the spiritual factor. The basic concern with security, however, is ours no less than theirs.

Of course, that concern must be balanced against others. *Knesset Yisrael* needs not only security but spirituality – and ultimately, the former for the sake of the latter. Those who, by dint of knowledge and inspiration, are able to preserve and enrich our moral vision and spiritual heritage, contribute incalculably to the quality of our national life; and this must be

considered in determining personal and collective priorities. Hence, while
we of the hesder yeshivot feel that military training and subsequent reserve
status for men should be virtually universal – spiritual specialization being
reserved, at most, for a truly elite cadre[2] – the length of post-training service
should be justifiably briefer than for those unable or unwilling to make a
comparable spiritual contribution. The military establishment, I might add,
generally understands this. Junior officers, concerned with keeping good
soldiers in their units, sometimes complain about this apparent inequity.
However, higher-level commanders, more keenly aware of the total picture
and the longer term, recognize the value of the spiritual aspect of hesder
as inspirationally significant, for *bnei yeshiva* as well as their comrades,
in the event of war. It should be emphasized, however, that from a Torah
perspective, the justification for abbreviated service does not rest solely
or even primarily upon the yeshiva's stimulus to bravery. It is grounded in
the intrinsic and immeasurable value of Torah per se – indeed, in the faith
and hope that it moves us toward the realization of the prophetic vision,
לֹא בְחַיִל וְלֹא בְכֹחַ כִּי אִם בְּרוּחִי אָמַר ה' צְ־בָאוֹת: "Neither by force nor by might but
by My spirit, saith the Lord of hosts."[3]

The case for hesder rests, then, upon several simple assumptions. First,
during the formative post-secondary years, a *ben Torah* should be firmly
rooted in a preeminently Torah climate, this being crucially important both
for his personal spiritual development and for the future of a nation in
critical need of broadly based spiritual commitment and moral leadership.
Second, the defense of Israel is an ethical and halakhic imperative, whether
because, as we believe, the birth of the state was a momentous historical
event and its preservation of great spiritual significance, or because, even
failing that, the physical survival of its three million–plus Jewish inhabitants is at stake. Third, in light of the country's current military needs,
and admittedly these should be reassessed periodically, yeshiva students
should participate in its defense, both by undergoing basic and specialized
training, thus becoming part of the reserves against the possibility, God
forbid, of war, and by performing some actual service even during periods
of uneasy peace.

The need for their participation is based upon several factors. By far the most important, although it relates more to training than to peacetime service, is the fact that in the event of war the Israeli army may very well need every qualified soldier it can muster. And lest one think that the number of hesder youths is militarily insignificant, let it be noted that, while indeed they may not seem all that many, nevertheless, the boys currently enrolled in hesder, not to mention those who have moved on to the reserves, can man over four hundred tanks – surely no piddling figure. This factor relates to training more than to peacetime service; but with respect to the latter as well, both common fairness and self-respect dictate that the Torah community make some contribution even if it be justifiably smaller than that of others.

The notion, held by many at one major yeshiva, that *Bnei Torah* should prepare for a possible war but need do nothing to prevent it, fails to recognize the importance of deterrence. It should be emphasized that, with respect to aiding others, prevention is at least the equivalent of relief, halakhically and not just proverbially. The *mizvah* of *hashavat avedah* includes deterring loss as well as restoring it.[4] The highest level of *tzedakah*, the Rambam tells us, takes the form of preventive sustenance, even if it does not cost the "donor" one single penny.[5] The rationale behind the position in question – in practice, it entails six months of training but no service thereafter – presumably rests upon the assumption that prevention can be supplied by others; or, as some put it, that so long as anyone is walking the streets or working on a civilian job, there is no excuse for pulling boys out of a *bet ha-midrash*. This view is not without foundation.

In determining whether and when the study of Torah should be set aside in favor of a *mizvah, efshar la'asota al yedei aherim,* the extent to which it can be realized by others, is a crucial factor.[6] However, that possibility should be real and not merely theoretical; and in assessing it, their readiness to take up the slack should presumably be considered. It is by no means certain that I may compel others, directly or indirectly, to assume my share of a common task so that I can continue my studies.[7] Further, the problem acquires a wholly different dimension when what is at issue is not just the distribution of time and effort but the possibility of danger; and this element is unfortunately present even in time of presumed peace.

Consequently, in determining the duration of peacetime service, we are driven back to balancing conflicting communal needs, and this is the basis of its abbreviation in hesder. It should be clear, however, that the concept of *efshar la'asota* provides no mandate for categorical dispensation. Those who strike this balance and conclude that they owe no peacetime service whatsoever are, of course, entitled to their position. But I must confess that I, for one, do not find the notion of a free of charge state morally engaging.

The ethical moment aside, a measure of service is, for many, a matter of self-interest, and not only because it is, after all, our own homeland that we are defending. Service enables the individual soldier to avert the moral and psychological onus of the drone, and it enables the religious community as a whole to avoid both the reality and the stigma of parasitism. It helps build personal character, on the one hand, and opens channels of public impact, on the other, by producing potential leaders attuned to the pulse and the experience of their countrymen. To be sure, the prospect of secular criticism should not routinely be the decisive factor in determining religious policy. Nevertheless, it cannot be totally ignored. Hazal, at any rate, did not regard *Hillul Hashem* and *Kiddush Hashem* lightly.

If the rationale underlying hesder is relatively simple, its implementation is anything but. I described it at the outset as the most difficult of the options open to a yeshiva high school graduate, and, seriously taken, it is precisely that. The difficulty is not incidental. It is grounded in the very nature and structure of hesder, and is threefold. First, there is the problem of dual commitment: the possible loss of motivation and momentum, and the division of time, energy, and attention inherent in the fusion of the study of Torah with any other enterprise, whether academic, vocational, or what have you. From this perspective, the question of hesder meshes with the much broader problem of the relation of the active and the contemplative life, of Torah and *derekh eretz*, of the sacred and the secular. As such it admits of no easy solution. דרשב"י אמר אלו הוינא קאים על טורא דסיני בשעתא דאתיהיבת תורה לישראל הוינא מתבעי קומי רחמנא דיתברי לבר נשא תרין פומין חד דהוי לעי באוריתא וחד דעבד ליה כל צורכיה, "If I had been present at Mount Sinai," said Rabbi Shimon bar Yohai, "I would have asked of the Merciful One that two mouths should be created for every person, one with which to study Torah and one with which to attend to all his [other] needs."[8] His wish is deeply shared by hesdernikim and their masters; but it remains a wish.

With reference to hesder, specifically, there is an additional problem: the conflict of values, lifestyle, and sensibility between *bet midrash* and boot camp, especially in a predominantly secular army. The danger is not so much that students will lose their faith and become nonobservant. On this score, yeshivot hesder have a track record at least as good as their immediate Eastern European predecessors.[9] It is, rather, a problem of possible attrition, the loss of refinement and the dulling of moral and religious sensitivity that may result from exposure to the rougher aspects of a possibly dehumanizing and despiritualizing existence. As the Ramban noted, the qualities of aggressiveness and machismo which are so central to military life naturally run counter to the Torah's spiritual discipline. Commenting upon the *pasuk,* כִּי־תֵצֵא מַחֲנֶה עַל־אֹיְבֶיךָ וְנִשְׁמַרְתָּ מִכֹּל דָּבָר רָע "When thou goest forth in camp against thine enemies, then thou shalt keep thee from every evil thing," he observes:

והנכון בעיני בענין המצוה הזאת, כי הכתוב יזהיר בעת אשר החטא מצוי בו. והידוע
במנהגי המחנות היוצאות למלחמה, כי יאכלו כל תועבה, יגזלו ויחמסו ולא יתבוששו
אפילו בניאוף וכל נבלה, הישר בבני אדם בטבעו, יתלבש אכזריות וחמה כצאת מחנה
על אויב. ועל כן הזהיר בו הכתוב, ונשמרת מכל דבר רע.

And what seems correct to me with respect to this *mizvah* is that the verse enjoins with regard to a period during which sin is rife. It is known of the behavior of warring camps that they eat every abomination, rob and plunder, and are not even ashamed of fornication and any villainy. The most decent of men by nature may become invested with cruelty and wrath as the camp goes out to engage the enemy. Hence, the verse enjoins, "And thou shalt keep thee from every evil thing."[10]

Situations less drastic than actual war are less threatening, but these, too, can have an impact. As the Ramban's interpretation clearly implies, the difficulty can be overcome, but a genuine and conscious effort is needed in order to avoid moral corruption and spiritual corrosion.

Probably the greatest difficulty, however, concerns neither the practical ramifications of the diffusion of effort nor the grappling with potentially inimical influences. It concerns the very essence of hesder: the maintenance of a tenuous moral and ideological balance between its two components. At issue is a conflict of loves, not just of labors. On one level, this is simply the problem of religious Zionism writ large. A hesder yeshiva seeks to instill profound loyalty to the State of Israel, but at the same time inculcates spiritual perspectives and values that are to serve as the basis for a radical critique of a secularly oriented state and society. The problem acquires another dimension, however, when that loyalty includes the readiness to fight and die. Moreover, it involves, on a second level, issues specifically related to a student-soldier. Like all yeshivot, a yeshivat hesder seeks to instill a love for Torah so profound and so pervasive as to render protracted detachment from it painful, and yet it demands precisely such an absence. It advocates patriotic national service even at some cost to personal development, and yet prescribes that students serve considerably less than their non-yeshiva peers.

These apparent antinomies are the result of the basic attempt to reconcile conflicting claims and duties by striking a particular balance: one that should produce an aspiring *talmid hakham* who also serves rather than a soldier who also learns; one that perceives military service as a spiritual sacrifice – we do *not* want students to be indifferent to their loss – but proceeds to demand that sacrifice; one that encourages a hesdernik to excel as a soldier while in the army but prescribes his return to the *bet ha-midrash* before that excellence is fully applied or perhaps even fully attained.

From the yeshiva's perspectives, these antitheses are fully justified. Indeed, they constitute the very essence of hesder as a complex and sensitive balance. However, preserving this balance, with its many subtle nuances, entails traversing a narrow ridge; and here lies the primary difficulty, existential and not just practical, of hesder. Small wonder that many only achieve the balance imperfectly. It is, however, in those who do succeed in attaining the balance, and who, despite the difficulty, are genuinely at peace with themselves, that hesder at its finest can be seen. And it is inspiring to behold.

These problems are very real. They pose a formidable educational challenge; and while they are by no means insuperable, as is attested by the history of yeshivot hesder, we ignore them at our peril. Moreover, it is precisely the adherents of hesder, those of us who regularly grapple with its sophisticated demands, who are most keenly aware of the problems. Nevertheless, although our centuries of statelessness tend to obscure this fact, hesder is the traditional Jewish way. What were the milieux of Mosheh Rabbenu, of Yehoshua, of David, of Rabbi Akiva, as Hazal conceived and described them, but yeshivot hesder? The mode of integrating military service with the study of Torah may very well have differed from our own. Hazal described Yehoshua as being reproached for having omitted a single evening of communal *talmud Torah* in his camp;[11] and as an army, we are unfortunately quite far from this standard. Nevertheless, the principle is very much the same.

Indeed, in the Ramban's view, the institution can be traced back to our very fountainhead. In explaining why Avimelech was so anxious to conclude a treaty with Yitzhak, he conjectures that it may have been due to the fact

...שהיה אברהם גדול מאד ורב כח, שהיו בביתו שלש מאות איש שולף חרב ולו בעלי ברית רבים, והוא גם בן חיל אשר לבו כלב האריה ורדף ארבעה מלכים גבורים מאד ונצחם, וכאשר ראו הצלחתו כי היא מאת הא־לקים פחד ממנו מלך פלשתים פן יכבוש ממנו מלכותו... וכמעשה אבות עשו בנים, כי היה יצחק גדול כאביו ופחד המלך פן ילחם בו בגרשו אותו מארצו:

that Avraham was very great and mighty, as he had in his house three hundred sword-wielding men and many allies. And he himself was a lion-hearted soldier, and he pursued and vanquished four very powerful kings. And when his success became evident as being divinely ordained, the Philistine king feared him, lest he conquer his kingdom.... And the sons emulated the fathers, as Yitzhak was great like his father, and the king feared lest he fight him because he had banished him from his land.[12]

This account of lion-hearted patriarchs and their sword-wielding disciples may fall strangely upon some ears. Although we do not like to admit it, our Torah world, too, has its vogues, and in some circles, much of the Ramban on Bereshit – the real Ramban, honestly read and unflinchingly understood – is currently passé.[13] The fact, however, remains: the primary tradition is hesder.

The reason is not hard to find. The halakhic rationale for hesder does not, as some mistakenly assume, rest solely upon the *mizvah* of waging defensive war. If that were the case, one might conceivably argue that, halakhically, sixteen months of army service is too high a price to pay for the performance of this single commandment. The rationale actually rests upon (a) the simple need for physical survival, and (b) the fact that military service is often the fullest manifestation of a far broader value: *gemilut hasadim,* an empathetic concern for others and action on their behalf. This element, defined by Shimon Ha-Zaddik as one of the three cardinal foundations of the world,[14] is the basis of Jewish social ethics, and its realization, even at some cost to single-minded development of Torah scholarship, is virtually imperative. The gemara in Avodah Zarah is pungently clear on this point:

ת״ר: כשנתפסו רבי אלעזר בן פרטא ורבי חנינא בן תרדיון, א״ל ר׳ אלעזר בן פרטא לרבי
חנינא בן תרדיון: אשריך שנתפסת על דבר אחד, אוי לי שנתפסתי על חמשה דברים.
א״ל רבי חנינא: אשריך שנתפסת על חמשה דברים ואתה ניצול, אוי לי שנתפסתי על
דבר אחד ואיני ניצול, שאת עוסקת בתורה ובגמילות חסדים, ואני לא עסקתי אלא בתורה
[בלבד]; וכדרב הונא, דאמר רב הונא: כל העוסק בתורה בלבד – דומה כמי שאין לו
אלוה, שנאמר (דברי הימים ב:יג): "וימים רבים לישראל ללא א־לקי אמת", מאי ללא
א־לקי אמת? שכל העוסק בתורה בלבד – דומה כמי שאין לו א־לוה.

Our rabbis taught: When Rabbi Elazar ben Prata and Rabbi Hanina ben Teradyon were arrested [by the Romans], Rabbi Elazar ben Prata said to Rabbi Hanina ben Teradyon, "Fortunate are you that you have been arrested over one matter, woe is me who have been arrested over five matters." Rabbi Hanina responded, "Fortunate are you that you have been arrested over five matters but are to be saved; woe is me who have been arrested over one matter but will not be saved. For you concerned yourself with both Torah and *gemilut hasadim,* whereas I concerned myself solely with Torah." As Rav Huna stated; for Rav Huna said, "Whoever concerns himself solely with Torah is as one who has no God. As it is written, 'And many days [passed] for Israel without a true God' (Divrei Ha-Yamim II, 5:13). What is [the meaning of] 'without a true God'? That one who concerns himself solely with Torah is as one who has no God."[15]

The midrash equates the renunciation of *gemilut hasadim* with blasphemy;[16] and the gemara in Rosh Hashanah states that Rabbah and Abbaye, both being descended from Eli, overcame the curse cast upon his house: "Rabbah, who engaged in the study of Torah, lived forty years; Abbaye, who engaged in Torah and *gemilut hasadim,* lived sixty years."[17] When, as in contemporary Israel, the greatest single hesed one can perform is to help defend his fellows' very lives, the implications for yeshiva education should be obvious.

What is equally obvious is the fact that not everyone draws these implications – and this for one of several reasons. Some (not many, I hope) simply have little if any concern for the State of Israel, even entertain the naive notion that, as one Rosh Yeshiva put it, their business could continue as usual with Palestinian flags fluttering from the rooftops. Others feel that the spiritual price, personal and communal, is simply too high, and that first-rate Torah leadership can only be developed in the monochromatic context of "pure" yeshivot. Still others contend that, from the perspective of genuine faith and trust in God, the yeshivot are the true guardians of the polity, and any compromise of their integrity is a blow at national security. These contentions clearly raise a number of basic moral, halakhic, and theological issues with respect to which I obviously entertain certain views. However, I do not wish, at this juncture, to polemicize. These are matters on which honest men of Torah can differ seriously out of mutual respect, and I certainly have no desire to denigrate those who do not subscribe to my own position. What I do wish to stress minimally, however, is the point that, for the aspiring *talmid hakham,* hesder is at least as legitimate a path as any other. It is, to my mind, a good deal more, but surely not less.

The point can be underscored by a brief glance at the relevant proof-texts most frequently cited by rigorous critics of hesder. Of course, those who oppose it because they have little use for the state, and presume that its dismemberment would not seriously endanger its inhabitants, need not look far for support. Given their assumptions, they can draw upon a plethora of sources that stress the overriding importance of *talmud Torah* and castigate the expenditure of time upon relatively insignificant purposes. I very much hope, however, that among our critics, this is a decidedly minority view; and I prefer to address myself to the position of those who do assign a measure of value to the state – and hence, of necessity, to its army – and whom the question of military service therefore confronts as an instance of the difficult, perhaps even agonizing, choice between conflicting values. In large measure – and I, for one, regard this as perfectly legitimate – the assignment of priorities is ultimately based upon the degree of importance attached to the two realms, as this determines the readiness to take respective risks; and, as previously noted, this in turn is a function of the much broader issue of the relationship of *talmud Torah* to the rest of human life. Nevertheless, much discussion of the issue quite properly centers upon specific authoritative texts, which, for this group of critics, must be such as do not simply espouse the study of Torah but address themselves to this dilemma directly; and I would like to briefly consider the more important of these.

While most of the relevant texts are aggadic, one *locus classicus* is purely halakhic, and it may best be treated first. The gemara in Bava Batra states that *talmidei hakhamim* are exempt from sharing the cost of municipal fortifications inasmuch as they "do not require protection."[18] Analogously, it is contended that they should be exempt from military service. One may state, in reply, that this claim raises a very serious moral issue. Can anyone whose life is not otherwise patterned after this degree of trust and *bittahon* argue for exemption on *this* ground? Is it possible to worry about one's economic future, in evident disregard of Rabbi Eliezer's statement that "whoever has bread in his basket and says 'What shall I eat tomorrow?' is but of little faith,"[19] and still not enter the army because one is presumably safe without it? I recall, some years back, admiring the candor of a *maggid shiur* who confided to me that he had moved from a neighborhood in which most young men served in Zahal to one in which they did not because, while he might be convinced intellectually that he ought not to serve in the army, he knew full well that he did not possess the depth of faith upon which such an exemption could only be granted. Hence, he felt too ashamed, especially as his sons were coming of military age, to remain in his old bailiwick. Perhaps not many would share this response, but the basic situation is probably not uncommon; and for many, at least, any argument based on this gemara is consequently problematic.

There is, however, no need to pursue this train of thought, for the basic analogy is quite tenuous on purely halakhic grounds. The payment in question is not inherently normative. It relates to no *mizvah* whatsoever. Rather, it derives solely from the obligation to help defray the cost of communal facilities from which one reaps benefit. This is obvious from the context; the impost is discussed in the same mishnah that deals with requiring tenants of a courtyard to pay for a gate or watchman's booth or both in order to keep out trespassers and onlookers, and both are cited by the Rambam in Hilkhot Shekhenim. Moreover, it is reflected in the fact that the sum is prorated according to the degree of benefit involved, with those subject to the greatest risk paying the most.[20] Hence, those who derive no direct benefit pay nothing. Tenants without cars do not generally pay for the upkeep of a building's garage, and those who have no television sets may be exempt from sharing in the cost of a central antenna.

The situation is radically different, however, with respect to an obligation precisely rooted in the responsibility to help others qua others. Does anyone suppose that one's duty to engage in a defensive *milhemet mizvah* "to help save [the people of] Israel from a foe who has descended upon them"[21] is based solely upon the fact that one is presently or potentially in danger? In the context of the egocentric ethic of a Mandeville or an Adam Smith, possibly. From a Torah perspective, however, this would be strange doctrine, the more so to the extent that we correctly perceive that such action is mandated by the general norm of *gemilut hasadim* and not just the specific commandment of defensive war.[22] Consequently, the gemara in Bava Batra provides no rationale whatsoever for totally exempting *talmidei hakhamim* from military service. *They* may not require protection but others do; and their duty to defend those who have no built-in armor remains.[23]

A second oft-cited source is the coda of Sefer Zeraim in the Rambam's *Mishneh Torah*. The Rambam first postulates the spiritual character of the tribe of Levi as explaining its being barred from a share in Eretz Yisrael and its spoils, and then goes on to expand upon this theme:

ולמה לא זכה לוי בנחלת ארץ ישראל ובביזתה עם אחיו? מפני שהובדל לעבוד את ה'
לשרתו ולהורות דרכיו הישרים ומשפטיו הצדיקים לרבים שנאמר "יורו משפטיך ליעקב
ותורתך לישראל", לפיכך הובדלו מדרכי העולם לא עורכין מלחמה כשאר ישראל ולא
נוחלין ולא זוכין לעצמן בכח גופן, אלא הם חיל השם שנאמר "ברך ה' חילו", והוא
ברוך הוא זוכה להם שנאמר "אני חלקך ונחלתך". ולא שבט לוי בלבד אלא כל איש
ואיש מכל באי העולם אשר נדבה רוחו אותו והבינו מדעו להבדל לעמוד לפני ה' לשרתו
ולעובדו לדעה את ה' והלך ישר כמו שעשהו הא־לקים ופרק מעל צוארו עול החשבונות
הרבים אשר בקשו בני האדם הרי זה נתקדש קדש קדשים ויהיה ה' חלקו ונחלתו לעולם
ולעולמי עולמים ויזכה לו בעולם הזה דבר המספיק לו כמו שזכה לכהנים ללוים, הרי
דוד ע"ה אומר "ה' מנת חלקי וכוסי אתה תומיך גורלי".

And why did not Levi partake of the patrimony of Eretz Yisrael and its spoils with his brethren? Because he was set apart to serve God, to worship Him and to teach His just ways and righteous ordinances to the masses. As it is stated, "They shall teach Jacob Thine ordinances, and Israel Thy law" (Devarim 33:10). Therefore, they have been set apart from the ways of the world: they do not wage war like the rest of Israel, nor do they inherit or acquire unto themselves by physical force. They are, rather, the Lord's corps, as it is stated, "I am thy portion and thine inheritance" (Bamidbar 18:20). And not the tribe of Levi alone but each and every person throughout the world whose spirit has uplifted him and whose intelligence has given him the understanding to stand before God, to serve Him, to worship Him, to know God; and he walks aright as he has cast off from his neck the many considerations which men have sought – such a one has been sanctified as the holy of holies, and the Lord shall be his portion and his inheritance forever and ever, and shall grant him his sufficiency in this world as he has granted to the kohanim and the Levi'im. As David, peace be upon him, says, "O Lord, the portion of mine inheritance and of my cup, Thou maintainest my lot" (Tehillim 16:5).[24]

At first glance, these lines seem to sanction, in principle, a *ben Torah's* total divorce from military service. In truth, however, they are of little, if any, relevance to our subject. On one level, there arises the obvious difficulty of squaring this statement both with the Rambam's personal history and with his repeated vehement critiques of those who exploit the study of Torah to worldly advantage by abstaining from all gainful activity in the expectation that they will be supported by the public treasury.[25] Even if we confine ourselves to this text, however, we shall find that its presumed sanction is weak, at best.

First, the initial postulate – that every Levite enjoys a dispensation from army duty, has no source in Hazal. On the contrary, it contravenes the evident purport of the mishnah in Sotah, אבל במלחמות מצוה הכל יוצאין, אפילו חתן מחדרו וכלה מחופתה "But in [case of] wars of *mizvah*, all go out, even a groom from his [wedding] room and a bride from her wedding chamber."[26] As has often been noted, if the Rambam's formulation is understood as a total bar on army service by shevet Levi, it seems, to be clearly contradicted by a gemara in Kiddushin.[27] Would or should *Bnei Torah* readily lean upon such a thin reed in order to exempt themselves from, say, the *mizvot* of lulav or shofar?

Second, it seems most unlikely that this statement is indeed all it is presumed to be. If the Rambam had truly intended to postulate a categorical dispensation for *bnei levi* or *Bnei Torah,* would he have presented and formulated it in this manner and context? Given his sharply honed discipline and sense of order, would he not have cited it in Hilkhot Melakhim u'Milhamoteihem (to cite the full rubric) together with all the laws of warfare rather than as a peroration to Sefer Zeraim? The implication is clear. What we have here is a hortatory coda, analogous to the conclusions of many of the books of the *Mishneh Torah* (which, of course, is to be given full weight as such, since it is, after all, the Rambam's), but is not to be confused with a clear halakhic mandate. It provides a vivid evaluation of an inspiring personality but does not dictate how it or others should act.

Even if this contention is rejected, however, the Rambam's statement remains largely irrelevant to the contemporary problem of hesder. For it should be noted, third, that the spirituality of the Levite does not preclude military service entirely. It only absolves him from waging war "like the rest of Israel."[28] At most, he can be exempt from the gamut of wars included within the *mizvah* of *milhamah* per se. This exemption has no bearing, however, upon his duty to help fight or prevent a defensive war that threatens the survival of his community and his peers. Is a spiritual order excused from saving human lives? To the extent that this obligation is rooted in the overall norm of *gemilut hasadim,* it encompasses everyone. The world of the *ben Torah,* too, rests upon three pillars. Of course, no one would suggest that all *bnei yeshiva* stop learning and turn to cardiology. There is, however, a clear difference between abstaining from specializing in humanitarian endeavors and forgoing a universal effort. And above all, the issue is not one of suspending *talmud Torah,* God forbid, but of balancing and complementing it.

Finally, even if we grant that the Rambam's statement does imply a categorical dispensation in purely halakhic terms, it remains of little practical significance. We have yet to examine just to whom it applies. A *levi* is defined genealogically. Those who are equated with him, however, literally or symbolically, are defined by spiritual qualities; and for these the Rambam sets a very high standard, indeed. He presents an idealized portrait of a selfless, atemporal, almost ethereal person – one whose spirit and intelligence have led him to divest himself of all worldly concerns and who has devoted himself לעמוד לפני ה' לשרתו ולעובדו לדעה את ה' והלך ישר "to stand כמו שעשהו הא-לקים ופרק מעל צוארו עול החשבונות הרבים אשר בקשו בני האדם before God, to serve Him, to worship Him, to know God; and he walks aright as the Lord has made him and he has cast off from his neck the yoke of the many considerations[29] that men have sought."

To how large a segment of the Torah community, or, *a fortiori,* of any community, does this lofty typology apply? Two percent? Five percent? Can anyone who has negotiated the terms of a salary, perhaps even of *naden* or *kest* or both, look into a mirror and tell himself that he need not go to the army because he is *kodesh kodashim, sanctum sanctorum,* in the Rambam's terms? Can anyone with even a touch of vanity or a concern for *kavod* contend this?[30]

Lest I be misunderstood, let me state clearly that I have no quarrel with economic aspirations or with normal human foibles. Again, least of all do I wish to single out *bnei yeshivot* for undeserved moral censure. I do feel, however, that those who would single themselves out for exemption from normal duties on the grounds of saintliness should examine their credentials by the proper standard.

Two other texts on this subject may be treated more briefly. One is

evidently critical of Avraham Avinu for having dispatched his students
to fight:

אמר רבי אבהו אמר רבי אלעזר: מפני מה נענש אברהם אבינו ונשתעבדו בניו למצרים
מאתים ועשר שנים? מפני שעשה אנגרייא בתלמידי חכמים, שנאמר (בראשית יד:יד):
"וירק את חניכיו ילידי ביתו".

Rabbi Abbahu said in the name of Rabbi Elazar: Why was Avraham Avinu
punished and his offspring enslaved in Egypt for two hundred and ten years?
Because he conscripted *talmidei hakhamim,* as it is stated, "He led forth his
trained men, born in his house" (Bereshit 14:14).[31]

The implications of this source seem clear but it, too, should not be
assigned decisive weight. In the ensuing lines, the gemara quotes alternative explanations for Avraham's punishment.[32] Moreover, the midrash
cites the comments of several tannaim and amoraim who all regarded
the mustering of his disciples favorably.[33] Third, Rabbi Elazar's criticism
is limited to conscription, with its almost inevitable encroachment upon
personal dignity. The term he uses, *angarya,* refers elsewhere to forced
labor or the requisition of goods;[34] and a parallel explanation of Assa's
punishment deals with conscription for construction without reference
to military service.[35] Hence, this gemara can only support an argument
against Zahal's subjecting *bnei torah* to a coercive draft. It says nothing of
their duty to serve as a matter of choice.

Lastly, we may note a more explicit source, it, too, positing a causal
nexus:

Rabbi Abba b. Kahana said: If not for David, Yoav could not have waged
war; and were it not for Yoav, David could not have engaged in Torah. As it
is written: "And David executed justice and righteousness unto all his people.
And Yoav the son of Zeruyah was over the host" (Shemuel II, 8:15–16). Why
did David execute justice and righteousness unto all his people? Because
Yoav was over the host. And why was Yoav over the host? Because David was
executing justice and righteousness unto all his people.[36]

Admittedly, in this gemara the case for spiritual exemption and the
division of functions is apparently more clearly articulated. Here, too,
however, several comments are in order. First, the gemara introduces

this comment with the observation that it runs counter to the prevalent thrust of the preceding discourse. Second, the engagement in Torah of which it speaks does not refer to purely contemplative study alone but to implementation through the molding of a just and fair society. Above all, however, this source is of little use to our critics on the right because of its protagonist. If they really wish to posit David, the heroic and sensitive soldier-scholar-poet-votary so graphically portrayed by Hazal in numerous contexts, as the prototype of the contemporary Israeli *ben torah*, I shall have little quarrel with them.

There is, then, no halakhic, moral, or philosophic mandate for the blanket exemption of *Bnei Torah* from military service. These categorical claims having been laid to rest, however, and their presumed authoritative basis neutralized, we are still confronted by the practical difficulty of weighing conflicting needs – of striking a balance, on both the personal and especially the communal plane, between the spiritual and the material, and of assessing the risks inherent in pressing one at the expense of the other. And we need to do this with reference to both ideology and fact, determining not only whether hesder is desirable but the extent to which, in one form or another, it is feasible. On this level, that of the practical formulation of public policy rather than the principled invocation of personal prerogative, there is room for disagreement – and, quite conceivably, for pluralist solutions.

Even assuming such pluralism, however, the composition of our educational mix must be carefully considered. I fully appreciate the contribution of non-hesder yeshivot to our spiritual life; I grant that they contain some individuals who at present serve their country well by devoting themselves to Torah exclusively, and this not because they might make poor soldiers but because of their spiritual potential. Much as I would like the great majority of their students to modify their course out of personal conviction, I have no desire to legislate them out of existence or into yeshivot hesder.

I realize that some of the arguments I have raised against full exemption might be pressed by others against the abbreviation of service; and that just as I would vindicate the latter on the basis of spiritual need, so may others justify the former for the same reason. Nonetheless, I feel strongly that, at the very least, the current proportion of hesder to non-hesder yeshivot is totally out of kilter. Surely, we dare not acquiesce in the protracted spiritual desiccation of *bnei torah* at a critical juncture in their lives. However, the ethical alternative should not be a self-determined carte blanche exemption. Hesder, conceived and implemented not as a compromise but as a bold response to a difficult dilemma, should be the standard rather than the exception. It is the direction which, upon searching examination of the issue, Torah leadership should seek to promote as a norm, not as a deviation.

In making any assessment of hesder, it is important that we approach the subject with full awareness of the military ramifications, a point not always sufficiently heeded. The story is reliably told of a leading Rosh Yeshiva who, at the height of the controversy over *giyus banot,* "the drafting of women," back in the fifties, attended a wedding near the Israeli-Arab border in Jerusalem. At one point, gunfire was suddenly heard and he scurried under a table, exclaiming passionately, *"Ribbono shel Olam,* I want to live! There is much Torah which I still wish to learn and create!" Whereupon a rather insensitive observer approached him and asked, *"Nu, rebbe, was sagt ihr itster wegen giyus banos?"* (Well, rabbi, what do you say now about *giyus banot?*). And he kept quiet. I cite the story not because I favor the induction of women – under present circumstances, I very much oppose it – or to impugn the memory of a truly great man, but in order to point out that, at a certain distance, one can lose sight of the simple truth that a Jewish soul must inhere within a Jewish body.

This nagging truth persists, however, and its appreciation is central to an understanding of an institution designed to reconcile the conflicting claims of spirituality and security, of *talmud Torah* and *gemilut hasadim,* of personal growth and public service. The dilemma posed by these claims is not of our choosing. The response, however, is; and in this respect, yeshivot hesder are a conspectus of our collective anomaly: a nation with outstretched palm and mailed fist, striving for peace and yet training for war. For the foreseeable future, this is our situation. While our position is more promising than in the past, we are far from being genuinely secure and can hardly afford to weaken our defenses complacently. Hence, in the context of our "station and its duties" (to use F. H. Bradley's term), hesder is, for *Bnei Torah,* the imperative of the moment. May God grant us a better station. In the meantime, however, if it is to become no worse, we must keep both our spirits and our guard up. Animated by vision and yet chary of danger, we of yeshivot hesder pray that He may grant us the wisdom and the courage to cope with the challenges of the time. Fully appreciative of both the price we pay and the value of that which we safeguard in return, we approach our task with responsibility and humility; and, impelled both by commitment to Torah and compassion for our people, we strive to fulfill it with a sense of broader spiritual and historical vision. Standing in tears atop Har Ha-Zeitim, the bleak sight of *kol ha-mekudash me-havero harev yoter me-havero* (that which is more sanctified than its neighbor is more desolate than its neighbor)[37] stretching before him, what would the Ramban have given to head a yeshivat hesder?

Notes

1. Avot 3:21.
2. The broader question of the morality of self-determined specialization that entails focusing upon some duties to the neglect of others deserves fuller treatment in its own right. The example of Ben Azzai, who proclaimed that whoever did not procreate could be likened to a murderer, and yet remained a bachelor with the explanation "What can I do? My soul yearns for Torah; the world can be preserved by others" (Yevamot 63b), is of course familiar, as is the dichotomy of Issachar and Zevulun. The problem requires further study, however.
3. Zekharyah 4:6.
4. See Bava Mezia 31a and Rambam, Hilkhot Gezelah ve-Avedah 11:20. Cf. Sanhedrin 73a.
5. See Hilkhot Matnot Aniyim 10:7.
6. See Mo'ed Katan 9b and Rambam, Hilkhot Talmud Torah 3:4. This only applies to *mizvot* that entail the attainment of a given objective but are not incumbent upon a particular individual. With respect to a personal *mizvah,* one is required to suspend study in order to perform it.
7. The definition of *efshar,* and especially whether a situation in which I indirectly compel someone to do A by doing B is to be regarded as such, is also relevant to another confrontation. The gemara in Kiddushin 32a cites virtually the same formula as a guide to a person faced with the dilemma of choosing between serving his parents and performing a *mizvah.* Quite possibly, however, the definition may not be identical in both areas.

8. Yerushalmi, Berakhot 1:2.

9. I recall discussing the matter some years back, before I had so much as seen a yeshivat hesder, with my late rebbe, Rav Yitzhak Hutner zt"l (who later rejected hesder for his own Israeli yeshiva on quite other grounds, because he felt it would interfere too seriously with learning). He virtually scoffed: "*Kalye veren! Einer ken kalye veren sitzendig in kandy store!*" (To go bad! One can go bad sitting in a candy store!). He did, however, feel that the sense of *tzeniut* was often adversely affected.

10. Devarim 23:10.

11. See Megillah 3a.

12. Bereshit 26:29

13. Of course, no one admits to dismissing him in so many words. However, the gap between the Ramban's perspective and that of much recent *parshanut,* particularly with reference to the human element in Bereshit and the balance between realistic and idealized, if not hagiolatrous, interpretation, is very broad.

14. See Avot 1:2.

15. Avodah Zarah 17b. The gemara prescribes no specific measure for *gemilut hasadim.* Presumably, however, it refers to a significant commitment. We can hardly suppose that Rabbi Hanina disregarded this area entirely. See also Maharal of Prague, *Netivot Olam,* Netiv Gemilut Hasadim, chap. 2.

16. See Kohelet Rabbah 7:4.

17. Rosh Hashanah 18a. Again, I presume that Rabbah, too, engaged in hesed, but only minimally.

18. Bava Batra 7b.

19. Sotah 48b.

20. See the whole discussion, Bava Batra 7b, Rishonim ad loc., and Rambam, Hilkhot Shekhenim 6:1, who accepts the position that the primary criterion of risk is proximity to the danger zone rather than the value of the threatened property. Quite conceivably, the payment is also a function of the ability to pay. The *sugya,* however, neither presents nor precludes this factor. It only relates to means as possibly determining the degree of benefit rather than the capacity to pay for it.

21. Rambam, Hilkhot Melakhim 5:1.

22. One may ask just why the Mishnah did not classify payment for fortifications as aid. The question of who should pay for public services, the beneficiaries or the whole community, is general and complex, and certainly deserves treatment in its own right. However, the Halakhah's decision in this case is clear. In any event, one cannot infer from a situation in which the burden is cast upon residents who evidently can afford the facility to one in which, by the very nature of the *mizvah,* it is incumbent upon the general community. I take it for granted, although this is admittedly a rather murky criterion, that if the residents could not afford the fortifications, the others would have been taxed to pay for them.

23. There is a second Halakhah that exempts *talmidei hakhamim* even from paying taxes that

maintain services and facilities which they need; see Bava Batra 8a and Rambam, Hilkhot Talmud Torah 6:10. However, this exemption, essentially similar to the one widely granted religious institutions today, only precludes the community's imposing upon them. It does not pertain to their possible obligation to perform certain vital functions. Moreover, it would appear from the gemara and from Rambam – who cites the general exemption in Hilkhot Talmud Torah but nevertheless felt constrained to set down the specific dispensation from paying for defense needs in Hilkhot Shekhenim 6:6, accompanied by the explanation "that *talmidei hakhamim* do not need defense because the Torah guards them" – that defense is excepted from the overall exemption. Evidently, if the *talmid petur* notwithstanding, this exception applies to vital needs (e.g., road maintenance, according to the Rambam [loc. cit.]; water supply, according to Rashi [Bava Batra 8a, s.v. *lekarya patya*]; or, in general, "that which is necessary for human life," as the *Shulhan Arukh* formulated it [Yoreh De'ah 243:2]), and thus its application to defense is natural.

Finally, it should be noted further that the scope of any exemption drawn from the gemara in Bava Batra depends upon the definition of *talmid hakham*, a question that arises in various halakhic contexts. See, with respect to our problem, Rav C.F. Tchursh, *Keter Ephraim* (Tel Aviv, 5727), pp. 172–174, and the many sources he cites. It may very well be, with respect to this definition, that we should distinguish between the general exemption and that for defense. The former is a personal *petur gavra* that may very well depend upon one's level and qualifications. The latter is grounded in one's adherence to Torah which affords him protection; and to this end, effort and commitment may be more important than accomplishment.

24. Hilkhot Shemittah ve-Yovel 13:12–13.

25. The best-known is to be found in *Mishneh Torah*, Hilkhot Talmud Torah, 3:10. See also *Perush Ha-Mishnayot*, Avot 4:5. For a full discussion of the issue, much of it centering upon the Rambam, see *Sefer Ha-Tashbets* 1:142–148.

26. Sotah 44b.

27. See Kiddushin 21b.

28. The construction, *v'ein orhin milhamah kishear Yisrael*, could mean not only that they do not wage war on a par with others, but that they do not wage it at all. Even on that interpretation, however, I think the statement would only refer to *milhamah* as an independent category but not as an instance of hesed.

29. The phrase *hishvonot rabbim* which I have rendered as "many considerations" is drawn from Kohelet 7:29. The JPS version translates "many inventions," but I find this overly intellectual, and it misses the element of worldly self-interest, perhaps even tinged by manipulative machinations, contrasted with man's primal rectitude, that is clearly implied by the context.

30. I am familiar with the contention that even if the exemption properly applies to only a select few, it must, in practice, be granted en masse, either because those few cannot be identified *ante facto* or because they need all the others as a supportive and stimulating environment. Given our national exigencies, however, I do not find it convincing.

31. Nedarim 32a.
32. Elsewhere, the Ramban suggests yet another explanation: the reason for the punishment was Avraham's decision to go to Egypt in a time of famine rather than remain in Canaan. This, states the Ramban (Bereshit 12:10), constituted a lack of sufficient trust in God.

   One may add that to the modern mind – unschooled in the theological reading of history, oriented to liberal individualism, and unattuned to the concept of causality, especially as it relates to reward and retribution, as expressed by Hazal – the whole discussion may seem strange. This subject requires much fuller elucidation than can be given. I would only state, very generally, that the causal relation should be perceived as correspondence, the meshing of a person with a complex as it impinges upon him, rather than as a linear interpretation, in quid pro quo terms, of the complex as a whole.
33. See the various views cited in Bereshit Rabbah 43:2.
34. See *Arukh Ha-Shalem* and *Otzar Lashon Ha-Talmud,* s.v. *angarya.*
35. See Sotah 10a.
36. Sanhedrin 49a.
37. From his famous letter to his son, in *Kitvei Ha-Ramban,* ed. Rabbi C.B. Chavel (Jerusalem, 1963), p. 368.

Chapter 8

The Human and Social Factor in Halakhah

Any comprehensive overview of the concern for the human and social factor within Halakhah needs to relate, perhaps both substantively and historically, to several planes. We need to consider, first, the primal halakhic core. What is its presumed, and possibly avowed, *telos*? And how "friendly" is its codex – how rigorous its demand and how permissive its latitude? Secondly, we must examine the halakhic process, from a historical (albeit not from a historicistic) perspective. In part, this is simply a complementary extension of the initial phase. Pursuant to an analysis of the scope and nature of the concern for man implicit in the *d'oraitha* bedrock of Torah, we could similarly probe the character and content of its *d'rabbanan* accretions. In part, however, it presents us with an independent challenge – examination of whether and how sensitivity to the human and social factor has impacted, legitimately, upon the formulation and implementation of Halakhah.

The first question itself bears a dual aspect, relating to both intent and content. With respect to the former, the Torah itself describes its regimen as destined to enhance human good:

ועתה ישראל מה ה׳ א־לקיך שאל מעמך כי אם ליראה את ה׳ א־לקיך ללכת בכל דרכיו ולאהבה אתו ולעבד את ה׳ א־לקיך בכל לבבך ובכל נפשך. לשמר את מצות ה׳ ואת חקתיו אשר אנכי מצוך היום לטוב לך.

And now, Israel, what doth the Lord thy God require of thee, but to fear

159

the Lord thy God, to walk in all His ways, and to love Him, and to serve the
Lord thy God with all thy heart and with all thy soul; to keep for thy good
the commandments of the Lord, and His statutes, which I command thee
this day?[1]

A similar chord is struck in familiar texts in Hazal. In a general vein,
we are told:

רצה הקב"ה לזכות את ישראל לפיכך הרבה להם תורה ומצות שנאמר ה' חפץ למען
צדקו יגדיל תורה ויאדיר

The Holy One, blessed be He, desired to give Israel merit, therefore He gave
them much Torah and many *mizvot*, as it is said (Yeshayahu 42:21), "The
Lord was pleased, for the sake of His righteousness, to make the Torah great
and glorious."[2]

And, at the pragmatic and utilitarian level, several halakhot are explicated in light of the assumption, התורה חסה על ממונן של ישראל.[3] (The Torah
was concerned with [unnecessary expenditure of] Israel's money.)

At bottom, however, such prooftexts are inconclusive, as they leave
open the critical issue of the definition of key terms. *Lezakot* could range
from material bounty to spiritual purgation. To which sphere does *letov
lakh* refer, the mundane arena of psychosocial benefit or the posthumous
olam shekulo tov?[4] We are therefore driven to move from teleology to
substance, to encounter the fabric of Halakhah proper. We would need to
examine, on the one hand, whether, and to what extent, its corpus promotes
and/or mandates affirmation or denial; its consonance with the realization
of natural desire or aspiration; where its norms, taken collectively, stand on a
scale of asceticism. On the other hand, we would have to analyze the extent
to which there is allowance for deviation, on human and social grounds,
in particularly trying circumstances; to test, in effect, the scope of the
Rambam's assertion with respect to the dispensation of *pikuah nefesh*:

הא למדת שאין משפטי התורה נקמה בעולם אלא רחמים וחסד ושלום בעולם ואלו
האפיקורוסים שאומרים שזה חילול שבת ואסור עליהן הכתוב אומר גם אני נתתי להם
חוקים לא טובים ומשפטים לא יחיו בהם.

Hence you learn that the ordinances of the Law were meant to bring upon
the world not vengeance, but mercy, lovingkindness and peace. It is of

heretics – who assert that this is nevertheless a violation of the Sabbath and therefore prohibited – that Scripture says, "Wherefore I gave them also statutes that were not good, and ordinances whereby they should not live" (Yehezkel 20:25).[5]

Such an examination, even if exhaustive, would hardly produce a definitive response. So much depends on the eye of the beholder and upon the standards employed. Moreover, the elements of the halakhic order are, in this respect, widely divergent, exacting rigor seemingly reflected in some and general acceptance in others, so that an observer can focus upon components highlighting his own emphases while apologetically parrying others, apparently inconsonant with them. And, of course, one's conclusions might be subtly multifaceted, postulating dialectical interplay, the concept of intermediate constriction as leading to ultimate human efflorescence, or both.

The last, broadly speaking, was the position of the Rav ל״צז. He repeatedly – alternately and, at times, even concurrently – developed twin themes. On the one hand, at both the ethical and the religious planes, he celebrated inhibition and restraint. At times, he almost identified *yahadut*[6] with denial and sacrifice, through which the Jew both heroically attains spiritual catharsis and submissively bonds with the *Ribbono shel Olam*. On the other hand, he consistently rejected asceticism and emphasized that Halakhah neither accepted nor rejected the world but affirmatively mandated its sanctification through disciplined channeling of physical and passional experience. His emphasis fluctuated, and the relation between the respective elements underwent changes. But the basic adherence to this dual motif remained fairly constant, and it served as one of the linchpins of his thought.

Even barring definitive conclusions, then, an analysis of the degree of halakhic concern with human and social reality and aspiration would bear valuable fruit. On balance, it would sharpen our insight into the substance and spirit of *devar Hashem*. At the very least, it would delineate attitudinal parameters framing possible conceptions of the place of human and social concerns within Halakhah. And it would reinforce our sense of the role, within *yahadut*, of Halakhah, as a ballast countering possible hashkafic excesses of either ascetic rigor or affirmative exuberance. Whatever instinctive or ideological reservations a purist may have about sexuality, these cannot exceed a certain point in light of the simple normative dictum – particularly as applied to a spiritual elite:

תשמיש המטה מעונג שבת הוא לפיכך עונת תלמידי חכמים הבריאים משמשין מלילי
שבת ללילי שבת.

Sexual relations are considered a form of Sabbath pleasure. Therefore, scholars who are healthy set aside Friday night as the night when they fulfill their [weekly] conjugal duties.[8]

Valuable as such a discussion might be, it is not, if I understand my mandate correctly, the focus of this paper. My primary concern shall not be the bedrock Halakhah, quintessential *devar Hashem,* but *ba'alei Halakhah, hakhmei hamesorah* in whom it is embedded and through whom it is developed, implemented, and transmitted. And I shall narrow the discussion still further by largely ignoring the basic phases of halakhic discourse – exegesis, hermeneutics, and analysis – and instead concentrating, with particular emphasis upon the post-Hazal era, on its latter stages of decision and *hora'ah.*

Hora'ah is comprised of two elements: *psak* and *pesikah,* respectively. The former refers to codification, the formulation of the law pertinent to a given area; and it is most characteristically manifested in the adoption, on textual or logical grounds, of one position in preference to others. As such, it is, essentially, the concluding phase of the learning process proper, whether on a grand or a narrow scale, and its locus is the *bet midrash. Pesikah,* by contrast, denominates implementation. It bespeaks the application of what has already been forged in the crucible of the learning experience to a particular situation. It does not entail the definitive postulation of the law governing a delimited area or its detail, but, rather, the concurrent and coordinate meshing of all aspects, possibly drawn from widely divergent spheres, obtaining in a concrete situation. Its venue is, publicly, the *bet din* or, privately, the meeting of inquirer and respondent. It does not necessarily demand of the *posek* that he take a stand or break fresh ground. Its challenge lies in the need to harness knowledge and responsibility at the interface of reality and Halakhah.

The human and social factor is relevant to Halakhah at its various levels; and the point can be briefly illustrated by the example of *shalom* – perceived not only in moral and hortatory terms, with primary reference to the Aggadic sphere, but as a halakhic element. At the teleological plane, it is described in one context as the impulse for the entire Torah. In the wake of Abbaye's query to Rav Yosef, as to why the Mishnah in Gittin ascribes the sequence of *aliyot* to the quest for synagogal harmony, and hence of *d'rabbanan* origin, when it could presumably be accorded *d'oraitha* status, as a fulfillment of the commandment of *vekidashto,* that we sanctify and entitle *kohanim* and *leviyim,* the gemara cites a brief discussion:

א״ל דאורייתא ומפני דרכי שלום כל התורה כולה נמי מפני דרכי שלום היא דכתיב דרכיה דרכי נועם וכל נתיבותיה שלום.

He answered: [This law] does derive from the Torah, but its object is to promote peace. [He objected:] But the whole of the Torah is also for the purpose of promoting peace, as it is written (Mishlei 3:17), "Her ways are ways of pleasantness and all her paths are peace!"[9]

It then goes on to present an alternate explanation, clearly implying that the basis of the rejoinder had been accepted.

What in the gemara is advanced, en passant, in the course of discursive debate, was posited by the Rambam in definitive terms; and furthermore, was linked to specific halakhot. As the coda to *Sefer Zemanim,* he elaborates upon a *din* cited from a gemara in Shabbat:

היה לפניו נר ביתו ונר חנוכה או נר ביתו וקדוש היום נר ביתו קודם משום שלום ביתו שהרי השם נמחק לעשות שלום בין איש לאשתו. גדול השלום שכל התורה ניתנה לעשות שלום בעולם שנאמר דרכיה דרכי נעם וכל נתיבותיה שלום.

If [a poor man] needs oil for both a Sabbath lamp and a Hanukkah lamp, or oil for a Sabbath lamp and wine for Kiddush, the Sabbath lamp should have priority, for the sake of peace in the household, seeing that even a Divine Name may be erased to make peace between husband and wife. Great indeed is peace, forasmuch as the purpose for which the whole of the Law was given is to bring peace upon the world, as it is said, "Her ways are ways of pleasantness, and all her paths are peace" (Mishlei 3:17).[10]

The stark contrast between the situation at issue – concern lest domestic tranquillity be perturbed should a member of the household bump himself in the dark – and the grandiloquent generalization only serves to sharpen awareness of harmony as a value.

At the plane of substantive content, we may regard the quest for harmony as the underpinning of a number of halakhot, if not of whole halakhic areas, *mid'oraitha*. From a certain perspective, the mandate of *bet din* is not only juristic but social, and its primary function in that connection is the preservation of comity.[11] Or, to take an individual example, the laws of *harhakat shekenim* are intended not only to avert inflicting damage, but positively, to promote interpersonal civility.[12] And, of course, the point is fully explicit as regards *takkanot d'rabbanan,* with respect to which the link is variously formulated. It may be viewed, as in the Yerushalmi's[13] explanation of *eruvei hazerot,* as an impetus to promote camaraderie, in positive terms. It may be the source of ordinances, instituted *mipenei darkhei shalom,* intended to forestall possible friction.[14] And, more sharply, it may underlie halakhot legislated *mishum eivah,* with an eye to averting potential enmity, not only between Jew and Gentile but within the Jewish community proper, whether the resentment of a mate[15] or the vindictiveness of a parent.[16] The primary chord, the need to preserve and enhance interpersonal and communal harmony, is uniformly clear, however.

The element of *shalom* is likewise in force as an overriding factor, preempting the "normal" Halakhah. In Hazal, this aspect, at the level of particular implementation rather than general legislation, only appears explicitly vis-à-vis *d'rabbanan* ordinances. However, the Rama extended it to the *d'oraitha* level as well. Invoking an Aggadic account of Achitophel's extension of the license presumably implicit in the erasure of the divine name in order to establish marital reconciliation, he daringly elevates this to the status of general procedural principle:

למדנו מכאן דמותר לשנות לשנות מפני השלום ומותר לעבור על "מדבר שקר תרחק" (שמות כג:ז) גם דוחה לא תעשה שבתורה שהיא "לא תעשון כן לה' א-לקיכם" (דברים יב:

ד) שהיא אזהרה למוחק השם כדאיתא בספרי פרשת ראה ומנאוה הרמב"ם ז"ל (ספר
המצוות, לא תעשה סה) והסמ"ג במנין המצות (לאווין ג) ואם כן אומר שהוא הדין שדוחה
לאו של מוציא שם רע, דמותר להוציא שם רע אם כוונתו לשמים ולתכלית טוב כדי
לעשות שלום.

> We have learned from here that it is permissible to modify [the truth] for the
> sake of peace, and it is permissible to violate the injunction, "Thou shalt dis-
> tance thyself from falsehood" (Shemot 23:7). [The consideration of peace] also
> overrides the Biblical prohibition of "Thou shalt not do thus to the Lord thy
> God" (Devarim 12:4), which bans the erasure of God's Name, as is explained
> in the Sifri to parashat Re'eh and counted by the Rambam and the Semag in
> their respective enumerations of the *mizvot*. Since this is so, I say that it is
> also the case that [peace] overrides the prohibition of defamation; in other
> words, it is permissible to defame another if one's intention is for the sake of
> Heaven and for a good cause, [namely,] to promote peace.[17]

In certain respects, the application is ironic, inasmuch as the over-
ridden *issur* is that of slander, presumably itself predicated, *inter alia,* by
the concern for preserving peace and reducing acrimony. Moreover, as a
routine operative principle the use of so amorphous and highly subjective
criterion to dispense with any *lo ta'aseh* is potentially subversive. However,
these reflections only reinforce awareness of the weight the Rama assigned
to *shalom* as a halakhic category.

That weight is, finally, relevant, although not always manifestly so, at
the plane of decision. In a sense, this point is manifested in Rava's resolution
of the question as to how one who can only afford either a candle for his
home or wine for *kiddush* should choose, with the statement, נר ביתו וקידוש
היום נר ביתו עדיף משום שלום ביתו. (a candle for his home is preferable, because
of the peace of his household)[18] Strictly speaking, however, this is not quite
a decision, as Rava confronts options but not opinions. However, the same
theme is indeed encountered in *hora'ah*, narrowly defined, as exemplified
by the Rosh's determination that educated judicial opinion could substitute
for hard evidence,

> כי על ידי המשפט יש שלום בעולם, ולכך נתנו כח לדיין לשפוט ולעשות מה שירצה
> אף בלא טעם וראיה כדי לתת שלום בעולם.

> For by means of judgment there is peace in the world; therefore they empow-

ered the judge to adjudicate and to do as he pleases, even without offering a
reason or a proof, in order to foster peace in the world.[19]

Illustrations apart, however, the cogency and legitimacy of a "human"
approach to *psak,* appears, to many, problematic. They would have us
believe that the ideal *posek* is a faceless and heartless supercomputer into
whom all of the relevant data is fed and who then produces *the* right answer.
Should this standard not be met, the shortfall is to be regarded as a failing,
the lamentable result of human frailty – in Bacon's terms, a manifestation
of the besetting "idols" which hamper and hinder the capacity for reasoned
judgment. On this reading, the process of *pesikah,* properly conceived
and executed, bears no semblance to an existential encounter between
seeker and respondent. It entails, rather, the application of text to problem,
the coupling of code and situation. This conception does not necessarily
preclude reckoning with the specific circumstances of the question and
questioner, as these may very well be part of the relevant objective data.
The prevailing tendency, however, would be to dwarf this factor; and as
to the human aspect of the *meshiv,* that would be obviated entirely. He,
for his part, is to be animated by the precept that אין מרחמין בדין, (we do not
have mercy in judgment) and hence, to pass on the merits of the issue with
imperviously stony objectivity.

Purist proponents of this approach often cry it up as the "frum" view
of *pesikah.* In reality, however, this portrait of a *posek* is mere caricature,
limned by those who, at most, *kar'u v'shanu,* but certainly *lo shimshu.* As
anyone who has been privileged to observe *gedolim* at close hand can
readily attest, they approach *psak* doubly animated by responsibility
to Halakhah and sensitivity to human concerns. The balance between
norm and need may be variously struck. There certainly are ideological
differences among *poskim* over how much weight to assign the human
factor – although, as Rav Avraham Schapira once noted, the classical
meshivim are likely to be among the more lenient, inasmuch as inquirers
are disinclined to turn to *mahmirim.* In principle, however, recognition
of this factor is the rule rather than the exception; and responsa include
frank acknowledgments of this theme. Writing to a colleague who had

dissented from a lenient *psak* he had rendered with regard to an *agunah*,
Rav Haym Volozhiner asserts:

וראיתי שברוב דברינו כוונתינו הולך אל מקום אחד אלא שכת"ר נוטה אל החומרא מחמת
שאין הדבר מוטל עליו ואף אני כמוהו לא פניתי אל צדדי היתרים העולים מתוך העיון
טרם הועלה עלי עול ההוראה והן עתה שבעוה"ר בסביבותינו נתייתם הדור מחכמים
והעלו על צוארי עול ההוראה מכל הסביבה שאינם מתירים בשום אופן בלתי הסכמת
דעתי הקלה וחשבתי עם קוני וראיתי חובה לעצמי להתחזק בכל כחי לשקוד על תקנת
עגונות והשי"ת יצילני משגיאות.

And I saw that in most matters, we were of like mind, except for [the fact that]
his honor leans towards stringency, since the matter does not depend upon
him. Likewise, before the yoke of practical decision was thrust upon me, I too
did not incline toward the leniencies arising from [legal] analysis. In our great
sins, however, the generation has been orphaned of sages, and now the yoke of
practical halakhic decision-making has been thrust upon me, for in our entire
region they do not free [*agunot*] in any manner without the concurrence of
my meager opinion. Therefore I have taken counsel with my Maker, and feel
obliged to gird all my strength and devote myself to remedying [the situation
of] *agunot*. And may the blessed Lord save me from error.[20]

And does not the whole history of coping with *agunot* reflect this
concern?[21] To anyone familiar with that history, the point is self-evident; but
no less an authority than the *Mass'et Binyamin* provides express witness:

ובאמת שהארכתי יותר מדאי בענין זה במקום שהיה לי לקצר מפני שידעתי דרך קצת
חכמי דורינו יצ"ו דרך ישכון אור להסתלק מכל ספק שבעולם והכל לשם שמים כי מיראת
הוראה ואם לא שיעלה בידם הלכה פסוקה וברורה עד שלא יפול בה שום דבר מחלקי
הסותר ודרכם דרך טובה וישרה בכל שאר הוראות אמנם בעיגונא דאיתתא לא כן עמדי
רק אנכי הולך בעקבי הצאן הרועים הקדמונים והאחרונים שבקשו צדדים (ו)צידי צדדים
בכל מאמצי כחם להקל בעיגונא דאיתתא וכמו שהבאתי דבריהם למעלה.

In truth, I have written too expansively on this matter, when I should have
been brief. [I did so] because I know that the way of some of the sages of
our generation, may the Lord preserve them, is to follow the shining path
and to avoid any doubt in the world, [refusing to rule on halakhic matters]
unless they can determine a clear and unequivocal ruling, untinged by any
contradictory considerations. They do this for the sake of Heaven, out of a
fear of rendering halakhic decisions. This is a good and a straight path in all
other areas of halakhic decision-making; but regarding *agunot*, such is not

my position. Rather, I follow the well-trodden path of the earlier and later shepherds, who sought with all their strength all manner of considerations, primary and secondary, to be lenient in matters pertaining to *agunot*, as I have cited above.[22]

Or, to take a far more limited issue, we are privy to the pained determination of the same *meshiv* who, upon losing his vision, found himself grappling with the Bet Yosef's conclusion that a blind person could not qualify for an *aliyah*:

כי זה עתה לעת זקנתי חשכו הרואות בארובות ותכהנה עיני מראות ולפי אשר עלתה במחשבה של הרב ז"ל יגרשני מלהסתפח בנחלת ה' ותורת אמת חיי עולם לבלתי אחשב במנין הראויין לעלות ולכן אמרתי וגמרתי בלבי חלילה לי מעזוב את דרך עץ החיים ומלאחוז בענפיה אהבתי זאת התעודה מימי קדם קדמתה משפטה ודתה וגם לעת זקנתי בל אשליכה ובה אתהלכה ואפתח בדבר הלכה לראות על מה עשה לי הרב ככה.

For now, in my old age, my eyes have become dim, and according to [the Bet Yosef's] opinion I should be banished from sharing in the Lord's inheritance (for the Torah of truth is eternal life), and I should not be counted among those suitable for an *aliyah*; therefore I said and determined to myself, "Heaven forfend that I depart from the path of the Tree of Life and cease grasping its branches! I have loved this law from earliest youth; it has always enjoyed primacy [in my life]. Even in my old age I shall not discard it, and I shall walk in it[s path]." [Thus,] I commenced halakhic research, to determine why the [Bet Yosef] has done this to me.[23]

It is, here, the *posek*'s own anguish, and with reference to a religious, as opposed to a mundane, need. But it is nonetheless profoundly human and bears ample witness to the rightful place of sensitivity within the process of halakhic decision. And would we have it otherwise? Does anyone truly yearn for a *dayyan* who approaches an *agunah* and a *blitztrop* with the same degree of equanimity?

Hazal certainly did not. The operative rule, כדי ר' פלוני לסמוך עליו בשעת הדחק, (Rabbi So-and-So is worthy of being relied on under exigent circumstances)[24] is clearly predicated upon the assumption that a *posek* can recognize an hour of need and may strive to respond to it. Implicit in this formulation is the concept of differential *psak,* the principle that divergent answers may be given to the identical halakhic question, depending upon attendant human and social circumstances; and it is this concept which holds the key to the advocacy of sensitivity in halakhic decision.

And yet, whatever its precedents, the question of the moral and religious validity of this approach persists. Presumably, it cannot be grounded in the preempting of Halakhah by alternate normative or pragmatic considerations. One recalls, by analogy, Newman's striking declaration: "The Catholic Church holds it better for the sun and moon to drop from heaven, for the earth to fail, and for all the many millions who are upon it to die of starvation in extremest agony, as far as temporal affliction goes, than that one soul, I will not say, should be lost, but should commit one venial sin, should tell one wilful untruth, though it harmed no one, or should steal one poor farthing without excuse."[25] Contemporaries may find it difficult to believe this sentence was not written by a virulent critic of Roman Catholicism but by one of its leading nineteenth-century spokesmen – indeed, by one of its most *liberal* spokesmen, and, *mirabile dictu,* in a work addressed to Anglicans, at that. The statement rings harsh if not cruel, and it aroused Kingsley's strident ire. And yet, the very harshness of the dictum serves to point up the dimensions of the problem to which, in context, it addresses itself.

The difference between temporal and eternal bliss is one of kind rather than duration. As the metaphysician holds that timeless eternity is not to be confused with infinite time, so the moralist contends that no amount of mundane joy can equal a single grain of transcendental bliss. Since he "regards this world, and all that is in it, as a mere shade, as dust and ashes, compared with the value of one single soul," he "considers the action of this world and the action of the soul simply incommensurate, viewed in their respective spheres." The difference between them being qualitative rather than quantitative, no measure of physical or emotional good can compensate for even the minutest spiritual evil. Hence, once a normative duty has been established, it becomes inviolate. Moral and religious law defines principles of right and wrong, and henceforth – except insofar as that law itself provides for dispensations – these can be sacrificed to nothing.

Given its premises, Newman's position, paradoxically harsh as it may seem, is grounded upon an inexorable logic. The Church is right in insisting that it "would rather save the soul of one wild bandit of Calabria, or whining beggar of Palermo, than draw a hundred lines of railroad through the length of Italy or carry out a sanitary reform, in its fullest details, in every city of Sicily, except so far as these great national works tended to some spiritual good beyond them."[26] Even in a moment of crisis, can one sacrifice bliss of *hayyei olam* upon the altar of *hayyei sha'ah*? How, then, can the same halakhist issue varied responses to an identical question?

The clear answer is that while, of course, for the committed Jew, Halakhah, as a normative order, can never be superseded by external pressures, a specific Halakhah may be flexibly applied – and, in a sense, superseded – by the internal dynamics of the halakhic system proper. And this, in two distinct, albeit related, ways. The first entails recourse to a phalanx of factors, of human and social import, which affect decision as acknowledged halakhic elements. At the apex stands, of course, *pikuah nefesh,* but other factors, local or general, of lesser gravity, also abound. These include physical and psychological pain, financial hardship, social harmony, and human dignity, sensitivity to any or all of which can affect *psak* measurably.

Yet, while the modus operandi concerning these factors – the measure of a *posek*'s awareness, how they are defined, and how liberally they are applied – may be of crucial practical significance, they do not constitute, philosophically, the heart of our problem. For their inclusion in the halakhic equation means that, even at the formal and technical level, two supposedly identical situations are, in effect, not identical at all. Our primary concern is therefore the second route – the latitude allowed a *posek* for differential decision even when all things are indeed, formally and technically, even.

That latitude is grounded in the pluralistic aspect of Halakhah. The halakhic order comprises three distinct tiers. There is, first, an ideal, and presumably monistic, plane, the Torah which is *bashamayim*. It is to this that the gemara in Bava Mezia alludes when it ascribes to the *Ribbono shel Olam* a position with respect to an issue in *taharot,* ספק בהרת קדמה לשער לבן (a case where it is unclear whether the bright spot preceded the white hair)[27].

There is, as the final stage, the definitive corpus, the genre of the *Shulhan Arukh,* which, having decided among various views, posits – again, monistically – what is demanded of the Jew. Intermediately, however, there is the vibrant and entrancing world within which exegetical debate and analytic controversy are the order of the day, and within which divergent and even contradictory views are equally accredited. The operative assumption is that, inherently and immanently, the raw material of Torah is open to diverse interpretations; that *gedolei Yisrael,* all fully committed and conscientiously and responsibly applying their talents and their knowledge to the elucidation of texts and problems, may arrive at different conclusions. License having been given to them all to engage in the quest, the results all attain the status of Torah, as a tenable variant reading of *devar Hashem:* אלו ואלו דברי א׳לקים חיים ("Both these and those are the words of the living God").[28]

In one sense, this pluralistic conception is most immediately relevant to the *gadol* himself, possibly authorizing him to act in accordance with his own dissenting lights, even in the face of a prevalent consensus.[29] However, it has ramifications for others as well. Were pure monism the order of the day, no degree of trauma – unless it constituted an acknowledged halakhic basis for dispensation – could justify deviating from standard norms. Against our grain, we would have to bow to Newman's trenchant logic. However, the introduction of the principle of *elu v'elu* alters the situation radically. Positions espoused by one *talmid hakham* are not only defined as a parcel of Torah with regard to himself. Within certain limits, they attain that status for adversaries as well. Time spent by Bet Hillel analyzing a view of Bet Shammai would be credited as a fulfillment of the *mizvah* of *talmud Torah; a fortiori* so, with respect to later *poskim* who had confronted both views before accepting one.

It is this concept which undergirds the legitimacy of recourse to minority opinions *bi'sh'at hadchak.*[30] Inasmuch as these opinions are not simply dismissed as erroneous but procedurally rejected – in practice, we can't have it both ways – they are very much alive, held in reserve where they can be culled from the shelf in a crisis. In effect, the principle of כדי ר׳ פלוני לסמוך עליו בשעת הדחק (Rabbi So-and-So is worthy of being

relied on under exigent circumstances) states, that while a given view has
been accepted *l'halakhah,* as part of our third tier, in an emergency we
envision ourselves back at our middle tier, sans decisive resolution, and,
hence, as authorized to heed another view. Moreover – and this is no less
remarkable – under the pressure of circumstance, we are not bound by
the general directive of *sefeka d'oraitha l'humra,* but are entitled to follow
a lenient minority.[31]

This license raises obvious questions. How liberally and by whom can
it be exercised? From how far back can discarded *shittot* be extracted – from
the Mishnah, the gemara, Rishonim, early Aharonim? Which views, if
any, might indeed be treated as error, and on what basis? At the practical
plane, these issues need to be clarified, but that task lies beyond my present scope. Here, I content myself with an account of the principle and its
rationale, as a manifestation of concern for the human and social element
within *pesikah.*

It is sometimes thought that the Rav was opposed to this approach.
To the best of my knowledge, this assumption is primarily based upon a
page drawn from *Mah Dodekh Midod* in which he emphatically rejects the
notion that psychosocial elements are factored into the halakhic process
and affect its course. Several sentences in this vein are admittedly sharp
and sweeping. And yet, careful examination of this tenuously balanced
passage reveals that its primary thrust is not denial of human considerations but insistence upon the autonomy of Halakhah. Commiseration
is acknowledged as a legitimate factor stimulating the *posek*'s quest for
a solution but is barred as a component of the halakhic process proper,
once that has been set in motion:

אולם זיקת־הגומלין של הלכה ומאורע אינה מתרחשת בתחום חשיבת ההלכה הצרופה,
כי אם במעמקי נפשו של איש ההלכה. המאורע הוא מניע פסיכולוגי הדוחף את החשיבה
הצרופה למסלולה. ברם ברגע שהיא מתחילה להתנועע במסלולה המסוים היא מבצעת
את תנועתה לא בכניעה למאורע, כי אם מתוך ציות לחוקיותה הנורמאטיבית־אידיאלית
המיוחדת לה.

However, the mutual connection between law and event does not take place
within the realm of pure halakhic thought, but rather within the depths of

the halakhic man's soul. The event is a psychological impetus, prodding pure thought into its track. However, once pure thought begins to move in its specific track, it performs its movement not in surrender to the event, but rather in obedience to the normative-ideal lawfulness particular to it.[32]

It is a nice distinction, and I confess that I am not certain it can be readily sustained in practice. In any event, it leaves the fundamental perspective I have outlined previously intact.

Moreover, the Rav's own experience as a *posek* – admittedly, not his primary task – over the years reflected this outlook. And I might add a salient recollection. During the mid-sixties, YU launched the Rogosin Institute for Jewish Ethics. One of its primary projects, under the direction of my late brother-in-law, Rav Professor Yitzhak Twersky zt"l, was a group enterprise which entailed ferreting out and analyzing *teshuvot* in which the ethical moment figured significantly, either by dint of the topic or by the impetus of the response. I recall vividly how the Rav appeared at one of the opening sessions, warmly endorsed the project, and enthusiastically recounted how Reb Lippa Mirrer had gone to great lengths in order to overcome prima facie considerations which had seemed to portend an almost certain *issur* for the wife of a *kohen*.[33]

The autonomy so dearly and rightly cherished by the Rav is of course vital; but insofar as we deal with human and social elements which are related to the internal dynamics of the halakhic process proper, it remains largely intact. In this respect, one factor is, however, critical: the degree of self-conscious awareness that a *posek* brings to his encounter with extraneous considerations. Where that level is low, the danger of distortion is great. A *talmid hakham* needs to examine himself and his situation candidly, to ascertain that whatever cultural forces, possibly unknown to predecessors, he confronts and perhaps absorbs, are filtered through the prism of his Torah personality and do not simply seep through the pores of his semi-conscious being. To be sure, intellectual historians revel in emphasizing that it is precisely with respect to unquestioned assumptions that the most significant change, subtle and incremental, takes place; and, within certain proportions, some shift in the parameters of thought cannot be denied. Hopefully, however, here, too, there is a filter, more relevant to attitudes than to perception. As the body rejects certain grafts, so the soul; and the nobler the soul, the more selective its system. Be this as it may, however, the counsel regarding a *posek's* active inclusion of human and social factors within his deliberations is that of controlled and critical sensibility.

Recognition of the possibility of differential *psak* leaves open the question of the circumstances under which recourse to it is valid, advisable, and perhaps even mandatory. Clearly, on so delicate an issue we can hardly expect unanimity, possibly not even a clear consensus. A number of variables are involved, and each is susceptible of a broad spectrum of definition. Inasmuch as the issue turns on the balance between the halakhic order and human need, any resolution hinges on the degree of flexibility – in light of hermeneutic and/or analytic canons and the *modus operandi* of the system – assumed with respect to Halakhah, on the one hand, and the importance ascribed to personal or communal travail, on the other. Even the most caring and sensitive *posek,* confronted with genuine tragedy, may rule *l'humra* because, despite his most profound commiseration, he cannot traverse what are, on his conception, the bounds of the halakhic universe; because he cannot make a travesty of a *din* in order to relieve a personal crisis.

The issue is most keenly perceived at the individual level, but, to the extent that it involves the formulation of standards, may be general as well. How is *pikuah nefesh* to be defined? How great and how immediate must danger be? And how is *nefesh* itself, in this context, to be understood? What of *sakanat eiver,* of derangement, of apostasy? Can endangered public safety, even where no loss of life is in prospect, be viewed as its equivalent? What degree of pain invokes the license of *za'ar* and how great a loss justifies the license of *hefsed merubeh*?

These are immanent questions, to be honestly and conscientiously confronted; and surely we have no right to demand of a *posek,* almost as a matter of moral and personal right, the most comforting answer. The notion that "where there is a rabbinic will there is a halakhic way" both insults *gedolei Torah,* collectively, and, in its insouciant view of the totality of Halakhah, verges on the blasphemous. What we do expect of a *posek* is that he walk the extra mile – wherever, for him, it may be – harnessing knowledge and imagination, in an attempt to abide by his responsibility to both the Torah with which he has been entrusted and to his anguished fellow, whose pangs he has internalized. For insensitive *pesikah* is not only lamentable apathy or poor public policy. It is bad Halakhah. To the extent that *kevod haberiyot*, for instance, permits a "violation," be it of a *d'rabbanan* injunction, actively, or of a *d'oraitha*, passively, failure to act on that principle undercuts a spiritual ideal. The Rav was fond of quoting the *Hafez Hayyim* to the effect that interruption of *keri'at shema*, where enabled, *mipenei hakavod*,[34] was not permissible but mandatory. Human dignity – the Rav would have preferred the term, "human sanctity" – is hardly a neutral matter.

Poskim, especially in the modern era, are often reluctant to invoke broad axiological *heterim* when they can construct more narrowly based decisions, in which local and possibly technical factors are more prominent. *Pesikah* can congeal into *psak*, and a decision issued, with trepidation, in light of special circumstances, may then enter the halakhic world as a precedent. The danger is particularly acute at a time when many, within and without the pale of commitment, seek to pounce upon every such *psak* in order to promote an ideological agenda. We should realize, however, that such reserve may exact a practical and educational toll, as awareness of certain values and their place within Halakhah may become jaded. Be this as it may, we can recognize the position of the human and social factor within halakhic decision as firmly secure. And, were visible evidence necessary, surely, the two greatest *poskim* of our generation, Rav Mosheh Feinstein and Rav Shlomo Zalman Auerbach zt"l, are prime exemplars.

Differential *pesikah* requires the raison d'etre of a human or social desideratum. With an eye to Mill and Moore, in defining it, we obviously need to distinguish between the desired and the desirable. I would not, with reference to our context, rule out entirely assigning weight to the former. As there is a concept of subjective need, *asher yehsar lo*, with respect to *tzedakah*, so that the *mizvah*[35] may encompass supplying a fallen aristocrat with a servant and conveyance, so empathetic concern for one's fellow may include taking into account matters which, for most, might entail mere comfort and convenience but, for him, constitute genuine present want. Clearly, however, our focus is the desirable – not just what a person or community wants but what they should want.

Movement from is to ought may raise, in the *posek*'s mind and heart, basic moral, hashkafic, and halakhic issues, possibly conerning his existential stance vis-à-vis certain halakhot; and these, in turn, greatly expand the horizons of our discussion. Some cases, tragic as they may be, induce, in the *posek,* profound commiseration, but little tension. The situation of an *agunah* whose husband has disappeared in battle, for instance, is palpably and uniformly perceived as pitiably bad. Trapped in a web of circumstance, she is bound by a norm whose inherent value a committed Jew readily comprehends but which, for her, has tragic ramifications. The situation might be somewhat different, however, in the case of a *kohen* who had fallen in love with a divorcee – or, worse still, who had become a *ba'al teshuvah* after marrying her. In this case, a *posek* could find himself torn between empathy for the young couple and appreciation of the ideal of *kedushat kehunah,* even in its devalued contemporary form.[36] He might lament the lack of an escape hatch which could provide dispensatory relief. But his appreciation of the norm per se and of the weight assigned it as a value is beyond question. However, in a third situation, that of *kiddushei ketanah,* betrothal of a minor daughter by a vindictive father, he, almost certainly, would not only regard the *mekadesh* as a scoundrel but would regret that the institution exists. He would not, *has veshalom,* sit in judgment upon the license or question its morality. היתפאר הגרזן על החצב בו אם יתגדל המשור על מניפו? (Should the axe boast itself against him that heweth therewith? Should the saw magnify itself against him that moveth it?) He would, however, candidly assume that what had been apt and perhaps even necessary in a given sociohistorical setting was no longer ideally suited to his own. The assumption would certainly not exempt him from mastering the relevant halakhot nor dim his enthusiasm for analyzing the nuances of *devar Hashem* as, in accordance with Hazal's authoritative exegesis, initially formulated. It might, however, in his mind and in ours, raise certain pertinent questions.

With respect to the last example, this might be particularly so, inasmuch as our *posek* evidently does not stand alone. Rav Yehudah in the name of Rav (or possibly, Rav Elazar) possibly had similar reservations and, hence, issued a prohibition: אסור לאדם שיקדש את בתו כשהיא קטנה עד שתגדל ותאמר בפלוני אני רוצה (It is forbidden for one to give his daughter in betrothal when a minor; [rather, he must wait] until she grows up and states, "I desire so-and-so.").[37] *Baʿalei hatosafot*[38] state that, due to changed historical circumstances, the *issur* was not observed in their society; and the Rambam softened the impact of Rav's injunction somewhat by substituting for *assur* the milder admonition, *ein raʾuy laʿassot ken.*[39] Be this as it may, the fundamental issue raised by Rav's innovation is clear. What are we to assume, what did he assume, about the previous situation? In which respect and on what basis was the change justified, if not necessitated? Did the danger that the betrothed daughter would not be pleased with her father's choice only surface in Rav's time? And if it preexisted, why had there been no previous concern about it? Was his sensibility more sharply honed than that of the Torah?

The question is general, and can be raised with reference to almost any *takkanah,* of human or social import. On the very same *daf* in Kiddushin, we hear of an analogous injunction, again cited by Rav Yehudah in Rav's name:

אסור לאדם שיקדש את האשה עד שיראנה שמא יראה בה דבר מגונה ותתגנה עליו ורחמנא אמר ואהבת לרעך כמוך.

A man may not betroth a woman before he sees her, lest he [subsequently] see something repulsive in her, and she become loathsome to him, whereas the All-Merciful said (Vayikra 19:18), "But thou shalt love thy neighbor as thyself."[40]

Had the concern for amity been heretofore ignored? Or, to take a later example, how are we to regard Rabbenu Gershom's ban upon polygamy, and how do its before and after relate?

Theoretically, several explanations may be suggested. One is that historical circumstances had, in a given instance, indeed changed. The fabric or structure of the community had been altered or the mindset of its members had been transformed so that phenomena which had previously been regarded favorably or apathetically now were resented, with the hardship engendered bearing redress. Alternatively, it might be contended that while a given procedure, for reasons we can only conjecture, had been enabled by the Torah, it had *ab initio* never been truly sanctioned, morally, but only permitted, if not quite at the level of לא דברה תורה אלא כנגד יצר הרע,[41] ("The Torah but related to man's evil inclination") then in a similar vein. From this perspective, the *takkanah* would constitute spiritual progress, as a collective *kaddesh azmekha b'mutar lekha* ("Sanctify yourself with what is permitted to you"). Finally, change could be ascribed to the refined sensibility of reformers who, in effect, challenged the ethos upon which heretofore fully approved elements had been grounded.

The last is grist for the mill of secular *maskilim* but, virtually by definition, is, to the committed Jew, unconscionable. It ascribes injustice to Torah and rebelliousness to *hakhmei hamesorah,* and we patently and vigorously deny both. Each of the preceding interpretations is, however, fully tenable. Assuming a stable standard, revised circumstances might militate a *takkhanah* regarding the applicable halakhot. The societal change might be for the better, as I suppose we would regard the yearning for interpersonal harmony in Rav's examples. Or it might be for the worse. *Mid'oraitha,* a parent is not obligated – unless, possibly, under the overarching rubric of *tzedakah* – to provide for his young;[42] and this, notwithstanding the allusion to such failure in a pasuk in *Eikhah* (4:3) as the epitome of cruelty. Presumably, the Torah here relied upon natural instinct. When that proved insufficient, the resultant social and moral lacuna required a *takkanah.* Or again, *pruzbul,* so dear to the hearts of secular historians as a paradigm of progressive reform, was, rather, defined by the Mishnah as the result of moral and religious decline:

כשראה שנמנעו העם מלהלוות זה את זה ועוברין על מה שכתוב בתורה... התקין הלל פרוזבול.

When he saw that people were avoiding lending each other money, thus transgressing what is written in the Torah, Hillel enacted *pruzbul.*[43]

Whatever the course of change, however, a *takkanah* of this vintage serves to reinforce the initial corpus and reassert its formal and axiological thrust.

The second alternative is equally tenable. The possibility that, in the course of halakhic history, the moral bar might be raised, cannot, *a priori*, be precluded. Our unflinching commitment to Torah and its values need not entail assent to the proposition that its charge is, in every area and in every respect, maximal. Our firm faith in *Torat Hashem temimah* need not assume that, at the formal normative plane, *temimut* has always been demanded of us, across the board. Quite the contrary. As the Ramban's famous portrayal of a *naval bireshut hatorah* (a scoundrel with Torah license) and comparable pronouncements clearly predicate, there may be room for complementing or supplementing its demands; and this, not only in order to plug loopholes, but by way of elevating the whole front. This endeavor may be communal no less than personal, and certain *takkanot* may be viewed as initiatives in this direction. In making specific judgments, we must of course be highly cautious. We need to check our own standards so as to ascertain that they are an outgrowth of the *ben Torah* in us and not simply an expression of an ephemeral Zeitgeist; and we need to examine the relevant evidence, internal and/or external, in order to determine whether our reading of the previous and later phases is sustainable. Granted this caveat, however, this interpretive mode is clearly possible.

For some, the issues are considerably complicated, philosophically and practically, if the focus is shifted from the primal Torah datum to its subsequent development through the interpretive and legislative endeavors of Hazal and their successors. They contend, first, that these labors were significantly influenced by extraneous factors – personal mindset, ambient culture, current assumptions, or contemporary attitudes; second, that many of these are inconsonant with the modern temper; and, third, that, in consequence, some halakhot are no longer binding.

The argument is familiar and appears in various contexts and guises. However, as committed *Bnei Torah*, we reject both the premises and the conclusion – particularly, with reference to Hazal. Certainly, they had predilections and attitudes. However, our faith in them inspires us with confidence that the halakhic process was governed by halakhic factors, that halakhic decision rested on halakhic grounds. We have neither the right nor the desire to suggest that their judgment was diverted or warped by extraneous factors. We trust that they were fully aware of what they were doing and totally responsible to *ammitah shel Torah.* The last thing we want to do is presume to understand them better than they understood themselves; to contend that while they may have thought they were pursuing one course, impelled by a given impetus, we, firmly ensconced in our social-scientific panopticon, know it was really another. The claim to superior retrospective insight is not uncommon in other contexts; but as to the critical transmitters – artificers of *Torah she-be'al-peh,* we shall have no truck with it. We shall impugn neither the wisdom nor the integrity of Hazal.

But, it will be rejoined, granted that Hazal were indeed doing what they thought they were doing – formulating halakhot in light of exegetical and logical principles – don't certain attitudes predispose to applying those principles in a given way and toward a specific end? In limited value-laden areas – *tefillah,* for instance – quite possibly. Even if that be the case, however, it is essential, in this connection, to bear a critical point in mind. The attitudes themselves are directives. ברוך שבחר בהם ובמשנתם. ("Blessed is He who chose them and their teachings") *Emunat hakhamim* relates not only to the normative corpus but to the axiological realm as well. Hazal are, for us – if I may invert Ben Jonson's phrase – not only commanders but guides. We follow in their footsteps not only out of deference to the formal and technical authority of the ultimate arbiter but because we recognize and are overawed by their greatness. They are, to adapt Justice Jackson's formulation, both right because final and final because right. Hence, their attitudes – no mere intrusive graft but an organic outgrowth of the *gavra rabba* in them, can indeed provide the proper infrastructure for certain halakhot.

Hazal's factual perceptions are, relatively speaking, more historically conditioned. Their reading of human nature, in its permanent metaphysical aspect, retains its full force; but observations of given sociological tendencies may be more relative and of lesser normative status. In an age of rampant speculative investment, no one is bound to a mercantilist ethos by dint of the gemara's assumption that property is only sold in distress – כל דמזבין איניש אי לאו דאניס לא הוה מזבין, ("Whatever a person sells, he would not have sold had he not been under compulsion".)[44] and presumably, no dispute should be adjudicated on the basis of avowedly anachronistic readings, insofar as their factuality is crucial. Hence, in certain areas, cautious reappraisal may very well be in order. There is, however, nothing in this process to undermine the halakhic order or to challenge its architects.

The situation is patently different, however, as regards attitudinal elements and practical implications of alleged obsolescence. Here, the gauntlet is patently and assertively thrown and we, for our part, reject both the critic's factual premises and his legal conclusions.

Even if one were to grant that some halakhot were grounded in attitudes, at least partially ascribed to various influences, and if one were to acknowledge license to confront the attitudes, it hardly follows that the halakhot in question can be dismissed cavalierly. We still have to deal, with respect to legislated *takkanot,* דבר שבמנין צריך מנין אחר להתירו[45] with the weighty issue of the scope of the concept of, the principle that a law retains formal validity unless and until abrogated by an authority comparable to that which had promulgated it; with respect to exegesis and interpretation, with the authority imbedded in, and derived from, the reality of פשטה הוראתם בכל ישראל. ("Their decision has spread throughout Israel")[46] Of course, in certain instances, historical change may be such that the current situation, given its different character, had never been subsumed under the presumed original Halakhah. To take a relatively non-controversial example – one which entails the abrogation of leniency rather than of stringency – the late medieval *Terumat Hadeshen* defended the view that a woman ought not to go to the *mikveh* on Friday night, at least where she could have gone previously. This runs counter to a Mishnah in Bezah which had explicitly stated that Bet Hillel held that utensils could not be immersed on Shabbat, but that human immersion was permissible.[47] The reconciliation given is that, on Rava's view, the distinction is grounded in the concern that the utensil's immersion appears to resemble its repair while, with respect to a person, it may simply be regarded as bathing. This distinction, contends the *Terumat Hadeshen*, is no longer valid, inasmuch as, in fifteenth-century Germany, no one bathes on Shabbat; hence, the dispensation for *tevilah*[48] is likewise rescinded. Or again, it is surely arguable that the halakhot concerning the exchange of coins of various metals do not apply if one changes nickels for a quarter, as Hazal dealt with multiple currencies and the United States has only a single currency, albeit with units of different metals.[49] However, where the case remains essentially similar, but only attitudes have changed, the Halakhah remains binding. Obviously, the line between the two categories is not always clearly drawn and may be the subject of controversy. Here, I simply note the direction relevant discussion might pursue.

What has been suggested with respect to Hazal is similarly applicable, albeit to a lesser extent, of subsequent *hakhmei hamesorah* whose views have been incorporated in the standard halakhic codex. Them, too, we hold in dual esteem, seeking from them both guidance and command; and they, too, we trust, were generally able to evaluate critically influences to which they were exposed, on the one hand, and to base their halakhic conclusions upon elements genuinely germane to *devar Hashem*, on the other. Admittedly, later *poskim* enjoy lesser standing than that of Hazal, with respect to being either right or final. We may take license, attitudinally, to explain the proscription of *kil'ayim* differently from the Ramban;[50] and it is not inconceivable that, at some point, fully responsible and fully committed *gedolim* will reexamine the Mahari Mullen's position regarding women's wearing *zizit*.[51] With respect to halakhic issues which verge upon public policy, particularly, we might feel that, at times, response to events has impacted upon the course of decision. Nevertheless, broadly speaking, our commitment to Halakhah and its authority entails faith in the integrity of the halakhic process and its outcome.

In conclusion, let me add three brief comments. In dealing with the human aspect of *psak*, I have focused upon the personal plane. It is at that plane that, ordinarily, the most critical issues are likely to arise – that potential tragedy may be most acute and pain most sharply experienced.

The same basic considerations obtain equally, however, in the public sphere. Hardship may be differently conceived, scope compensating for intensity; but the overarching approach would be quite similar. In a sense, a fresh qualitative dimension is added here, inasmuch as we deal with the well-being of a *zibbur* as such and not only with multiple individual problems. Hence, economic factors, at a level short of privation, which might not have been decisive at a personal plane, may nonetheless carry the day in the public sphere. But again, the governing halakhic and hashkafic elements are essentially similar.

Reference to the public sector serves to introduce a second comment. I have spoken throughout of sensitivity to the human or social factor as a basis for leniency. With regard to decisions a *posek* is called upon to render vis-à-vis an individual, this is indeed, ordinarily, although not invariably, the case. In the communal arena, however, concern over the human factor may rather stimulate *humrah*. Decisions made at this plane, even of the nature of *pesikah,* are less ad hoc in character and take a more panoramic view of public policy. Part of that policy surely involves sustaining the human aspect of a society and enhancing its moral fiber; and that may militate stringency as well as leniency. The Meiri noted this point with reference to concern for maintaining adherence to *din Torah* generally; but, for our purposes, his comment can be focused upon our particular topic. Apparently somewhat puzzled, as was Rabbenu Tam, by Rav's statement that appointees to the *sanhedrin* should know *letaher et hasherez min hatorah,* (how to purify a creeping thing according to the Torah)[52] he explains:

ויראה לי בפירוש דבר זה שאם יראו תקלות יוצאות בדורותיהם באיזו דין תורה יצאו לחדש דינין ולהוסיף ולגרוע להוראת שעה וליתן סמך לדבריהם מן התורה ובדומה לזה כתבו הגאונים בדיני התלמוד שיש ביד רבנים או גאונים לחדש גזרות ותקנות דרך כלל או דרך פרט להסיר איזה ענין מכוער לפי מה שיראה בזמנו בסמך מועט ועל דבר כיוצא בזה כתבו גדולי המפרשים לא נתן התלמוד אלא לבעלי הקבלה המומחית או לבעלי הסברה הנכונה ושקול הדעת הצלול להיות גורעים ומוסיפים ודורשים אלא שפרגוד זה נגעל בפני רוב בני אדם ואין ראוי לכך אלא מופלג בדורו בידיעה וחריפות ופלפול מיושר ודעת מיושבת.

It would seem to me in explanation of this matter that if they see in their generation stumbling blocks emerging from certain Torah laws, they will innovate laws or add or subtract, [enacting] temporary measures and bringing support for them from the Torah. Similarly, the Geonim have written in their principles of the Talmud that rabbis or geonim possess the authority to innovate decrees and regulations, on a general or particular level, to remove unseemly matters as they see fit in their time, with only minimal support [from the sources]. On a similar matter, the greatest of commentators (i.e. Rabad) wrote: The Talmud has not been given over to anyone to detract or add or derive [laws], except for those who possess expert traditions or those who possess proper analytic skills and clear and deliberate judgment. However, this curtain has been drawn before the majority of people, and only one who is outstanding in his generation in his knowledge, sharpness [of thought], straightforward argumentation, and calmness of mind is worthy [of penetrating the curtain].[53]

Parts of the passage are striking and require further analysis. The balance of initiative, concern, and caution which characterize it is clear, however; and equally clear is the fact that its application can expand obligation rather than relieve it.

Finally, we need, in candor, to avoid merely stonewalling realities or sidestepping issues. No one questions the fact that, in some instances, our primary sources and our primal attitudes diverge. Moreover, it is not our baser predatory instincts but our nobler spiritual self which is engaged. And the problem is not one of *hukkim* as opposed to *mishpatim*. On the contrary, *akhilat hazir u'levishat sha'atnes,* (the eating of pork and wearing of *she'atnez*) with respect to which the Torah has constructed an arena and has established the ground rules for working within it, pose relatively little philosophic difficulty. That is more likely to arise, if at all, where Halakhah has confronted areas immanent in the human condition and has legislated with respect to them. Broadly speaking, *Hoshen Mishpat* and *Even Ha'ezer* are fraught with greater difficulty than *Orah Hayyim* or *Yoreh De'ah.*

These concerns, related to the larger issue of moral conscience and normative fealty – are real. We encounter elements which we describe, not only euphemistically but genuinely, as difficult; and the art of halakhic living is, at times, not so much discovering the answers as knowing how to live with the questions. Hence, our commitment to Torah and, *a fortiori,* to its integrative *mesorah,* constitutes an article of faith and embodies *emunah,* genuinely conceived. The facile conjectural assertions of historicistic critics, steeped in the mindset and vocabulary of relativistic multiculturalism and limited by tepid appreciation and admiration of Hazal, are well-known. However, to *Bnei Torah* – even to those willing to entertain the validity of some particular statements – as a general onslaught their approach is wholly untenable. Each of us, who is halakhically knowledgeable, could compile a shorter or longer list of cruces, of directives which, had we authored the definitive codex, would never have been written. We did not, and are not presently authorized to do so; and each of us, who is halakhically committed, abides by *devar Hashem,* even when we have not fully comprehended or, possibly, not yet fully internalized, its total message. Even as we cope – at times, even as we agonize – our commitment remains firm and vibrant, and our passionate conviction, *ashreinu mah tov helkeinu,* in every sense of *tov,* abides, keen and deep. In practice, our response may be multiple. Where we can, we seek recourse to proper adaptive change. כי באמת קשה הדבר לתקנת המדינה, Reb Hayyim Ozer wrote to Rav Herzog, שהגנב יפטור את עצמו בכפל ומודה בקנס יהי' פטור לגמרי וע"כ שבכגון זה צריך לתקן תקנות המדינה. ("Truly, it would impede the proper running of a state were a thief to exempt himself from a [punitive] double fine, for [Torah law dictates that] one who confesses his crime is exempt from paying a fine; therefore, in such a case it is necessary to enact regulations of the state".)[54] Where we cannot, we live and work, animated by the humility and honesty of Reb Akiva Eiger's poignant plea – וה' יאיר עיני ("And may God enlighten my eyes".)

Notes

1. *Dev.* 10:12–3; see, especially, Ramban, *ad loc.*
2. Makkot 23b.
3. Rosh Hashanah 27a.
4. See Rashi, *Dev.* 10:13 and Maharal, *Tiferet Israel*, ch. 5.
5. *MT*, Shabbat 2:3.
6. See, e.g., *Divrei Hagut V'ha'arakhah* (Jerusalem, 1982), pp. 270–1.
7. See, e.g., *Uvikashtem Misham* in *Ish Hahalakha, Galuy V'nistar* (Jerusalem, 1979), pp. 207–215.
8. Rambam, *MT*, Shabbat 30:14. The context in which the Rambam places this Halakhah underscores the fact that at issue is an aspect of the *mizvah* of *oneg* and not only the fulfillment of obligation to a spouse.
9. Gittin 59b. It is not clear from the text as to whether the rejoinder is Abbaye's. Whether *vekidashto* applies with respect to a *levi* is in dispute; see *Tur Orah Hayyim,* 201. If not, the gemara's question is confined to *kohen.*
    For a parallel discussion, see Yevamot 21a.
10. *MT, Hannukah* 4:14. Rashi, Shabbat 23b, assumes the *ner* discussed in the *sugya* is a Shabbat candle. However, no mention of this appears in the *sugya,* and the Ritva, *ad loc.,* explains that an ordinary week-day candle is intended. This clearly appears to have been the Rambam's view as well.
    Some manuscripts omit the word בעולם. The omission reduces the statement's sweep but not its substance.
11. See Sanhedrin 6b. I take it for granted that R. Elazar, who rejects *pesharah* as an option for *bet din,* does not deny their role in preserving comity, but only holds that it is superseded by the obligation to absolute truth.
12. See *Teshuvot Harosh,* 108:10. I assume here that these ordinances are *mi'doraitha.* This point is in dispute, however. See Rabbenu Hananel, Sanhedrin 7b, and *Be'urei Hagera, Hoshen Mishpat,* 155:8.
13. See Yerushalmi, Eruvin, 3:2 and 7:9.
14. In some instances, inasmuch as this extraneous factor is the basis, the legal force of whatever is mandated may be reduced, and the ownership generated by it limited. See Gittin 61a, *Shebuot* 41a, and Bava Mezia 12a.
15. See Ketubot 66a and 96a.
16. See Bava Kamma 87a–b.
17. *Teshuvot Harama,* 11. The Rama goes on to cite the concepts of *averah lishmah* and *eit la'assot lashem.* These terms seem to divert the discussion in another direction, the net effect being the raising of problematic hashkafic and halakhic elements, on the one hand, but significantly circumscribing the scope of the license, on the other.
18. See Shabbat 23b.

19. *Teshuvot Harosh*, 107:6 (in Yudlov's ed., p. 444).
20. *Hut Hameshulash*, 8.
21. See Yitzhak Zev Kahana, *Letakkanat Agunot* (Jerusalem, 1947), passim.
22. 109. The principle that leniency should prevail with respect to *agunah* appears in Hazal, notably, as regards the dispensation with the need for two proper witnesses; see Yevamot 88a and Rambam, *MT, Gerushin,* 13:29.

    It is strikingly counterbalanced, however, by the far-reaching *humrah* of *mayyim she'ein lahem sof*; the seeming contrast requires some thought.
23. *Ibid.*, 62.
24. See, *inter alia,* Berakhot 9a and Shabbat 45a.
25. John Henry Newman, *Lectures on Certain Difficulties Felt by Anglicans in Submitting to the Catholic Church* (London, 1850), p. 199.
26. *Loc. cit.*
27. See Bava Mezia 86a.
28. See Shalom Rosenberg, *Lo Bashamayim Hee* (Alon Shevut, 1997), passim; and see, particularly, the bibliographic note, p. 9n.
29. See Rosh, *Pesakim* Sanhedrin 4:6; and cf. my remarks in "Legitimization of Modernity," in *Engaging Modernity,* ed. Mosheh Z. Sokol (Northvale, 1997), pp. 11–14.
30. My discussion is based on the assumption that minority views can also be relied upon in crisis, even if the issue is a *d'oraitha* injunction. This is disputable, however. See the references cited in *Encyclopedia Talmudit,* 9:260.
31. See, however, Niddah 9b, where the gemara states that the principle of *bi'sh'at hadehak* suspends the normal canons of *pesikah* – e.g., the provenance of majority opinions – but does not apply when a minority view has been explicitly and categorically rejected.
32. Rav Yosef Dov Soloveitchik, *Divrei Hagut V'ha'arakhah* (Jerusalem, 1982), p. 77.
33. The *teshuvah* cited is in *Malbushei Yom Tov, Even Ha'ezer,* 7.
34. I have been unable to track down where the *psak* appears, but my recollection on this point is clear.
35. See Ketubot 67b.
36. It is doubly devalued: 1) halakhically, as the status of *meyuhas* is generally lacking; and 2) experientially, inasmuch as the positive aspect of *avodah* is relatively muted, and the confining prohibitions are dominant.
37. Kiddushin 41a.
38. S.v. *assur.* See also Mordecai, Ketubot, 179.
39. *Ishut* 3:19.
40. Kiddushin 41a. The Rambam, *loc. cit.*, again substitutes *ein ra'uy* for *assur.*
41. See Kiddushin 21b; and cf. *Teshuvot Harambam,* ed. J. Blau (Jerusalem, 1960), p. 374.
42. See Ketubot 49–50.
43. *Shebi'it,* 10:3.
44. Bava Batra 47b.

45. Bezah 5b. This is, of course, a very broad subject in its own right, whose proper treatment is well beyond my present scope.

46. See *Abodah Zarah* 36a.

47. See Bezah 17b–8a, where four reasons for the prohibition concerning utensils – and hence, implicitly, for the dispensation concerning persons – are suggested. It is not clear which prevails, *lehalakhah* – or whet her, indeed, one needs to choose between them; see Rif and Rosh, *ad loc.* However, the Rambam, Shabbat 23:8 adopted Rava's view with regard to *shabbat* (but cf. *Yom Tov,* 4:17–8), and it is to this that the *T.H.* relates.

48. See Resp. 256–7. The logic of this contention should presumably proscribe *tevilah* on *shabbat* even if there had been no opportunity to immerse earlier. However, the *T.H.* does not push the argument this far.

49. See Bava Mezia 44a–5b.

50. See his comments on *Ber.* 1:11 and *Vay.* 19:19, in which he bases the injunction upon a highly static view of the physical world and upon a very limited and conservative role for man within it.

51. See *Sefer Ha'agur, Hilkhot Zizit,* 27. The *psak* runs counter to the view prevalent amongst Rishonim, and the explanation for it suggested by the Rama, *O.H.* 17:2 הואיל ואינו חובת גברא, is rather difficult.

52. See Sanhedrin 17a. For Rabbenu Tam, see *Tosafot*, s.v. *sheyode'a.*

53. *Bet Habehirah,* Sanhedrin, p. 55.

54. Quoted in Rav Y.A.H. Herzog, *Hahukkah L'Israel Al Pi Hatorah* (Jerusalem, 1989) 2:75n.

Chapter 9

The Rav at Jubilee: An Appreciation

Any account, testimonial or critical, of the significance of a major spiritual figure must refer to two intersecting axes: the vertical and the horizontal.[1] On the one hand, he is to be perceived within his own field, as a laborer in its vineyards – relating, in part, to current peers, but, as a link in a historical chain, to be measured, primarily, against his predecessors and successors. On the other hand, he is to be regarded within the ambience of his broader contemporary milieu, with which he interacts and upon which he presumably impacts.

This point is particularly salient with respect to *morenu ve-rabbenu*, the Rav זצ"ל, inasmuch as this dichotomy dovetails with a second distinction, pertinent to the Rav generally, and to his first major work, *Ish Ha-Halakhah*, in particular. The Rav always had a penchant for positing antitheses and antinomies; and one of these – classically rooted in Hazal and the Rishonim, and constituting a major crux of general religious thought – was the relation of talmud and *ma'asseh*. Throughout *Ish Ha-Halakhah*, a dual – at times, even an ambivalent – attitude obtains with respect to this issue. At one juncture, we read:

וכשהרבה ממושגי ההלכה אינם מקבילים אל התופעות הריאליות, אין איש ההלכה מיצר
ודואג כלל. משאת נפשו, היא לא הריאליזציה של הלכה, אלא הקונסטרוקציה האידיאלית
שניתנה לה מסיני, וזו קיימת לעולם ועד.

And when many halakhic concepts do not parallel phenomena in the real

189

world, the *Ish Ha-Halakhah* is not at all concerned or worried. His desire is
not the realization of Halakhah, but the ideal construct given it at Sinai, and
this exists forever.

Indeed, disengagement is idealized even with reference to Torah activity proper, so that abstinence from *psak* is not just reluctantly countenanced
but virtually celebrated:

יסוד היסודות ועמוד המחשבה ההלכתית המה לא ההוראה למעשה, אלא קביעת הלכה
עיונית. לפיכך השתמטו ועדיין משתמטים אישי ההלכה היותר גדולים מלכהן בכהונת
רבנות בישראל, ונספחים על הסיעה של יראי־הוראה... ההלכה – לא המעשה; היצירה
האידיאלית – לא הריאלית, מייצגת שאיפת בעל ההלכה.

The essential foundation and pillar of halakhic thought is not practical
halakhic decision-making, but the determination of theoretical Halakhah.
It is for this reason that the greatest *Ishei Ha-Halakhah* avoided and still
avoid serving in rabbinic posts, and attach themselves to the party of those
who fear to make such decisions... The [theoretical] Halakhah – not its
implementation; abstract creativity – not the actual, represent the desire of
the master of Halakhah.

This formulation is fully consistent with the Volozhin tradition's
emphasis upon *Torah lishmah* and also with an ardent interest in the
abstruse abstractions of neo-Kantian metaphysics and epistemology.
Elsewhere, however, a very different chord is struck. At one point, talmud
and *ma'asseh* are defined objectively as twin coordinates of halakhic
existence:

אם אדם מישראל חי על פי הלכה (וחיים על פי ההלכה – פירושם: הכרת ההלכה כשהיא
לעצמה, והיקשה אל העולם הריאלי – התגשמות ההלכה), אז גאולה תהיה לו.

If a Jewish person lives in accordance with Halakhah (and living according
to Halakhah means recognizing Halakhah [as an area] unto itself, and
analogizing – to the real world – the embodiment of Halakhah), then "there
will be a redemption for him."[3]

Indeed, at one point, realization seems to be regarded as the ultimate
telos, to which instrumental study is possibly subordinate:

אין איש ההלכה שואף לעולם טרנסצנדנטי, לשכבות "עליונות" של הוויה זכה וטהורה,

כי הלא העולם האידיאלי, משאת נפשו וילד שעשועיו של איש ההלכה, נוצר רק לשם
התגשמות בעולם הריאלי הזה.

Halakhic man does not long for a transcendent world, for "supernal" levels of a
pure, pristine existence, for was not the ideal world – halakhic man's deepest
desire, his darling child – created only for the purpose of being actualized
in our real world?

On the subjective plane, similarly, practical implementation is
described as a desideratum of halakhic man – perhaps as *the* desideratum:[5]

איש ההלכה מגשים את התורה במעשה, בלי ויתורים ופשרות... כי הלא התגשמות
ההלכה היא משאת נפשו וחלומו הנהדר. (איש ההלכה, עמ' 97)

Halakhic man implements the Torah without any compromises or conces-
sions, for precisely such implementation, such actualization is his ultimate
desire, his fondest dream.

This antithesis – ultimately, I believe, unresolved in the essay – is
reflected in the Rav's life. As he and his father זצ"ל spent days and long
winter nights by the hearth of the Khaslavitch *bet ha-midrash*, poring over
the niceties of הולכת הקטורת ביום הכיפורים or of התפסה בשבועה, could any flight
of the imagination have led either to envision him as battling, in later
years, for the welfare of as yet un-unionized *shohetim*, scraping to meet
weekly Maimonides School salary deadlines, or regularly addressing con-
ventions of the Rabbinical Council of America or the Mizrachi? Yet both
aspects, the contemplative and the active, engaged the Rav throughout;
and each, as well as their interaction, must be discussed in any survey of
his achievement.

Between the distinctions I have posited there is, to be sure, no correspondence. There is, however, a measure of correlation, the world of
ma'asseh being viewed primarily with reference to the contemporary, while
that of talmud looks before and after. Beginning, then, with the vertical
axis, we focus initially upon the Rav's place on the historical continuum
of *hakhmei ha-mesorah*. His role in this capacity is itself dual, spanning
the realms of Halakhah and *mahshavah*. I believe that his position with

respect to both differs markedly, however. Any objective description of the Rav as a gadol in the world of learning begins perforce by referring to his place in the Brisker tradition – begins, that is, by positing that in this sphere, he did not so much innovate a course as pursue one. In a meaningful sense, therefore, the element of *hiddush* – as measured, say, against the achievement of the Rav's grandfather, Reb Hayyim, or of a Rabbenu Tam – is constricted.

This is said without the slightest intent of deprecation. By definition, genuine methodological innovation in any field is unusual – all the more so in the Torah world so oriented to mesorah; and it would be singularly rare for a person reared, as the Rav was, in a highly self-conscious and articulate tradition, at a stage when one could still meet its founder. Moreover, excessively frequent sharp methodological shifts are, from an overall perspective, not only unlikely but undesirable, the value of novelty being very much a function of its historical context. Surely, however, such radical originality is not the litmus test of intellectual greatness, either in the Torah world or elsewhere. Does anyone challenge the credentials of the Rash of Sens and the Rashba simply because they trod, respectively, in the footsteps of the Ri and the Ramban?

If the Rav did not found a tradition, he certainly proved himself, within the parameters of the Brisker mode in which he was reared, a remarkable *mehaddesh*. Over the years, the Rav's creative powers repeatedly awed talmidim and, more than any other factor, charged the atmosphere of so many *shi'urim*. The fusion of imagination and precision, of energized sweep and rigorous discipline, continually resolved cruces and informed insights. At its most electric, however, it enlarged the bounds of the halakhic empire by enriching its lexicon with fresh concepts. Ideas such as the *safek* of *tarti de-satri* – doubt resulting from unresolved tension between conflicting elements rather than lack of knowledge – or of *mizvot* whose *kiyyum* is inwardly experiential, although their implementation entails a normatively mandated physical act, may perhaps be retrospectively traced to inchoate precedents. Unquestionably, however, as developed concepts, they bear the Rav's stamp, and it was he who implanted them in the Torah world.

Moreover, his creative energies ranged far afield. He was instrumental in significantly extending the scope of *lomdut,* particularly with respect to many areas of Orah Hayyim. What the Rav said of Reb Hayyim – that he had transmuted the siddur from the preserve of shamashim and ba'alei batim into the domain of *talmidei hakhamim*[6] – was even truer of himself.

And yet, at bottom, the Rav's achievement in the realm of Halakhah, remarkable as it was, bore fruit in a familiar field, one Reb Hayyim had tilled and sown; and he acknowledged this readily and gratefully. The situation is quite different with respect to the sphere of *mahshavah.* The areas of experience explored, the mode and level of inquiry, the resources employed, the problems formulated, above all, the ideas and emotions expressed – these indeed constitute, conjunctively, a new departure. As regards Halakhah, the Rav's achievement had analogues among the panoply of his peers – especially among those who moved in a common ambit and, hence, paralleled some of his *hiddushim.* None, however, even remotely approached the range and depth, the subtlety and complexity, of his *mahshavah.* And it was truly his – neither an extension nor an expansion of an existing defined tradition, but genuine innovation. After one has peeled away some of the homiletic component, for which there was ample precedent, so much of his work – and particularly the entire constellation – remains remarkably original as regards both form and substance. Raw material, of course, he mined from many sources; but he was in no sense eclectic, and the product bore the imprint of his innermost thought and being. If there have recently been significantly comparable antecedents in the Torah world, I am unaware of them. Only Rav Kook, with whose views the Rav agreed in certain areas but from which he diverged sharply in others, provides any basis for comparison; and both his primary concerns and his philosophic focus were very different. Some aspects of the Rav's work had analogues in the general culture, and this is obviously of interest to students of his thought or to intellectual historians at large. However, for *Bnei Torah* in quest of spiritual direction, this fact does little to alter our perception of the uniqueness of the Rav's total hashkafah and experience.

His contribution was especially significant at the interface of his two primary interests: his attempt to formulate and enunciate a philosophy of Halakhah. The attempt was not novel; but its being undertaken by a gadol of the first rank, endowed with rigorous philosophic training,[7] is – at least, in the modern period – most striking. In approaching the issue, the Rav evidenced traces of both rationalism and fideism – and yet, in the spirit of *naʾaseh ve-nishma*, transcended both. While seeking, in a sense, to interpret Halakhah in terms of general categories, he had little propensity for *taʾamei ha-mizvot* in the tradition of, say, the *Sefer Ha-Hinukh* or Rav Samson Raphael Hirsch. For one thing, he eschewed the recourse to utilitarian considerations, if not the outright apologetics, that often typify this tradition. Rather, he persistently stressed that while the halakhic regimen is, as the Torah describes it, ultimately *le-tov lakh,* its message, both short-term and intermediate-term, is one of demand and sacrifice. Beyond this, however, he had no predilection for explaining – much less, explaining away – the nitty-gritty of minutiae, and manifested no sense of responsibility to do so. He preferred broader vistas – addressing himself to overarching concerns, delineating underlying assumptions and ultimate goals, positing values and direction, defining the nature and thrust of Halakhah as a normative order. In doing so, he sought, in the spirit of a much-cherished analogy to modern science, to focus upon the "what" rather than the "why." He insisted upon rigorously analyzing a Halakhah in its own legal terms as a prerequisite to philosophizing about it; and he radically differentiated between rationale as extraneous to a *mizvah* and that which may be of its woof and warp.

The enterprise is admittedly, at times, delicately balanced. The Rav vehemently rejected the intrusion of subjective pseudo-philosophic explanations as an instrument of interpreting objective halakhic material. And yet, with respect to *mizvot* whose halakhic essence has moral or theological import – *tefillah* is a prime example – the Rav's own *hiddushim* clearly reflect his philosophical orientation. He insisted, vigorously, upon the autonomy of Halakhah, regarding as quasi-heretical any attempt to ascribe its content to historical, sociological, or psychological factors. And yet, by definition, the very notion of a philosophy of Halakhah entails viewing – although not, of course, judging – *devar Hashem* through the prism

of universal categories. Moreover, the use of detail – to which recourse
may be had to buttress a thesis, but which can be neutralized, fideistically,
as technical and inscrutable when inconsonant with it – opens up the
charge of selectivity.

These issues are legitimate concerns, and certainly need to be addressed
in any serious analysis of the Rav's work. Still, delicate or not, balance
there is. The fundamental difference between a philosophical orientation
grounded upon Halakhah and one imposed upon it is clear. Even if the
distinction is overly fine, as applied to borderline cases, it is conceptually
sharp. Fine though the line may be, the Rav at times regarded it as a Rubi-
con. Unless mandated by the raw halakhic data, he was consistently wary
of sacrificing formal to teleological considerations. Whether with respect
to *bein adam la-makom* or *bein adam la-havero,* he categorically rejected
any inclination to substitute contextual for normative thinking – unless,
again, there was built-in flexibility in the halakhic base. Hence, he enriched
our Torah world with a philosophic perception that is both authentic and
insightful. The Rav's was an authoritative voice, elucidating the substance
of Halakhah in all its ramifications, and relating it to general axiological
and human concerns, whether personal or collective. In so doing, he broke
fresh ground and put us all very much in his debt.

Sheer novelty or even singularity apart, what, in the Rav's thought and
expression, so powerfully gripped us? In part, of course, the force of his
charismatic personality – especially as we have, at times, been alternately
overwhelmed and enchanted by it, in the course of mesmerizing *derashot*
and stimulating *shi'urim.* Ultimately, however, his hold upon us was far
more substantive. W. B. Yeats once commented that a person writes rhetoric
about his struggles with others and poetry about his struggles with himself.
As an orator, the Rav had no peer in the Torah world. But it is the poet
in him that so touched and enthralled us. He opened for us new vistas of
spiritual experience, vistas within which the drama of human existence,
in the form of confrontation with oneself, the cosmos, and, above all, the
Ribbono shel Olam – all in the context of halakhic existence in its most
rigorous Brisker formulation – is charged with hitherto unperceived force
and meaning. It is not as if we had engaged in the quest of וביקשתם משם

and had faltered. We had simply never thought in those categories. It is not as if we had felt tremulous anxiety as lonely men and women, but in a minor chord. Mired in the pursuit of mundane daily concerns of faith, most of us had simply never confronted that reality. The Rav did. What we had missed, he experienced, in terms of the dichotomy so cherished by him, at both ends of the scale: *gadlut ha-mohin,* the depth and force of a powerful mind mastering its environment and impacting upon it, and *katnut ha-mohin,* the simplicity of the child – not as the epitome of intuited holistic existence idealized by the Romantics, but as the archetype of a helpless humble spirit groping toward his Father and seeking solace in Him and through Him.

Something of that experience he communicated to us through various channels; and in so doing he sensitized us to the need for a fuller dimension of our own *avodat Hashem.* Flashes of what he saw and showed both engage and haunt us; chords of what he heard and said resonate in our ears; strains of what he felt palpitate in our hearts. Beyond detail, however, we have been gripped and stirred by דמות דיוקנו של רבינו "the usage of our master" – magisterial but sensitive, winsome but ultimately inscrutable – and his spiritual odyssey. At home we have, hanging on the wall, one picture of the Rav with an engaging smile on his face; another of him bent over pensively, with a somber, almost brooding, expression. In looking at the latter, I am frequently reminded of Wordsworth's portrayal of the statue "Of Newton with his prism and silent face, / The marble index of a mind for ever / Voyaging through strange seas of thought, alone."[8] Only not just a mind but a soul, not just thought but experience, and above all, not marble, but a passionate human spirit.

From the realm of talmud, broadly conceived, we move to that of *ma'asseh.* Some of the Rav's activity in this sphere might be perceived as *askanut* – quasi-political, in a sense, and yet of genuine spiritual import. Two instances spring to mind immediately. The first is his stand vis-à-vis the Conservative and Reform movements. Hearing some current dilettantes, one might get the impression that the most eloquent and vigorous statement the Rav made with respect to the non-Orthodox was his protracted silence about the Synagogue Council of America. But those who remember the fifties accurately know better. Who issued the radical *psak* that if one had to choose between forgoing *tekiat shofar* and hearing it in attendance at a mixed temple, he should opt for the former? Who, in the public mind, gave Orthodoxy intellectual respectability and credibility in its confrontation with other movements? To whom did *metukkanim shebahem,* right-wing Conservative rabbis seeking to stem the tide of tinkering with Halakhah – whether with respect to Gentile wine or women being called up to the Torah – turn for guidance? Of course, the Rav knew, as we ought to know, that many in the deviationist movements, rabbis and laymen both, are genuine *mevakkeshei Hashem,* sincerely seeking the *Ribbono shel Olam* in the context of *yahadut* as they perceive it; and to them he accorded both respect and understanding. But as a custodian of tradition, he was, in thwarting institutionalized revisionism, adamantly unwavering. One can truly apply to him the Ramban's encomium of the Rambam, in his letter to the Northern French rabbanim:

מי הכה הצדוקים אשר היו כגבורים חוסים, מי נתן הכיתוסים לשוסים, הלא הרב ז"ל כי ה' עמו.

Who defeated the Zadokites, who were as strong as warriors? Who gave over the Boethusians to the despoilers? Was it not the Rav, may his name be a blessing, for the Lord was with him.[9]

The second instance concerns interfaith rather than intracommunal relations, although it, too, had internal ramifications. I refer, of course, to the Rav's adamant stand against Jewish-Christian theological dialogue. Concerned, in the wake of Catholic overtures encouraged by the thaw in anti-Semitism mandated by the Second Vatican Council, that the sense of the singularity and uniqueness of *Knesset Yisrael* might become jaded, both within and without the Jewish world, the Rav fought vigorously against incipient ecumenism. He, and only he, had both the stature and the courage to restrain those who, whether *leshem shammayim* or otherwise – the prospect of having one's picture with the Pope appear on the front page of the *New York Times* is no mean temptation – sought the warm embrace of our erstwhile contemners; and the policy he enunciated – assent to dialogue about moral or social issues but rejection of discussions of faith and dogma – has stood the Orthodox community in good stead. In retrospect, some may feel that the Rav's anxiety about missionary impulses and possible mass apostasy was exaggerated. Be that as it may, the episode – and it was more than that – boldly manifested the Rav's engagement in communal affairs and the leadership he exercised in that capacity.

Even in the realm of *ma'asseh*, however, sociopolitical activity was not the Rav's forte. His primary practical role was realized through the interface of talmud and *ma'asseh* – through teaching, which Aquinas aptly defined as the ideal fusion of the active and the contemplative life. This interaction probably lies at the heart of the gemara's discussion, as understood by Rashi, about the comparative merits of talmud and *ma'asseh*. Resolving an apparent contradiction about their respective priority, the gemara concludes: לא קשיא, הא למיגמר, הא לאגמורי (This is not a problem: one statement refers to studying, and one to teaching.) Rashi explains: למיגמר לעצמו, מעשה עדיף, אבל לאגמורי לאחריני עדיף ממעשה. (When it comes to teaching himself, action is preferable, but teaching others is preferable to action.)[10]

Presumably, the intent is not simply that teaching is more meritorious, qua talmud, than *ma'asseh*, but rather that, in effect, it incorporates both, in the spirit of Hazal's formulation:

תורה ללמדה, זו היא תורה של חסד; שלא ללמדה זו היא תורה שאינה של חסד.

Torah to teach: this is the Torah of Hesed; not to teach: this is the Torah which is not of Hesed.[11]

As regards the Rav, then, his primary practical contribution was as *morenu ve-rabbenu*, our master teacher. And this in two respects. First, in the narrow sense of exposition, explication, and instruction. He often, albeit at times with a note of conveniently feigned self-deprecation, described himself as a melammed; and that he was, without peer. His capacity for formulating pivotal questions with an eye to the relation between principle and detail, his sheer pedagogic skill in stimulating curiosity and insight;

above all, his fertile and suggestive solutions – these left their imprint upon students over the span of half a century.

He addressed himself to this task with conscious dedication – dictated, in part, by his professional responsibilities as a *rav ha-'ir* or as a Rosh Yeshiva, but, driven far beyond what these duties required by the impetus of mission, that pervasive sense of *shelihut* of which he often spoke so fervently and so eloquently. This was primarily manifested in the course of regular *shi'urim* whose sheer scope is strikingly impressive, but it also impinged upon his *harbazat Torah* as a whole. It largely influenced, for instance, the choice of topics for the Yahrzeit *shi'urim* so heavily tilted toward Orah Hayyim, and almost wholly devoid of more abstruse areas such as Kodashim, that had been his father's forte and, in a sense, his own first love. I vividly recall how one year, several decades back, he began to prepare a Yahrzeit *shi'ur* to deal with *kinyan hazer*, but then dropped the idea, out of concern that the infrastructure might not be sufficiently familiar to many in the audience. In a similar vein, when his interest in publication intensified in later years, he firmly encouraged the assignment of primacy to writings that would best serve the general Torah public, rather than to those geared to his indigenous "lomdische" constituency.

In the Rav's thought and experience, his role as *moreinu ve-rabbenu* went in tandem with a second – that of *meturgeman*. He once remarked to me that it is the basic function of *marbizei Torah* in each generation to render its content into the language and categories of their contemporaries; and there is no question but that this facet was an integral component of any self-portrait he limned. That rendering was, of course, interpretation rather than mere translation; and very much in the spirit of the gemara in Kiddushin:

תניא, רב יהודה אומר, "המתרגם פסוק כצורתו, הרי זה בדאי, והמוסיף עליו, הרי זה המחרף ומגדף, אלא מאי תרגום תרגום דידן."

R. Yehudah says: Whoever translates a verse literally is a liar, and one who adds to it is a blasphemer and a libeler. What then is translation? Our Targum.[12]

As a halakhic entity, *Targum didan* is related to an area much

developed by the Rav, *Keri'at Ha-Torah*. Explicating a *pasuk* in Nehemyah
that describes the Torah reading upon the return from exile, the gemara
explains:

אמר רב חננאל אמר רב, "מאי דכתיב, 'ויקראו בספר תורת האלקים מפורש ושום שכל
ויבינו במקרא'? 'ויקראו בספר תורת האלקים,' זה מקרא, 'מפורש,' זה תרגום, 'ושום
שכל,' אלו הפסוקים, 'ויבינו במקרא' זה פיסוק טעמים," ואמרי לה, אלו המסורות.

R. Hananel said in the name of Rav: What is [the meaning of the verse]:
"And they read in the book of the Torah of God, distinctly, and they gave the
sense, so that they understood the reading"? "They read in the book of the
Torah of God": this refers to the reading tradition; "distinctly": this refers to
Targum; "and gave sense": this refers to the verses [i.e., the punctuation]; "they
understood the reading": this refers to the cantillation, and some say: these
are the traditions of spelling.[13]

In this connection, the Rav repeatedly developed a distinction
between the *keriah* of mid-week or of Minhah on Shabbat, primarily
geared to maintaining continual contact with Torah as a vivifying force,
and that of Shabbat morning, intended to provide not only inspiration but
instruction and direction.[14] Hence, he contended that *targum* was confined
to the latter, as a vehicle for the realization of public *talmud Torah,* for which
an intermediary interpreter could be pivotal, in line with the prescription
of an oft-quoted Yerushalmi:

כשם שניתנה על ידי סרסור, כך אנו צריכים לנהוג בה על ידי סרסור, עאל רבי יהודה
בר פזי ועבדה אילה, "אנכי עמד בין ה' וביניכם בעת ההוא להגיד לכם את דבר ה'"

Just as it [the Torah] was given by means of an agent, so must we behave
with it by means of an agent. R. Yehudah bar Pazzi entered [the synagogue]
and made as to ask this question [answered it by reciting the verse]: "I stood
between the Lord and between you at that time to tell you the Word of the
Lord."[15]

The Rav was central to our weekday and Shabbat *keriah* – both as our
link to the mesorah, infusing us with the substance of Torah, and through
creative explication, halakhic and philosophic, relating it to the realities of
the modern world. This dual integrated function of *rav-meturgeman* was
a difficult and delicate enterprise. Interpret too literally, and you run the

risk of ossification and obscurantism – הרי זה בדאי; range too far afield, and you raise the specter of blasphemous deviation – הרי זה מחרף ומגדף. Only *Targum didan,* traditional creative exposition, in the hands of a thoroughly responsible and richly innovative master, hits the mark. And we are all deeply in the Rav's debt for his having embarked on this undertaking.

The Rav's dual role as spiritual mentor was, for him, a source of immense gratification. However, it was also, perhaps inevitably, a cause of considerable frustration. The frustration centered, primarily, on the sense that the full thrust of his total *keriah-targum* was often not sufficiently apprehended or appreciated; that by some, parts of his Torah were being digested and disseminated, but other essential ingredients were being relatively disregarded, if not distorted. In a moment of striking candor, when my colleague, Rav Yehuda Amital, first visited these shores almost twenty years ago, the Rav commented to him: "You know, I have devoted *talmidim* – very devoted *talmidim.* If I were to announce a *shi'ur* at two o'clock in the morning, they would come *en bloc.* And yet, deep in their hearts, they think I'm an apikoros." The remark was laced with characteristic humor and confined, presumably, to a select group. Nevertheless, it gave vent to a genuine, if painful, sentiment.

The ideological fault aside, however, he often felt – and this, with respect to a far broader group – that even among *talmidim,* some of his primary spiritual concerns were not so much rejected as ignored; indeed, that spirituality itself was being neglected. Like the Rambam, he was persistently perturbed by religious vulgarization, practical or conceptual, and by shallow ritualization of either the modern or the "frum" strain; and the tension between the subjective and the objective, between action, thought, and experience, was a major lifelong concern. The sense that he was only partially successful in imparting this concern gnawed at him, and impelled efforts to redress the imbalance; but these, too, were only partly successful. After his wife's death in 1967, he initiated intensive *shi'urim* for *talmidim* who would come to Brookline to learn during the summer. One day (around 1969–70), he stunned the group by announcing that, inasmuch as he found them spiritually desiccated, he would now, in addition to the regular *shi'urim* on the *masekhet,* learn the *Likutei Torah,* of the Ba'al Ha-

Tanya, with them; and he started, the following day, with the section on אני
לדודי ודודי לי. "But," he confided to me subsequently, "it didn't really help."

The most forceful expression of this sentiment is to be found in
a brief essay which I regard as the single best introduction to the Rav's
thought – all the more so as it bears the stamp of total genuineness, having
been conceived and composed during and shortly after his bout with cancer
in the winter of 1959–60. After lamenting that the current Torah world
has produced aspiring *talmidei hakhamim* who are intellectually asser-
tive but experientially deficient, he goes on to assign part of the blame to
himself:

> לפיכך אני מצהיר כי יש בידי להצביע על אחד האחראים למצב הנוכחי, והוא אני בעצמי.
> אני לא יצאתי ידי חובתי כמורה דרך והוראה בישראל' חסרו לי הכוחות הנפשיים שמורה
> ורב זקוק להם' או נטול רצון הייתי ולא הקדשתי את כל אשר לי למשימתי. בשעה
> שהצלחתי, במידה מרובה או מועטת' כמלמד ומורה במישור "גדלות המוחין" – תלמידי
> קיבלו ממני הרבה תורה וקומתם האינטלקטואלית התחסנה והלכה וגדלה במשך השנים
> שבילו במסיבתי – לא ראיתי ברכה מרובה במישור החווייתי. לא עלה בידי להיות עמהם
> חיים משותפים, להתדבק בהם ולהעניק להם מחום נפשי. דברי, כנראה, לא הציתו את
> שלהבת י-ה בליבות רגישים. חטאתי כמרביץ תורה שבלב הנמסרת בכוח המעטת הדמות
> עד כדי "קטנות המוחין". אתי תלין משוגתי.

And therefore I affirm that I can identify one of those responsible for the
present situation, and that is none other than myself. I have not fulfilled my
obligation as a guide in Israel. I seem to have lacked the ability – the personal
power – required of a teacher and rav, or perhaps I lacked some of the desire
to fulfill the role completely, and I did not devote myself completely to the
task. To a greater or lesser degree, as an educator and teacher on the plane
of *gadlut ha-mohin,* "mental greatness", my students have received much
Torah learning from me, and their intellectual standing has strengthened
and increased during the years they have spent with me – but I have not
seen much growth on the experiential plane. I have not succeeded in living
in common with them, cleaving to them and bestowing some of my personal
warmth on them. My words, it would seem, have not kindled a divine spark
in sensitive hearts. I have fallen short [in my role] as one who spreads the
"Torah of the heart" – [a Torah] that is transmitted by the power of [the
teacher's deliberate] diminishing [of his own towering] stature, to the point
of *katnut ha-mohin.* And the failing lies with me.[16]

That, too is part of the Rav's legacy. Not just spellbinding *shi'urim,* magnificent *derashot,* and electrifying *hiddushim,* but the candid recognition of failure – failure transcended by its very acknowledgment. In his own personal vein, so aristocratic and yet so democratic, he has imbued us with a sense of both the frailty of majesty and the majesty of frailty. He has transmitted to us not only *Torat Mosheh Avdi,* but the midrashic image of Mosheh Rabbenu constructing and then dismantling the Mishkan daily during *shiv'at yemei ha-millu'im*[17] – whose import the Rav interpreted as the fusion of radical, almost Sisyphean, frustration with ultimate hope. He has initiated us, far from the admiring crowd, into the anguished quest – unlike Plotinus, he did not necessarily experience it as a flight (either an ascent or an escape) – of the alone for the Alone. He has left us not only memories of packed audiences, dazzled by his multifaceted powers, but the riveting sense of the message of the mishnah, so humbling and yet so inspiring:

מנין שאפילו אחד שיושב ועוסק בתורה' שהקב"ה קובע לו שכר? שנאמר, "ישב בדד וידום כי נטל עליו."

How do we know that even one who sits and occupies himself with Torah, the Holy One, blessed be He, sets a reward for him? For it is said, "He sits alone and is silent, for he has taken upon himself" (Eicha 3:28).[18]

The Rav repeatedly referred to this mishnah when expatiating upon the experiential character of *talmud Torah*; and the meeting envisioned by it may be regarded as the epitome of the Rav's talmud and *ma'asseh.* His quintessential aspiration was the fusion of spirituality and *lomdut.* We who come after cannot, retrospectively, imagine the past half-century without him. Prospectively, as dwarfs on a giant's shoulders, we feel charged to persist, impelled by his spirit, in the implementation of his goals – to learn, to teach, to realize. To the best of our abilities, we are called and we are pledged to continue, in the *bet ha-midrash* and in the community, his multifaceted enterprise – להגדיל תורה ולהאדירה.

Notes

1. I have given the title "An Appreciation" to this piece, a slightly expanded and embellished version, with appropriately revised tenses, of a talk originally delivered before the Orthodox Union Convention in 1992, on the occasion of the fiftieth anniversary of the Rav's becoming Rosh Yeshiva at Yeshivat Rabbenu Isaac Elhanan." It is presented, properly, as a labor of love and gratitude, rather than as a critical analysis – not even in the vein of Walter Pater's *Appreciations*. But I have aimed throughout for objective descriptive accuracy, although certainly not for a dispassionately objective tone.

    Readers who heard or read the hesped of the Rav זצ"ל, which I delivered a year and a half later, will, not surprisingly, note some overlap, although I did not have the earlier talk before me while preparing the latter, and certainly did not consciously strive to recall or reproduce it. Nevertheless, I have assented to the invitation from *Tradition* to publish this piece, on the assumption that its difference from the hesped warrants as much.

2. *Ish Ha-Halakhah: Golah va-Nistar* (Jerusalem, 5739), p. 31.

    With respect to the substance of this passage, several points may be noted: (1) The examples subsequently cited all refer to modes of dealing with deviant phenomena, whose failure to materialize, so that the relevant Halakhah can be applied, is obviously not to be lamented. It does not follow from this, however, that a *talmid hakham* may be equally apathetic about the fate of positive or even ideal elements. (2) Abstinence from *psak* out of *yir'at hora'ah* may not reflect indifference to implementation but, rather, responsible concern about it – and hence, anxiety over possible error. (3) The statement about the reluctance of *gedolim* to enter the lists of *psak* probably requires some qualification. It is true of some venues – nineteenth-century Lithuania, out of whose tradition the Rav sprang, possibly being a case in point – but as a historical generalization, it strikes me as somewhat sweeping.

3. Ibid, p. 41.

4. Ibid, pp. 35–36.

5. Ibid, p. 79.

6. See the account of Reb Hayyim's method in the Rav's hesped of his son, Reb Yitzhak Zev, "Mah Dodekh mi-Dod," *Divrei Hagut ve-Ha'Arakhah* (Jerusalem, 5742), pp. 79–80.

7. How much the formal philosophic discipline, as opposed to general cultural orientation, contributed to the Rav's overall *mahshavah* is worthy of study. In *The Halakhic Mind*, the impact is powerful; but, while published only recently, it is a relatively early work (1940s), and the question can be raised with respect to later phases.

8. "The Prelude," III, pp. 61–63.

9. *Kitvei Ha-Ramban* (Jerusalem, 5723) I, p. 341.

10. Bava Kamma 17a; Rashi, s.v. *le-migmar.*

11. Sukkah 49b.

12. Kiddushin 49a.

13. Nedarim 37b.

14. See *Shi'urim le-Zekher Abba Mari* זצ״ל (Jerusalem, 5743), I, c. 5–10.

15. Yerushalmi, Megillah 4:1.

16. From an article initially published in *Hadoar* (5720) and reprinted in בסוד היחיד והיחד ירושלים), תשל״ו), p. 420.

17. See Rashi, Vayikra 9:23.

18. Avot 3:2.

Chapter 10

The Rav זצ"ל in Retrospect: *Divrei Hesped*

I.

וַיְהִי רָעָב בִּימֵי דָוִד שָׁלֹשׁ שָׁנִים שָׁנָה אַחֲרֵי שָׁנָה וַיְבַקֵּשׁ דָּוִד אֶת־פְּנֵי ה' וַיֹּאמֶר ה' אֶל־שָׁאוּל
וְאֶל־בֵּית הַדָּמִים עַל־אֲשֶׁר־הֵמִית אֶת־הַגִּבְעֹנִים:

There was a famine in the days of David, year after year, for three years. David
inquired of God, and God replied, "It is because of Saul and because of the
blood-guilty house, in that he massacred the Gibeonites."

(Shemuel II 21:1)

The Gemara in Yevamot 78b explains the phrase "because of Saul" as referring to the fact that he was not properly eulogized. In this context, the
phrase has a double meaning. First, a eulogy must be carried out according
to the procedures detailed by Hazal, as set out in Yoreh De'ah 344, and
its contents must be suffused with Hazal's spirit and in consonance with
the manner of thought and response which they specified. Additionally,
however, both as part of the formal requirement of the eulogy and beyond
it, what is required is that the eulogy succeed in describing the deceased
in his true character, and, with an appreciation of, his true stature – to
bemoan the loss.

In regard to this examination of a personality, the Rav זצ"ל himself commented (on Bereshit 5:1): זֶה סֵפֶר תּוֹלְדֹת אָדָם "'This is the book of the events of man':[1] one must study a person like a book." Is there, then, a more urgent time than now, a time that requires us to observe the halakhot of reading a Torah scroll[2] – completely explicated, properly understood,[3] with a sensitivity and feeling for the subject's essential qualities, unique lineaments, and overall complexity? Is there a time when these requirements are more strongly in force than when his image rises before us, "when I stand there"?

It may be assumed that Saul, a king who fell in a bloody battle in which the people of Israel suffered a crushing defeat, in a period in which a stubborn struggle for the political leadership of the nation and its future path was being conducted, was not eulogized properly in two senses.

In the twilight era that began in the wake of Saul's defeat and death, in political confusion and social chaos, who had the strength and resources, or even the will and desire, to arrange a proper funeral and eulogy for one of whom it is written: "Shemuel took a flask of oil and poured some on Saul's head and kissed him, saying: 'God anoints you as ruler over His people, over His inheritance'" (1 Shemuel 10:1)? Second, in those days of perplexity and political change, whoever entered upon this task would most likely have lacked the discernment to trace precisely the lineaments of Saul's personality and accomplishments in their full scope. Consequently, he would have failed properly to assess the severity of the loss[4] and to bemoan it.

However, it was precisely Saul's persecuted antagonist, the "sweet singer of Israel,"[5] who surmounted the hostilities of the past, and in the first fruits[6] of his song raised a dirge:

הַצְּבִי יִשְׂרָאֵל עַל בָּמוֹתֶיךָ חָלָל אֵיךְ נָפְלוּ גִבּוֹרִים... שָׁאוּל וִיהוֹנָתָן הַנֶּאֱהָבִים וְהַנְּעִימִם בְּחַיֵּיהֶם וּבְמוֹתָם לֹא נִפְרָדוּ מִנְּשָׁרִים קַלּוּ מֵאֲרָיוֹת גָּבֵרוּ... אֵיךְ נָפְלוּ גִבּוֹרִים וַיֹּאבְדוּ כְּלֵי מִלְחָמָה:

Your glory, O Israel, lies slain on the heights,
How the mighty have fallen!...
Saul and Jonathan, beloved and cherished when alive, were not
separated in their death. Swifter than eagles, stronger than lions....
How the mighty have fallen, the weapons of war perished![7]

Nevertheless, still more remains unexplained than has been clarified; the dirge concentrates on only one aspect of the personality of the slain king, although one that expresses both his essence and his military role – that which is reflected in the reverberating expression, "how the mighty have fallen."

Did this expression really characterize the tragic image of this figure, anointed by God and present him in his full stature? Did it open a vantage point, no matter how limited, through which we might glimpse the struggles of his soul? Did it illumine the motives and meaning of his suicide? And beyond the personal aspect, did it succeed in giving voice to the national calamity, as deep as the sea, that occurred to the kingdom of Israel in that short space of time, to express the piercing feeling of sorrow that prevailed among all classes of the nation in the wake of the defeat?

Conscious of this prospect, we come, with fear and trembling, to eulogize our master and teacher, may his memory be blessed. With the first aspect, we can, relatively speaking, cope adequately. It is possible to set a time for the eulogy with due consideration for the prohibition against eulogies during the month of Nisan, and according to the determination of the Mishnah that "a person should not arouse [his relatives] to mourn or eulogize his deceased [relative during] the thirty days prior to the Festival" (לא יעורר אדם על מתו ולא יספידנו קודם לרגל שלשים יום).[8] At hand, we have the guidance of the Ramban in his *Torat Ha-Adam,* ranging from the broad injunction, "[Although our intention is for the deceased's honor,] we are forbidden to eulogize the deceased excessively, namely, much more than is his due. Rather, we eulogize him according to the honor due him and a bit more, as is the custom of eulogizers, but not excessively so," (ואסור לאפלוגי בהספדא ביקרא דשכבי טפי ממאי דחזי ליה אלא משבחים אותו לפי כבודו ויותר מכן כדרך המשבחים ולא בהפלגה יותר מדאי...)[9] to the specific directive that "as for a sage, noble, or gaon, we bring [his body] into the *bet midrash*, place the bier in the place where he was wont to preach, and his disciples and the Congregation of Israel eulogize him." (אבל חכם ואלוף וגאון מכניסין אותו לבית המדרש ומניחים את המטה במקום שהיה דורש וסופדין אותו תלמידים וקהל ישראל).[10]

Who among us, however, is capable of successfully meeting this second challenge, fulfilling the holy, obligatory, but impossible duty of properly eulogizing the Rav ל״ז, taking into account his essence and character, his qualities and accomplishments, his gestalt and values, his place and deeds? Certainly not I. In part, this is because I feel that I do not deserve the merit, the honor of eulogizing my teacher and father-in-law ל״ז. The honor of eulogizing the Rav ל״ז in this forum is the just desert of my brother-in-law, Rabbi Yitzhak Twersky, shlita, in whose house, and the house of the Rav's first-born daughter, Atarah, the Rav lived for the twenty-six years that have passed since the death of his wife ל״ז, and who, despite all the difficulties attendant thereto, served him with devotion, faithfulness, and efficiency. And in part, my reluctance stems from my deficiencies in regard to profundity of thought and imaginative grasp, linguistic precision and fine discernment, rich language and lofty thought; in short, lack of the requisite ability to express feelings and engage deepest sympathies. Only one person – a man who, among other things, was the greatest eulogizer of this century – could be said to have had the capability to properly eulogize the Rav ל״ז – the Rav himself.

Nevertheless, it is incumbent on us, his children who are his disciples, and his disciples who are his children, to attempt to fulfill the *mizvah* of eulogizing him, to the extent that our understanding allows, even though, from a certain point of view, we will fall short of the goal, as hard as we may try. And this is so, even though the danger exists that we may even, God forbid, come to denigrate the one we wish to praise. Our situation is reminiscent of R. Hanina's comparison of a person who lavishly praises the attributes of the Holy One, blessed be He, to someone who praises an earthly king for the silver coins in his treasury even though he possesses thousands upon thousands of golden dinars: is he not denigrating the king instead of praising him?[11] Despite our awareness of our shortcomings in thought and expression, our obligation is to praise, to give thanks – and, to our great sorrow – to mourn.

II.

But the Rav ל״ז himself has shown us the way, even as to our approach in eulogizing him. More than thirty years ago, in an act of exalted heroism – this was just a few days after he had been informed that he was suffering from cancer, even though no public announcement had yet been made – he eulogized his uncle, R. Velvel ל״ז. At the climactic moment – the crescendo still rings in my ears – he cried out, pounding on his shtender, "'Not so is My servant Mosheh'!"[12] Not so is my servant R. Yitzhak Zev! Uncle was not merely better, he was not merely greater – he was different! He was unique!"[13]

Afterwards, when the Rav ל״ז published his eulogy in Hebrew, he wrote:

> There were many sages in my uncle's generation, cedars of Lebanon, heads of the exile, and teachers of Torah to many. They were great in their Torah knowledge, masterful debaters in Mishnah, gemara, and Codes. Nevertheless, "Not so is My servant Moses" – not so R. Yitzhak Zev, the Brisker Rav, who was distinct and distinctive, unlike them in his approach and habits. The title Gadol Ha-Dor does not fit him and does not express his singular qualities. He was alone in his generation, preeminent in that gifted generation.[14]

If this could be said of R. Velvel ל״ז, who, after all, was not all that different from his father, R. Hayyim ל״ז, or his brother, R. Mosheh ל״ז – and, indeed, the special qualities attributed to him could more accurately be taken to characterize that which he so well typified, the dynasty and approach of Brisk in general, and not so much himself personally – the statement is all the more appropriate for the Rav ל״ז. In the full interplay of his power, his range and strength, his approach and methods, he was not only singular in his generation, but his like has not been seen in several generations. The many-colored coat of Yosef, each stripe rich in itself and at the same time part of an exquisite unified tapestry,[15] symbolized the unique standing of the righteous Yosef in the household of our patriarch, Yaakov. Analogously, the incarnation of the diverse spiritual richness that coalesced into the personality of our Master, the Rav ל״ז, had no like in our time.

By what means was this singularity reflected and expressed? The Torah twice testifies to the uniqueness of our Master Mosheh. In Baha'alotekha it says:

Not so is My servant Mosheh; he is the most faithful of My household. I speak to him face to face, and by vision and not by riddles; he beholds God's similitude.[16]

At the end of Vezot Ha-Berakhah it says:

No prophet like Mosheh has arisen in Israel, [one] whom God knew face to face, in regard to all the signs and wonders which God sent him to perform in the land of Egypt, to Pharaoh and all his servants and his entire land, and in regard to the mighty hand and all the great terror which Mosheh wrought in the sight of all Israel.[17]

The difference is clear, and so is its reason. The first passage refers to Mosheh's greatness as a prophet on the personal level – the power of the experience and the means that brought it about, the content and profundity of his comprehension, the constancy and manner of his standing in the presence of God, which characterized the encounter of the Master of Prophets with the Lord of All Worlds, as described in the *Mishneh Torah* in chapter 7 of *Hilkhot Yesodei Ha-Torah*, and from another point of view, in the *Guide of the Perplexed* II:35.

In contrast, the second passage concentrates on his communal role and designated function as leader and divine emissary, in the sight of all Israel and before the world and its denizens.[18] These two roles are mutually sustaining. Hence, an additional dimension of singularity, celebrated by *Knesset Yisrael* in the Yigdal hymn, "No one like Mosheh has arisen in Israel, a prophet who beholds His similitude," relates to this fusion and emanates from the conflation of passages. Despite this, the two passages are concerned with differing aspects of his role.

A parallel duality characterizes the great Torah authorities of all generations. The title "Light of the Exile," specifically applied to Rabbenu Gershom, defines the quality of a Torah authority, a *gadol ba-Torah*, within whom are hidden two aspects.

Ma'asseh Bereshit, the story of Creation, records the creation of light in two passages, pertaining, respectively, to the first day and the fourth. This bifurcation does not require great exposition. The creation of light on the first day refers to its creation in an absolute sense, as a primordial creation, without function and without relation to any other part of creation. "The Lord saw that the light was good"[19] – He observed it as an isolated phenomenon. As such, it has an independent value: "I saw then that the superiority of wisdom over foolishness is as the superiority of light over darkness."[20] On the fourth day, however, a new aspect was added: "The Lord placed them [the great lights] in the expanse of the heaven to light the earth and to rule over day and night, to distinguish between light and darkness."[21] That is, the light was embodied in corporate bodies and acquired their designated function. Not light (*or*) but enlighteners (*maor*).

Spiritual enlighteners, too, have a dual character; they embody the good and the beautiful, on the one hand, and leadership qualities on the other. And so, when we come to mourn their setting, we may employ two complementary cries: "I cry for this beauty that lies withered in the earth,"[22] and "Woe to the ship that has lost its captain!"[23] A person mourns the withering of the good and the beautiful not merely because it represents a loss to him, but from the pain attendant upon the descent of that dignity and glory to oblivion. Anyone who observes a Torah scroll being burned must tear his garment as a sign of mourning, even if he still has a veritable library of Torah works that can serve as a replacement. On the other hand, we are required to bemoan the terrible void that has opened up before our generation, and to proclaim the sense of loss that has seized us. "And the entire House of Israel will mourn the burning"[24] – that is, both the tragedy of the death and the subsequent loss.

III.

In respect to someone like the Rav ז״ל, who merited to be a successor of Mosheh Rabbenu, we need to examine, in the hour of eclipse, his singularity in both these areas, as a scholar of Torah and as a luminary of Torah. What was the quintessence of the beauty of the Rav ז״ל, "the light, which was good," the light in and of itself that the Rav manifested? First and foremost, was his greatness in Torah learning, to which he dedicated his strength and time, "to understand and perceive, to obey, to learn and to teach, to keep and perform and fulfill all the words of the learning of Torah with love";[25]

his involvement with all the minute details[26] of the "researches of Abbaye and Rava,"[27] and all their ramifications, in order to clarify and explain them in their utter profundity at the highest level. He was, in his generation, the representative of Brisk and Volozhin. In him, more than in anyone else, were wonderfully combined the drive for truth and responsibility to it, together with the boldness of originality and creative innovation. "To tell the truth," one of the children of the Griz commented to me over thirty years ago, "Uncle was more creative than Father."[28] "Uncle" here refers to the Rav's father, R. Mosheh ל״ז, and R. Mosheh saw his son not only as a successor equal to himself but as one who surpassed him.

As a gadol in Torah he was, in essence, a tower of light for his disciples, and through them for their disciples and the entire generation. At times he dazzled, at times he illuminated, at times he blazed with flashes of blinding insight. In part, he explained and developed concepts that were the common possession of the *bet midrash* in which he was schooled; in part, he sharpened them, poured new content into them, and placed them in new contexts. And in part, he produced new concepts[29] – as, for instance, of a category of doubt regarding two conflicting matters that issues from the balanced conflict between two certainties, and not from uncertainty itself, or the category of *mizvot* whose performance is physical, of relations to the limbs with which they are carried out but whose fulfillment relates to the area of "duties of the heart."

Unfortunately, a part of this light was hidden from many for a long time. I recall my own derelictions in this regard.[30] When I entered the class of Maran ל״ז more than forty-two years ago, I arrived at a time following a two-year period during which he had conducted *shi'urim* on Tractate Shabbat, and before that Tractate Pesahim. With my arrival began a period of two and one-half years during which he concentrated on Niddah and Mikva'ot, going over them twice in succession. In my stupid naivete, I thought that the central areas of Nashim and Nezikin were the proper areas of study for the classical Roshei Yeshiva and their heirs, that Kodashim had been appropriated by R. Velvel, and that the Rav's "home field" was made up of the tractates of Berakhot, Mo'ed, parts of Toharot (even though the Rav himself emphasized that his insistence on repeating

Niddah and Mikva'ot stemmed precisely from his feeling that he had not mastered them sufficiently) – and their "suburbs." To be sure, even then signs were not lacking that could have corrected this error, at least for one whose vision was not obtuse. I recall that during my first year at the Yeshiva, before Pesah, and before I had entered the Rav's *shi'ur*, several students took hold of him in the hall adjoining the study hall and begged him to deliver a *shi'ur* regarding the selling of hametz. He agreed, and clarified the entire matter on the spot, although the issue was one that required mastery of not only the essential issues of hametz but the entire area of the laws of acquiring possession (*kinyanim*), in its length and breadth, in a manner that to me, at least, was astounding.

Nevertheless, the error of restricting the Rav to specialized areas of concern was still widespread; the degree of obtuseness that this required became clear to me only later. His mastery of all areas of Halakhah was sure; there was not a field whose essentials were not absolutely clear to him and immediately available – *mehuddadim be-fiv.*[31] Indeed, the Rav ל"ז often focused upon presumably "lighter" areas, out of a deep conviction that it was essential to achieve a conceptual understanding of every part of the Torah, and not only those sections of which it is said that "whoever wishes to become wise should occupy themselves [with Seder Nezikin]";[32] and in this he discerned a personal challenge. Once he prefaced a *shi'ur* on Chapter Ha-Kore Omed[33] with the exclamation that the effort involved in mastering it in a conceptual manner was commensurate with the effort described in the verse "Who turns the rock into water, flint into springs of water."[34] But this was not because he lacked the requisite mastery in the traditionally "heavier" areas. There recently appeared a volume – its publication initiated and organized by my brother-in-law, Rav Haym Soloveitchik, and edited by Rav Haym Ilson and Rav Yitzhak Abba Lichtenstein – entitled *Hiddushei HaGram veha-Grid,* containing *hiddushim* on Seder Kodashin that the Rav ל"ז produced in conjunction with his father before he had reached his twenties. The work speaks for itself; but from it one may assess his creative power in other areas of Torah learning.

As far as erudition and precise knowledge of the details of the law are concerned, there may be those who will claim, probably with justice, that his generation included many who were more erudite than he. But we may adapt the appraisal of R. Haym Ozer (Grodzinski) that R. Haym (Soloveitchik) was more of a *baki* than the Rogochover (R. Yosef Rosen), even though the latter knew the whole Torah by heart. "R. Haym's Tosafot he didn't know!"[35] What the Rav ל"ז saw in the Rambam, and the conceptual worlds[36] he built upon what he saw, others, though they may have been able to recite the Rambam's words with wondrous accuracy, did not see and did not build.

The Rav's creativity began by formulating the right questions, continued by marking out the right modes of thought, and ended with the creation of a clearly defined content, although not always would he tie up all the loose ends pertaining to side issues. In learning, he was as dynamic as can be imagined; the light produced was not of particles but of waves.[37] In this week's Torah reading we read, "Nevertheless, a spring or a cistern wherein there is a gathering of water shall be clean."[38] In the world of Torah, there are *gedolim* who may be compared to a cistern, such as R. Eliezer b. Horkenos, whom his teacher, Rabban Yohanan b. Zakkai, termed "a plastered cistern that does not lose a drop."[39] And there are those who are conspicuous for their resemblance to an ever-renewing spring, as Rabban Yohanan b. Zakkai described R. Eleazar b. Arakh, another disciple listed in the same Mishnah, whom he termed an "overflowing spring." The Rav ל"ז was, in his essence, one of those powerful springs who never ceased his investigations, who never ceased striving, never tired of attempting to take the measure of a subject. He may be described in the terms presented by the baraita of Kinyan Ha-Torah,[40] "like a spring that does not cease and an overflowing stream."[41]

I recall that when the Rav ל"ז was in his sixties, I met one of his acquaintances, a veteran disciple of the Slobodka Yeshiva. He asked me what tractate the Rav was learning in his *shi'urim*, and when I replied, "Bava Kamma," he burst out with the exclamation, "Bava Kamma! At his age, who has the strength to do Bava Kamma? The European Roshei Yeshiva studied the key tractates of the yeshiva curriculum in their twenties and thirties, recorded their *hiddushim* in a notebook, and gave their future *shi'urim* in accordance with their notes. True, they studied all their lives.

But the clarification of key tractates they completed at an early stage of their study."

That was not the way of the Rav, ז״ל He did not rest on his laurels. He was never satisfied with merely polishing earlier insights. My brother-in-law, R. Haym, told me that as a young boy he studied Tractate Niddah with his father, and when they reached the *sugya* of Hadar Ka-Hazyah Be-Onot (9a), a certain point kept them from proceeding. The Rav ז״ל considered the matter for a long time, and Haym, in all innocence, said to him, "Papa, isn't this noted in the notebook in which you recorded the *shi'urim* you gave last year in yeshiva? Let's look at it." This suggestion earned him a look in which wonderment and rebuke were mixed, as though he had suggested something indecent. Dynamism of this kind can create problems, especially in the realm of halakhic decision-making, where the contradictions between one cycle of study and another have more than once created confusion. But the Rav ז״ל could behave in no other way – and did not wish to.

IV.

Notwithstanding everything that has been said so far, however, it is difficult to speak of the Rav's contribution in the realm of pure, abstract Halakhah (*ha-halakhah ha-tzerufah*) as great, essential, unique. The true revolution in this area was effected by R. Hayyim, and his successors – his sons, grandsons, disciples, and their disciples – continued in the conceptual world he had created and along the lines he laid down. This was so of R. Iser Zalman Meltzer, R. Baruch Ber Lebowitz, and R. Elchanan Wasserman, and so 'too' in regard to R. Mosheh and R. Velvel – and the Rav, ז״ל. The strain of "not so My servant Mosheh," in its fullest and sharpest sense, inheres in the range and variety of areas encompassed by his interests and in whose multifaceted interaction he created his spiritual and conceptual edifice.[42]

Alongside Halakhah, which constitutes the central beam of the structure he erected, were Aggadah, Kabbalah, philosophy, science, literature. In his range of interests he had no peer. I cannot judge whether his book, *The Halakhic Mind,* which deals with the interaction of Halakhah and

the philosophy of science, and especially physics, achieved its goal when
it was written half a century ago, or whether it has weathered more recent
scientific developments. Nevertheless, who among the masters of Torah of
recent generations could have dreamed of such a project? And how many
could even have understood its intent? Who else would have been capable
of analyzing or describing the experiences of "the lonely man of faith"? To
delineate the typology of the *Ish Ha-Halakhah*? From the point of view of
content and form alone, has anyone in our time produced the like of his
great eulogies? He may well have rivals in regard to specific components
of his spiritual and conceptual world, but none in regard to the breadth
of his range of interest.

The diversity of his areas of interest constitutes an additional barrier
to those who might wish properly to evaluate his contribution. In the letter
his father sent to one of those who was involved in selecting a chief rabbi
for Tel Aviv in 5695, R. Mosheh ז״ל praised both his greatness in Torah and
his accomplishments in secular sciences and general education. In light of
this, he went on to predict:

> He is the person who will captivate the land, spiritually and materially. His
> home will be a meeting-place for the wise, and he will exert influence upon
> all parties. These will seek Torah from his pronouncements, and those will
> be bound to him and accept his bidding, out of appreciation for his dignity
> and general wisdom, as experience has already demonstrated![43]

Unfortunately, this was precisely the problem, for this conjectured
admiration was, to a large degree, of "these" and "those" – and was therefore
only partial and deficient. In the yeshiva world, some saw the Rav ז״ל as
fitting in with the authors of *Birkat Shemuel* or *Masat Mosheh* – and no
more. In like fashion, among those interested in Jewish thought, some see
him as fitting in with Rosenzweig or Levinas – and no more. However,
in order to determine his true stature, a working knowledge of the fields
upon which he drew in his interweaving of the elements of his conceptual
system is absolutely necessary.

A seventeenth-century English philosopher suggested that no one
could understand prophecy without having been granted a measure

of prophetic insight. The same is true of lower degrees of insight. And inasmuch as the capacity for diversity is not very common, appreciation of the Rav's standing all too frequently falls short of the mark. Moreover, at times criticism, is heard from persons who are unable, because of their limited scope, to grasp the depth of the Rav's essence or thought. Yet his greatness remains manifest.

V.

Despite the multifaceted range of the Rav's spiritual work, it must be emphasized that it all stemmed from one root. My intent here is not to dwell on specific issues; this is not the place to deal with the relation between *hiddushei halakhah* and Jewish thought in general, or in the Rav's work in particular. I will content myself at this time with establishing one clear and central fact that he asserted forcefully and in no uncertain terms, and even, one might say, in an extreme fashion: the authority and independence of Halakhah as a construct in which both the objective and the subjective found a place. On this occasion, I refer primarily to the personal aspect, the inner and existential source of his work. The Rav ז"ל devoted himself to disciplined halakhic thought, precise and unyielding. Similarly, in the realm of general culture, he was especially attracted, from his early interest in Neo-Kantianism, to mathematics and physics. And yet, it seems to me that in his innermost self abode the soul of an artist.

This artistic soul pulsed within him even in respect to his concerns in the field of Halakhah. There is a divide in the world of Brisk between the theoreticians who determine its principles and apply them consistently and the artists who spread their wings and soar. If you will, there is a further division between painters and sculptors, on the one hand, and musicians, on the other. Among the Levites, the Rav ז"ל would have found his place among the singers – and this, not solely because of his powers of articulation and formulation. Expression was indeed an area in which the Rav excelled. After all, he was educated and created his first *hiddushim* in the shadow of R. Hayyim, who insisted that lack of clarity in elucidation and exposition betrays a lack of understanding. But the Rav strove for and achieved more than clarity in exposition. On the verse "He gave to Mosheh two tablets, stone tablets written by the finger of God, when He had finished speaking to him on Mount Sinai,"[44] the midrash records the following comment:

> Said R. Shimon b. Lakish: "Whoever expounds words of Torah [in a way in which] they are not pleasant for those who hear them – as a bride is pleasing to her bridegroom, it were better for him that he had not said them. Why? Because when the Holy One, blessed be He, gave the Torah to Israel, it was as beloved to them as a bride is beloved to her spouse. How do we know this? For it is said: "He gave to Mosheh when he had finished [*ke-khalloto*, interpreted as *ke-khallato*, 'as his bride']."[45]

This was the goal toward which he strove, and this is what he achieved.

However, his essential artistry was in substance, and not merely form – in the work of imagination in the field of Halakhah. His thought was not technical and functional, but creative. When he was still a precocious pre-*Bar Mizvah* youngster, his father sent a notebook filled with his *hiddushim* to R. Haym, who, in his enthusiasm, ran immediately out to show them to his close friend, R. Simhah Zelig Reuger, the rabbinic judge in Brisk. And in the Rav's later life, the subject of creativity, its delights and meaning, occupied and even fascinated him. The subject serves as a major facet of *Ish Ha-Halakhah*, it animates the continuing preoccupation with the phenomenon of repentance, and, among other things, stands at the root of his concern with the return to Zion and his identification with Religious Zionism, which is built on the glorification of man's role as an agent and mover in the vistas of history and nature, as a partner in the enterprise of terrestrial creation. And if this was his conception with respect to the active scene, all the more so with regard to the contemplative. The Rav זצ"ל did not merely glorify creativity; he embodied it.

Recognition of the poetic strain in the Rav's זצ"ל halakhic work is, to a degree, for those blessed with perceptive acuity.[46] More visible is his artist's eye in the field of Jewish thought. Here, too, however, we must be careful to make distinctions. For various reasons, the best-known of his essays here in Israel is without doubt "Kol Dodi Dofek." However, as will be recalled, this is a work which – aside from its middle third, which deals with the phenomenon of evil and suffering against the background of Job's travails – is richly endowed with a certain rhetorical grace, as we might well expect for a work that began as a Yom Ha-Atzma'ut address before a large audience. This style was, admittedly, close to his heart; the Rav himself was endowed with uncommon eloquence. At his best, especially in his mother tongue, Yiddish, the Rav ל״ז was a spellbinding speaker and preacher, capable of holding an audience of thousands for long hours. Moreover, he unquestionably approached the act of verbal expression fully conscious of his task. At the opening of his eulogy of R. Hayyim Heller ל״ז, he set down the principle that "one who gives a eulogy must be an excellent pedagogue, the instrument of cold, clear intellect but also an artist, the voice of the bewildering experience of a man who stands before something both hidden and awe-inspiring."[47] This is how he saw himself – and not only in his eulogies.

But the Rav's artistry was not restricted to the rhetorical plane. The Irish poet W.B. Yeats once remarked that one writes rhetoric about his struggles with others but poetry about his struggles with himself. In this respect, too, the Rav was a poet – in the depth, power and precision of his feeling, as well as his sensitivity to it, and not just in talent for expression. An introspective self-analysis, intertwined with the feeling of standing before God, was at the center of his consciousness. His essay "U-Vikkashtem Mi-Sham," published only some fifteen years ago, was written at the end of the Second World War; originally entitled "*Ish Ha-Elokim*," it was intended as a counterpart to "*Ish Ha-Halakhah*." He wrote it as one possessed. At times he sat down to write in the evening, he would continue without stop till dawn. My mother-in-law ל״ז, concerned for his health, would object, "Why? Can't it wait until tomorrow?" But he, deep in spiritual and emotional struggle, remained adamant.

His creative work was, in part, a lyrical poem, the expression of fear and love of the Lord of All Worlds, pursued by longing for Him. But primarily it was dramatic. Spiritually, and also practically, to some extent, the Rav ל״ז lived in a climate of counterpoint and confrontation. Near the end of "U-Vikkashtem Mi-Sham," there is a wonderful passage of self-revelation, describing how, as a small boy, he imagined a dispute between the Rambam and the Ravad:

I remember how, as a young boy, isolated and friendless, I was frightened of the world. The world was cold and strange; I thought that everyone was making fun of me. However, I had one friend – don't laugh at me – and that was the Rambam. How did we become friends? Simple, we met!

The Rambam was a frequent guest at our house. When my father and teacher still lived with his father-in-law, the pious gaon R. Eliyahu Feinstein in Pruzhan, Father would sit and study day and night. Around him gathered a group (not overly large) of young scholars and exceptional *bahurim,* who would eagerly attend his lectures.

Father's lectures were given in the parlor of grandfather's house, where my bed stood. I used to sit on my bed and listen to Father lecturing. He would always speak about the Rambam. This was the procedure[48]: He would open the gemara; read the *sugya.* Then he would say: "This is its interpretation according to the Ri and the Tosafists; now let us look at the Rambam, and see how he interpreted it." Father would always find the Rambam differing from the others and departing from the simple meaning of the text. Father would say, in complaint, "We understand neither the Rambam's assumption nor his way of explaining the *sugya,*" as though protesting to the Rambam himself: "Our master Mosheh, why have you done this?" Accordingly, Father would continue, "The Ravad's objections are correct."

Members of Father's group would jump up from their seats, each proposing a solution. Father would listen and refute each proposal in turn. "The words of our master are as hard as iron," he would say. Nevertheless, he would not surrender; he would lean his head in his bent hand and sink deep into thought. The group would fall silent, not daring to interrupt his meditations.

After a long time he would raise his head, slowly, slowly, and begin: "Gentlemen, let us see…" and begin to explain. At times he would talk at length, at times he would be brief. I would strain my ears listening to him, although I understood not a word of the matters under discussion. Nevertheless, two impressions coalesced in my young, simple brain. (1) The Rambam was surrounded by opponents and "enemies" who wanted to do him a bad turn. (2) Father was his sole defender. Were it not for Father, who knew what would happen to the Rambam? I would feel that the Rambam himself was present, here in the parlor, listening to father. The Rambam was sitting with me on my bed. What did he look like? I did not know exactly. But it seemed that his appearance before Father was most comely and handsome. He had the same name as Father – both were called Mosheh.

Father would speak with closed eyes; the students, tense, with eyes shut as well, would listen attentively. Slowly, slowly, the tension would lift. Father would stride along fearlessly; new hypotheses would be raised, halakhot would be formulated and defined with wondrous exactitude. New light shone. The difficulties were overcome; the *sugya* was interpreted properly. The Rambam emerged victorious. Father's face radiated joy. He had defended his "friend," our master Mosheh son of Maimon. A happy smile could be seen on his lips. And I too was part of that joy. I was happy, I was elated. I would jump up from my bed and run quickly to my mother's room with the exhilarating news: "Mother, mother, the Rambam is right! He defeated the Ravad. Father helped him. How wonderful Father is!

But not infrequently the Rambam's luck did not hold – his "enemies" surrounded him on every side; the problems were as hard as iron. Father could not understand his words. He tried to defend him with all his might, but salvation would not come. Father was sunk in thought, his head resting on his fist. The students, along with me and the Rambam, would wait with bated breath for Father's solution. But father would raise his head and say sadly, "*Teiku,* the Rambam's formulation is very difficult; there is no solution. We must leave it for another day."

The whole group, and Father among them, was sad. We were, as it were, tearfully taking leave of the Rambam.[49] A quiet melancholy settled on every face. Tears would flow from my eyes. I would even see tears glittering at the corners of the Rambam's eyes.

Slowly, I would go to Mother and say to her with a broken heart, "Mother, Father could not justify the Rambam's formulation; what should we do?" "Don't be sad," mother would answer, "Father will find an answer for the Rambam. And if he doesn't, maybe you will, when you get older. The essential thing is to study Torah with joy and enthusiasm."[50]

This dramatic imagination, which, in the springtide of life, so affected the fearful child in his bed, accompanied the mature gaon all his life. The "young boy, isolated and friendless," became the "lonely man of faith," in that both viewed reality through a prism of confrontation and struggle, of contention, "the heavenly creatures moved back and forth,"[51] rejecting easy solutions. This imagination easily found its place within the framework of a dialectal approach, nurtured it and was nourished by it; and in this way, enriched and deepened the profundity of the Rav's creations.

The nature of creativity, or, more precisely, of the creative man, was one of the central points of this struggle for understanding. But the Rav ל"ז was ambivalent about this confrontation – the creation confronting its Creator, not, God forbid, as a contender, but even as a partner. On the one hand, he admired the boldness and initiative; on the other, he recoiled from the thought of forcing God's hand.

The most striking expression of this attitude may be found in the distinction the Rav draws between Adam I and Adam II in "The Lonely Man of Faith." But the dualistic relationship – the confrontation between man's creative tension and his status as God's creation – is most clearly reflected in earlier essays, and most notably in connection with the very fortress of Torah creativity, the world of Halakhah.

The way of a *talmid hakham,* he explained in "On the Love of Torah and the Redemption of the Soul of Our Generation," is founded both on "intellectual achievement"[52] and on childlike simplicity and innocence.

> Intellectual achievement reaches its peak and then returns to its roots, to *katnut mohin,* to childlike innocence,[53] from which the morning dew of simple purity has not been eradicated. In place of the mature *talmid hakham* who stands on his own, is a child, given over to the authority of others, who has only a refreshing and rejuvenating directness and simplicity.[54]

He sounded the same theme in his eulogy, composed after his own recovery in 5720, of R. Hayyim Heller ל"ז, who indeed reflected this mixture of traits.[55]

> A strange polarity has descended upon the world of authentic Judaism. It is as though it swings between the two ideas of maturity and childhood. A mature man, whose intellect has risen to the highest level of knowledge of Torah-learning, whose thought is graced with vast powers, both fully developed and still bursting forth, with profundity, range, and acuity, is not yet entirely mature, for the soul of a child still abides within him. He is full of knowledge, refined intellect, great experience, and sober vision, crowned with years and spiritual greatness; yet at the same time he remains a playful child, a youngster whose innocent curiosity, natural enthusiasm and impetuosity, and soulful restlessness have not left him. He is old, yet young; a man touched by age, but also a toddler with curls black as a raven,[56] from whose eyes the dream of youth has not yet departed. If the man has grown old, and all together adult,

if the morning of his life has entirely passed, and he stands, in soul and spirit, at the noontide of life, bereft of the dew of youth, if all of him is adult – in his thought, his feelings, his desires, his faith, and his faithfulness, he cannot reach God. The adult is too cunning. He is guided by utilitarianism. Experience of God is not to be found among the mercantile. Only a child can break through the bounds and limits that separate calculations of ends and means from the Infinite.[57] Only a child in his simple faith and his enthusiasm that can ignite sparks is able to make the astounding leap to the bosom of God. "For Israel is a lad, and God loved him."[58] "Is Ephraim a darling child to Me? Is he a child that is cuddled? For as often as I speak of him, I remember him still; therefore My heart yearns for him."[59] Giants of Torah, geonim of Israel, became, as it were, young children when they reached the realm of faith. A young child with all his innocence. Their charm, their simplicity, their panic-stricken shudders, blazing spiritual elation, and their surrender to it. Wherever you find their maturity, there you find their childlikeness.[60]

However, it is clear that the bottom line was not intended as a negation of creativity – after all, the experience of duality is itself a creative act – but as a new confirmation of its worth, so long as it is connected to a self-abasement that expresses fear and an embrace that embodies love. The Rav ז״ל saw man as he saw himself, a tragic creature sunk in the reality of confrontation and struggle, but he was without a trace of radical pessimism. In his personality and in his being, that possibility was precluded by his consciousness of standing "before God," the stance the Rav took such pains to define with halakhic and philosophical precision as the embodiment and fulfillment of the phenomenon of the *mizvah* of joyfulness. The Rav did not manifest the external mannerisms of piety that writers of hagiographical biographies dote upon in their descriptions of other *gedolim*, even though his piety[61] was so profound a part of him that when he once inadvertently turned on a light on the Sabbath, he spontaneously burst into tears. Yet, the consciousness of always standing before God was at the center of his world. On other occasions and in other contexts, he concentrated on clarifying the relationship between this consciousness of God's presence and other basic matters in particular, prayer, the quintessential "standing before God," and *talmud Torah,* which brings God's presence to those engaged in it. Beyond all of these analytical deliberations, the consciousness that "I have placed God before me always"[62] filled and sustained his entire being.

VI.

How did the Rav's ז״ל leadership express itself? Unlike Mosheh, he did not achieve the status of a faithful shepherd "in the eyes of all Israel." Essentially, he was the captain of a ship whose passengers were the community whose social and ideological outlook was similar to his own. But for them, the leadership he provided was critical. We ought to examine its component parts.

In Israel, the first programs broadcast after his passing stressed his status as a *posek* accepted in all circles, and as the leader of Religious Zionism outside Israel. There is a certain truth to this, but only a partial one, and not merely because there were circles that did not accept his decisions. This simple description is not complete and comprehensive. True, he devoted not a little effort to halakhic decision-making, both as the spiritual leader of Greater Boston, especially in his first decade there, before he began his more concentrated activity in New York, but also because of his role as an advisor of ultimate resort for his students, and through them, for many of their congregants.

Whether from force of circumstance or his personal predilections, he did not conduct himself like the scholars he described in *Ish Ha-Halakhah*. In that essay he observed that "the greatest men of Halakhah have shirked and continue to shirk the responsibility of serving as rabbis in the broader Jewish community, and join those who count themselves as 'fearful of *psak*.' And if they are forced to violate this policy and to decide matters of practical Halakhah – this is only a minor duty to which these men of Halakhah do not entirely give themselves."[63] He, in practice, when invited to participate in halakhic decision-making, addressed the challenge in all seriousness, conscious of his responsibility. His approach to these decisions was typical of him and his heritage. Intermixed therein was a certain independence, based on his innovative analytic methodology, fused with profound sensitivity to the issues involved, with full consciousness of the need for *heart*. His guiding principle, with ramifications grounded in both of these factors, was this statement by his father, R. Mosheh ז״ל: "It is necessary to *pask'n* on the basis of the gemara and the Rishonim, and to control *psak* by means of the *Shulhan Arukh*."[64] The relative degree of flexibility embodied in these words enabled a type of *psak* that combined responsibility to halakhic truth with an attempt to come to terms with the human dimension involved. He was always impressed with the efforts of *gedolei Yisrael* to seek solutions that took the moral aspect of human needs into account, so far as the ability of the *posek* and halakhic flexibility allowed. And that typified his own approach.

Nevertheless, it would be erroneous and misleading to think that *psak* was the center of his personal world or communal activity. *Psak* was not his natural element; he did not take to it as a fish to water, as did his friend and relative, the Gaon R. Mosheh Feinstein ז״ל, or, the Gaon R. Shlomo Zalman Auerbach, ז״ל.[65] He saw his concern with halakhic decision-making, with the works of the *poskim*, as a continuation and broadening of his ongoing study, but he did not view it as an independent field of endeavor in which to specialize. Practical halakhic decision-making was his response to the needs of individuals or of the community, but did not call for the systematic cultivation that could have determined the course of his life.

One should view his organizational activities in parallel fashion. He had close contacts with the Jewish political world, especially early in his career, as a member of the Nesiut of Agudath Israel in the United States, and after World War II (presumably, because of it and as a consequence of it), as the shining jewel in the crown of the World Mizrachi Organization. He involved himself in these activities not as a response to pressure, and certainly not, God forbid, for self-glorification, but on principle. His work for these organizations was an expression of his belief that it was necessary to imbue all realms of life and society with sanctity and to overcome the challenges bound up with such activities. Beyond this, however, was a concern for his approach to communal leadership. True, he did not, in the long run, hold aloft the banner of the ideology that is now termed "Da'at Torah," which maintains that every political question has an essentially halakhic character, and is thus susceptible to the obligatory and exclusive decisions of the *gedolei Torah*. At first he inclined to this view, and even asserted it with enthusiasm. As he said, in his eulogy for R. Haym Ozer ז״ל,

The high priest who wore the holy diadem, who obtained God's favor even in cases of impurity affecting the Holy Temple, who would decide matters in regard to the technicalities of the minimum measures of *ketamim*,[66] and mikva'ot, regarding eruvim, or mixtures of milk and meat – the most technical areas of Halakhah – would also inquire of the Urim ve-Tumim; the same priest would decide with finality all questions involving the most serious communal or national problems, such as "Shall I attack or not?"[67] – issues of war and peace, of hope and despair, of our relations with the nations or with the reigning power."[68]

After a time, he abandoned this view, and in the course of decades he accepted and even sharpened the distinction between matters involving *mizvot* (*divrei mizvah*), which are to be decided by halakhic decision-makers, and other matters (*divrei reshut*), in which significant weight is attached to the opinions and authority of other leaders, or to private judgment. Nevertheless, although he rejected the decisive reach of rabbinic authority in political matters, he was insistent that such matters be determined from a perspective of refined spirituality and in consonance with Torah values. And he fully recognized that he was one of the few who could bring the proper measure of spirituality to bear upon Religious Zionism so as to ensure its standing as a Torah movement.

But even these concerns, far more so than matters of *psak*, were of peripheral importance to him. Essentially, he was not a man of affairs in the pragmatic sense of the term, and found it difficult to come to terms with purely means-oriented perspectives, even in relatively simple matters. He was a man of the spirit, down to the roots of his soul. He deemed matters of the spirit to determine their own existential category, even when they were not expressed in terms of Torah and *mizvot*. I recall that he once was visited by a certain wealthy man who was totally cut off from any religious life. Afterwards, when I asked him how the visit had gone, he said to me, with some surprise, "You know, he is a spiritual person."

Thus, the political leadership the Rav ז"ל provided, to the degree to which he did so, was not conspicuous in terms of direct communal action. And even in this area, his leadership consisted more of creating an atmosphere, pointing a way, imbuing the movement with requisite ethical overtones, establishing the proper scale of values – in short, with giving over his general Torah view, as opposed to inculcating a specific social theory or particular policy. And he was certainly removed from outright party politics. There is, of course, a connection and even an overlap between areas or aspects. In the Rav ל"ז's experience, as in that of others, there was no wall separating the world of the learned and the practical arena, and the sermons and lectures he gave at various Religious Zionist gatherings overlap both areas; but the central concern was always spiritual, not political.

VII.

The Rav's ל"ז luminescence enlightened, flashed, and illuminated by its radiation – radiation that was embodied in the world of action as instruction (*hora'ah*) in both its narrow[69] and broad senses. The Rav's self-image, with respect to his functioning, was bound up with activity at once intellectual and educational. On various occasions, he said that if asked, upon his arrival in the afterworld, to delineate his claim to eternal life, he would point to three factors: (1) he had studied Torah with his children, (2) he had founded the Maimonides School in Boston, and (3) he had, for a very long time, assumed responsibility for the economic solvency of an eminent *talmid hakham*. He always defined himself as a *melammed*, not, I hasten to add, from feigned humility – he well knew his worth – but from a realization of the greatness of the endeavor of teaching, which to his mind was truly "the work of heaven" not only because it was carried out for the sake of God, but because it was carried out *by* God. In addition, the Rav ל"ז saw in this role the fulfillment of the commandment of *imitatio Dei* – just as He teaches Torah to his nation Israel, so you too must teach Torah to Israel.[70]

To the fulfillment of this responsibility he brought both skill and artistry. Both in his day-to-day *shi'urim* in the yeshiva and in his appearances at public functions, the atmosphere was virtually electric – and not simply because he did not hesitate to castigate his students for negligence in mastering the relevant sources or mental laziness in analyzing them. His ability as a teacher was rare in the extreme – a mixture of clarity, exactness,

profundity, and innovation, in which he demonstrated the inverse of the
comment of his grandfather, R. Haym,[71] that is, the extent to which a clear
understanding expresses itself in clear exposition. He had the capability
and readiness to make this knowledge available to people of widely disparate levels of knowledge and understanding, from those at the heights
of Torah scholarship to those on its foothills, from accomplished *talmidei
hakhamim* to simple working Jews, from kollel fellows to high-school and
even primary school students. Those who knew him only from his *shi'urim*
in New York did not always appreciate his powers. But in Boston, where
he was more involved in the society of ordinary people, as well as in the
work of the Maimonides School, this quality of his was apparent to all.
Hazal say in a midrash that at the time of the Giving of the Torah, every
Israelite received a Torah suited to his own individual understanding and
absorptive capacity. Thus, too, as one aspect of the principle of "teach a
child according to his understanding,"[72] it is the master's responsibility to
teach his student, even though today this principle appears to lie beyond
the grasp of many. As a melamed, the Rav ל"ז functioned not only with
an abstract theoretician's adherence to an articulated policy, but with the
intuited approach of a born teacher.

The Rav's link with teaching involved yet another aspect of his personality: his love of Torah. It is hardly necessary to emphasize how central a
part of his existence this was. He often spoke about it, and wrote prolifically
on the subject. But his existential tie to Torah was deeply stamped on his
soul, well beyond the analysis and clarification of the concept of teaching
Torah. Toward the end of his life, he often spoke of this tie as having enabled
him to withstand the strain of the threefold bereavement he experienced
within a three-month period, when, in the winter of 5727, he lost his mother,
brother, and wife. But this intense love for Torah characterized his entire life
in a variety of contexts, and it crystallized within him a love for teaching
as well as a love for learning.

This found practical expression in the innumerable *shi'urim* he conducted, which provided him with personal satisfaction and, in essence,
reflected his devotion to both Torah and his students. On the part of the
recipients of this wealth, his devotion aroused not only astonishment at

the ability displayed but also admiration and veneration mixed with love. Nevertheless, on the part of a not-insignificant portion of his students, this bond with the Rav ל״ז was tinged with "the awe of your master,"[73] either from fear of that great fire or because they themselves had been singed by it. The Rav ל״ז demanded much of his students, as he demanded much from himself. If we did not always meet his demands, we were liable – in particular, during the first twenty years of his time at Yeshiva,[74] to be the recipients of his reproof and censure. But this was a reproof that stemmed from his bond to us and his feelings of responsibility for us. As the years passed, it became clear that it was precisely those who were closest to him who received the most severe tongue-lashings. But despite this, the stamp of fear imprinted by censure was clear. It was sharpened, moreover, by the Rav's overall mode of personal interaction. Despite his communal involvements, there was a strain of introversion in the Rav ל״ז, and it was not easy for him to give expression to his deeply rooted affection for his students in a way that would mitigate the fear he instilled. But despite all this, those students – and not necessarily the most seasoned – who succeeded in penetrating the barrier of "the awe of your master," experienced the depth of the mutual bond between a master and a disciple that the Rav ל״ז continually held up as being the very backbone of tradition. They understood that for the Rav ל״ז, the Rambam's admonition "The master is obligated to express his anger at them and verbally humiliate them in order to sharpen [their intellects and perceptions]"[75] was a complement to his demand that "a person must be concerned with his disciples [honor], and love them, for they are sons who give pleasure both in this world and in the world-to-come."[76] They felt in their very flesh the depth of the bond with them, beyond verbal caress, that animated him. And for their part, a broader but also deeper view aroused not only enthusiasm but also a tie of love for their master and for the man in him.

VIII.

Light and enlightenment. There was, however, yet another aspect to the Rav ל״ז in his relationship to his community. The Bible employs two contrary metaphors in describing God, although ultimately they are complementary. One, which we have concentrated on so far, is that of light: "For with You is the source of light, in Your light we see light."[77] The second is one of shade: "The one who dwells in the refuge of the Most High, and abides in the shade of the Almighty."[78] "God is your guardian, your shade at your right hand."[79] The same is true of the great: they serve as both light and shade.

This is true in two senses. In one respect, this applies on the heavenly plane, insofar as the merit of a great person serves to protect and shield his generation. In his comments on Caleb's words during the incident of the spies, "Their shade has turned away from them – God is with us; do not fear,"[80] Rashi, following the gemara in Sotah 35a, interprets the word "shade" as meaning "their protection and their strength: the decent people among them have died – Job, whose merit would defend them."

It is true in another respect, in regard to matters involving the community, or, to be more precise, *communities.* To the extent that there are deep-seated ideological divisions in *Knesset Yisrael,* a great Torah leader provides legitimization for the community that follows him, even when it constitutes a minority. "In R. Eliezer's town they would cut wood to make coals in order to produce iron [to produce a scalpel for use at a brit milah] on the Sabbath; in the town of R. Yose Ha-Galili they would eat fowl with milk."[81]

For more than two generations it was the Rav ז״ל, more than anyone else, who provided inspiration and an imprimatur for the perspective and the group that attempted to bridge the gap between Torah and general society and culture. He was far from adopting what is now called Modern Orthodoxy. On the contrary, he often levelled penetrating criticism at its aspects that smacked of shallow thinking, deficient halakhic obligation, or compromising, lukewarm religious experience. In his eulogy for R. Hayyim Heller, he intoned:

> Whenever I visited him in his apartment on the West Side of Manhattan, in the midst of its concentrated Jewish life, turbulent and perplexed – its synagogues, organizations, clubs, and all their appurtenances, I would always feel as though I had entered another world, as though I had penetrated a boundary that separated two separate realms of existence. One was the world of the earlier

generations – the Shakh, the Taz, and the Gra; and the other was the world of Modern Orthodoxy, bereft of wings for flight and lacking the roots that would enable it to penetrate deeply within religious experience.[82]

Nevertheless, in regard to the core issues of principle – a link to the secular world and its knowledge, wrestling with its challenge rather than isolating oneself from it, the importance of Zionism and the State of Israel – the Rav ז״ל was a pillar of cloud and fire for this camp. Its votaries did not always understand his approach, in all its complex balance. At times, either through boorishness or superficiality, or because of their own ulterior motives, they distorted his words and turned them to their own uses. However, his fundamental approach was clear and consistent. On his banner the Rav ז״ל inscribed the words of Caleb, "Let us arise and take possession of [the land], for we can overcome it,"[83] and this motto guided him all through his life as a communal leader.

It is well known that many great Torah authorities disagreed with this approach and with him. This is not the place, nor is it yet the time, to pass definitive judgment upon the standing of his path as a way of life for the future, as an option for the many. Time will tell what elements of his thought are valid for all times and climes, and what elements are to be considered only a temporary measure (*hora'at sha'ah*); history will judge. There is no doubt, however, that for those who clung to it and to him, the Rav ז״ל was a mighty oak, a shelter and a fortress in the face of arrows of criticism and vehement attack directed against a large community of loyally committed Jews. In his time and place, he led and protected an entire camp, and enabled it to rear its head and maintain its spiritual stature.

IX.

With respect to shade, we need to touch upon yet another aspect. The familiar scriptural references to this theme, "He abides in the shade of the Almighty," and, in the next verse, "my fortress and my refuge, in whom I trust,"[84] are both drawn from Tehillim 91, which Hazal termed "a song of mishaps" or "a song of plagues."[85] The emphasis is on shade as a barrier that protects those within against attacks from without. In another verse, however, which the community of Israel recited on Shabbat Hol Ha-Mo'ed Pesah, while the Rav's bier was yet before it, there is revealed an entirely different aspect of this word. "In his shade I delighted to sit, and its fruit was sweet to my palate."[86] "I delighted" – refers not to mere protection against mishap and disease, but to positive pleasure that arouses desire and longing; and this, in the context of Shir Ha-Shirim, which the Rav ז״ל interpreted, as did the Rambam, as a parable of the quest of the soul possessed with a mad desire, for God: "That is what King Solomon, peace be upon him, referred to parabolically: 'for I am sick with love,' and all of Shir Ha-Shirim must be seen in this light."[87] The delight in question clearly does not denote that absence of mishap and disease, but, rather, the pleasure of communing with the Lord of the universe, with the One "whom my soul loves." Two purposes and two experiences are encompassed within the framework of one phenomenon. In one verse King David beseeches: "Show me favor, O Lord, show me favor, for my soul trusts in You, and in the shade of Your wings I will shelter until misfortunes pass."[88] In another, he sings, "for You have been my help, and in the shade of your wings I will sing."[89] That selfsame sukkah may serve as "a shadow by day [protecting me] from heat, and a fortress and hiding place from storm and rain,"[90] and as a communion site, in which a Jews "sits in the faithful shade to welcome guests, rejoicing in this world and in the next."[91]

The same is true, *mutatis mutandis,* in regard to the *gedolei Yisrael* in whose shade dwell those who seek Torah and desire to cleave to God. Their company instills security and bestows bliss. As far as the Rav ז״ל is concerned, aside from the opportunity to absorb his Torah knowledge, we "delighted and sat," charmed by his personality. He had an uncommon magnetism. At his best, he had a sense of humor, sharp but also vivacious. Above all, he was crowned with glorious dignity – a "majesty" about which he often spoke in regard to others – that elevated him above others but did not sunder him from people.

Alongside the nobility and aristocracy that enveloped him was an exemplary simplicity. Until his twilight years, when, upon coming to New York, he required and received devoted care from students, he did not have attendants, nor did he want them. He made his own bed, answered the telephone himself, answered letters in his own hand, and when in the Yeshiva cafeteria, sat at a table like any of the students. He lived as a *talmid hakham* who had forgone the honor due him – not consciously, or self-consciously, but as a natural expression stemming from the roots of his character. He did not accept the contention that the honor due the Torah and its scholars must now be emphasized all the more inasmuch as people's link to Torah has weakened. The notion that a secular age was precisely the time to sharpen the sense that "Who are the true kings? The rabbis"[92] in the eyes of ordinary people and scholars, so that insofar as Torah scholars are kings and the representatives of the world of true values, the honor due them must not be yielded, was alien to him. All the more did he recoil from haughtiness, which blinds the eyes even of the discerning[93] to the point of demanding imaginary displays of respect, and which may even contain, as he was fond of remarking, a certain measure of "going with head held high" that, as Hazal noted, may keep the Divine Presence at a distance.[94] With enthusiastic self-identification, he used to tell the story of his grandfather, R. Hayyim who saw a group of saddened children as he was walking down a street in Brisk. He asked why they were sad, they replied that they wanted to play horse and rider but lacked a "horse" to ride on. Right then and there, he offered his own back for the purpose. This spirit animated the grandson as well.

Not that the Rav ל״ז lacked an awareness of the honor due one of his stature. He would talk of this at times, and when an academic chair was endowed for him at Yeshivat Rabbenu Yitzhak Elchanan in 5716, he produced a glowing *derashah* on the subject. He always distinguished, however, and profoundly so, between true honor – that due the *melekh ha-kavod,* related to the value of *kevod ha-beriyot,* as noted in the verse, "Therefore my heart rejoices and my honor is glad,"[95] and that honor whose pursuit takes a person out of the world.[96] In regard to God, R. Yohanan says at the end of tractate Megillah (31a), "Wherever you find the transcendence of the Holy One, blessed be He, there you find His humility [mentioned as well]." This combination, *mutatis mutandis,* also characterized the Rav ל״ז.

The humility spoken of by R. Yohanan is not a subjective feeling, but a readiness to enter into a relationship with "a contrite and humble spirit,"[97] despite one's exalted status. In this, too, the Rav ל״ז went his own way – not out of a condescending pity for "the wretched of the earth" but from a profound feeling for man's dignity. This feeling, based on Jewish sources but with universal dimensions, animated and inspired him, in matters large and small. His great love for Jews did not dim his appreciation for the "the image of God"[98] in all humanity or eclipse it. When a Catholic widow who worked in his home was caught in financial difficulties, he sprang to the task of arranging a collection for her. And in communal matters, this principle, along with his distress at the possibility of *hillul Hashem,* stood behind his zealous support for the unequivocal demand for a board of inquiry to look into the massacres at Sabra and Shatila.

The Rav ל״ז was a notable *ba'al tzedakah* who both gave and induced others to give. In accordance with the gemara in Sukkah (49b) that *tzedakah* is repaid only in proportion to the hesed in it, his charity was based on the moral and theological foundation of the recognition of others as being "in the image of God" and not merely on pity for the recipient's troubles. Not always did the Rav succeed in greeting others with a cheerful countenance.[99] At times, he was in a mood that could express itself in isolation or anger. But this was never an essential expression of his strongly held principles regarding the dignity of man. His theology was always based on that dignity – a basis which, by his own admission, often placed its stamp on his halakhic decisions.

X.

But now we miss the Rav ל״ז on every plane – personal and communal, theoretical and practical, ethical and existential. Especially, perhaps, the latter. As a Torah personality and an educator, he was greatly preoccupied by his efforts to design an experiential corpus that was at once a system of thought and a song, to disseminate and inculcate it, and above all, to forge a link between it and the purely intellectual sphere.

"And R. Levi said," we are told at the end of Mo'ed Katan (29a), "Whoever goes out of the synagogue and enters the study hall, and from the study hall to the synagogue, merits receiving the Divine Presence, as is written,[100] 'they will go from strength to strength, everyone appearing before God in Zion.'" In contrast, however, it is recorded at the end of Berakhot (64a) that "R. Levi bar Hiyya said: Whoever goes from the synagogue to the study hall and occupies himself with Torah merits receiving the Divine Presence," with no mention of the opposite transition – going from the study hall to the synagogue. It seems to me that there is no contradiction between the two statements. If a person entirely abandons the synagogue, the place of "the worship of the heart," when he leaves it for the study hall, and never occasionally returns to the synagogue, he will not merit receiving the Divine Presence. If, however, he succeeds in bringing the import of the synagogue with him to the study hall, its experience and meaning, this one-way transit will suffice to bring the Divine Presence.

The Rav ז״ל often dealt with the connection between these two centers; and in one of his Yahrzeit *shi'urim* he suggested a new approach to the subject. His point of departure was an apparent contradiction between two talmudic passages, a *sugya* in the first chapter of Berakhot (8a) and another in Megillah (26b–27a). In the first source we find:

> Said R. Hisda: What is [the reason] for the verse "God loves the gates of Zion more than the tents of Yaakov"?[101] God loves gates betokening Halakhah more than synagogues and study houses.... and Abbaye said: At first I would study in the house and pray in the synagogue; until I heard what R. Hiyya b. Ami said in the name of Ula: From the day the Temple was destroyed, all that God has in this world are the four cubits of Halakhah. Now I pray only where I study.

Following this source, the Rambam, who, on the Rav's view, probably did not have the words "and study houses" in his texts, codified, in Hilkhot Tefillah (8:3), "A house of study is of greater importance than a synagogue, and even though there were many synagogues in their city, many great sages would pray only where they occupied themselves with Torah."

On the other hand, at the beginning of the chapter "Bnei Ha-Ir" in Megillah (26b–27a), Amoraim disagree over the issue of whether the sanctity of a house of study is greater than that of a synagogue, or vice versa.

> Said R. Papi in the name of Rava: [One may convert] a synagogue into a house of study, but it is forbidden to convert a house of study to a synagogue. And

R. Papa in the name of Rava teaches the reverse.... Bar Kappara expounded: What is written, etc., "and he [Nebuchadnezzar] burned every large house in fire."[102] R. Yohanan and R. Yehoshua b. Levi [disputed the matter]. One said: "A place in which Torah is magnified, and the other held, a place in which prayer is magnified.

The Rav ז"ל propounded the following question in regard to these passages:

In either case we have a difficulty. If Abbaye held as did R. Yehoshua b. Levi, that the sanctity of a house of study is greater than a synagogue, he should have prayed there even before he heard Ula's statement. And if he disagrees with R. Yehoshua b. Levi and agrees with R. Yohanan, namely, that the sanctity of a synagogue is greater than that of a house of study, why did he transfer his prayers to the house of study?

His reply is illuminating.

It seems to me that the explanation for this is simple. The discussion in the *sugya* in Megillah with regard to which sanctity is greater, that of the house of study or that of a synagogue, has no connection with the question regarding prayer or its proper place. It relates only to the question of whether one may change a place dedicated to one purpose to the other. Even if we assume, with R. Yehoshua b. Levi, that the sanctity of a house of study is greater than that of a synagogue, and that converting a place of Torah to one dedicated to prayer is forbidden, because we must raise places from a level of lower sanctity to higher sanctity, and not lower them, it is nevertheless possible that prayer must be carried out in a synagogue. Each place is dedicated and set apart for its own purpose and *mizvah*. The synagogue is set aside for the fulfillment of the *mizvah* of prayer, and the house of study for Torah; and so, prayer has to be carried out in the place designated for that *mizvah*, namely, the synagogue; the *mizvah* will not be enhanced by carrying it out in a study hall, which is designated for a different *mizvah*. The function and, indeed, the essence of the house of study is expressed in the study of Torah and not in prayer.

With regard to the question of raising or lowering the sanctity of one for the other,[103] it is quite possible to conclude that the Halakhah legislates that the setting aside of a place for the *mizvah* of *talmud Torah* is greater than setting aside a place for the *mizvah* of prayer; and yet prayer must nevertheless be carried out in a place proper to it[, even if its sanctity is lower than that of the study hall]. The superiority [in sanctity] of [a place dedicated to] *talmud Torah* over [the sanctity of a place dedicated to] prayer has no influence on [the latter's] unique connection to prayer. Is there, for example, any enhancement of the *mizvah* of eating sacrificial meat of a lower degree of sanctity[, which may be eaten within the walls of Jerusalem,] in the Temple court [where only sacrificial meat of a higher degree of sanctity is ordinarily eaten]? Certainly not. The former may be eaten throughout Jerusalem, and eating it in a place of greater sanctity [the Temple court] makes no difference. The same may be said of prayer. It must be carried out only in the synagogue, which has been set aside for that purpose, and not in another place, even if the sanctity of the other place is twice as great.

Thus, no conclusion regarding the [*mizvah*] of prayer may be drawn from the debate between R. Yohanan and R. Yehoshua b. Levi. The innovation of R. Hisda and Ula was on an entirely different plane. A house of study is sanctified not only for the *mizvah* of *talmud Torah*[104] but also for the *mizvah* of prayer – and this to a greater degree than the sanctity of a synagogue. R. Hisda interpreted the verse "God loves the gates of Zion more than the tents of Yaakov," which deals with the sanctity of the Temple in Jerusalem over against the other sanctuaries and great high places, such as those at Shiloh, Nob, and Gibeon. He equated the [sanctity of] houses of study to [that of] Jerusalem, and [the sanctity of] synagogues to [that of] other sanctuaries. It is clear, in regard to Jerusalem and its relation to Shiloh, Nob, and Gibeon, that the sanctity of each was not different in substance from the others; Jerusalem was sanctified for the same *mizvot* as the others. The sanctity of Jerusalem did not include matters not subsumed under the rubric [of the sanctity of] Shiloh. The difference between them was one of the degree and nature of the sanctity, not of what *mizvot* it embraced. And the same is true of the difference between the house of study and the synagogue. The house of study is dedicated and set aside for prayer, just like the synagogue. Its essential dedication for study includes prayer. And that is what R. Hisda and Ula determined: the sanctity of prayer set within a framework of Torah is greater in degree than that of prayer alone. It was for this reason that Abbaye stated that when he heard the words of R. Hisda and Ula he began to pray in the place in which he studied. Ula's innovation was the concept that the four cubits of Halakhah constitute a continuation of the Temple, and partake of its sanctity. Thus, the sanctity of the house of study includes both, for it has been set aside for *both* Torah and prayer, as was the Temple itself.[105]

What is stated here, in the context of halakhic discourse, faithfully reflects the Rav's own conception of the range of these *mizvot* and his goal in regard to both. From the very beginning, he strove and taught toward the creation of a link in both thought and action between the synagogue and the house of study; for the fusion of the speculative and the experiential, the theoretical and the actual: for the comprehension of study as a meeting with the Divine Presence, and an emphasis on the dimensions of the service of the heart [i.e., prayer] within Torah study, the designing of the "crown of Torah" as the conjunction of the acumen of *lomdut* with personal sanctity. The matter was of great concern to him. Despite his desire and effort to link the two, he more than once expressed a feeling of failure and frustration in regard to the task of making his students aware of the experiential aspect of learning. In an article that he published in 5720, a short time after he recovered from cancer surgery, he complained that his students strove for greatness in Torah, and had the merit of learning and comprehending much, but they lacked the experiential link that was bound precisely with *katnut ha-mohin*. And in the continuation, in regard to his activity as their teacher, he added, in a confessional vein:

> And therefore I affirm that I can identify one of those responsible for the present situation, and that is none other than myself. I have not fulfilled my obligation as a guide in Israel. I seem to have lacked the ability – the personal power – required of a teacher and rav, or perhaps I lacked some of the desire to fulfill the role completely, and I did not devote myself completely to the task. To a greater or lesser degree, as an educator and a teacher on the plane of *gadlut ha-mohin*, the desire to achieve, my students have received much Torah learning from me, and their intellectual standing has strengthened and increased during the years they have spent with me; but I have not seen much growth on the experiential plane. I have not succeeded in living in common with them, in cleaving to them and bestowing some of my personal warmth on them. My words, it would seem, have not kindled a divine spark in sensitive hearts. I have fallen short [in my role] as one who spreads the "Torah of the heart" – [a Torah] transmitted by the power of [the teacher's deliberate] diminishing [of his own towering] stature, to the point of *katnut ha-mohin*. And the failing is mine.[106]

I doubt that he changed his evaluation in later years. During summer vacations, in the years after his wife's death, he would deliver *shi'urim* quite intently for a group of *talmidim* who came to Boston to learn. One year – I think it was 5729 – he announced to them one fine day that since they were spiritually desiccated, starting the next day he would add regular *shi'urim* in the *Likkutei Torah* of the Ba'al Ha-Tanya.[107] And indeed, he began to study the *derashah* of "I am my beloved's, and my beloved is mine" with them. "But, you know," he commented to me later, "I don't think it helped much."

However, for our part, we feel his loss sevenfold precisely on the plane of bringing the synagogue into the study hall. To our shame and sorrow, we have not sufficiently absorbed and internalized the lesson of "I am my beloved's, and my beloved is mine." We find it difficult not only to clarify and sharpen the answers, or to develop approaches; we have difficulty even elucidating *the questions*.

After R. Eliezer the Great passed on, the gemara in Sanhedrin (68a) tells us, his coffin was carried along the road. "R. Akiva met [the procession].

> From Caesarea to Lydda he beat his breast[108] until blood flowed to the ground. When the line formed [around the coffin for the eulogy, R. Akiva] began: "'My father, my father, the chariots of Israel and its horsemen!'[109] I have my coins but no moneychanger to exchange them." (As Rashi explains, "That is, I have many questions, but no one to ask.")

Such a situation is certainly vexing, but there is worse: when even the penny is lacking and there are no coins to exchange.

In regard to our involvement in the world of Halakhah, it is possible, to a greater or lesser degree, to compare our situation to R. Akiva's. We are on the road, we have progressed along the furrow: we have acquired from the Rav זצ״ל the tools and the concepts; we have penetrated at least to the perimeter of his world. But on the experiential and existential plane, we are bankrupt and lack vision. The sphere in which the Rav lived, the heights to which he soared, and the depths he plumbed, are simply beyond our comprehension. The penetration of his glimpse of eternity is beyond our understanding, our prosaic essence. We knock at the gate, but like blind men,[110] we cannot find the door. R. Hisda has taught us, "A person should always enter into a synagogue [at least as far as the width] of two doorways [before praying]."[111] But we, without the Rav's זצ״ל guidance, have difficulty finding the entrance "to the house in which Torah and prayer are magnified" together.

XI.

Woe, woe, to the beauty that is buried in the earth.[112] And woe to the ship – and to us, its passengers – which has lost its captain. Woe to the generation that is bereft of its light. In his shade we delighted to sit[113] and now, the tree has been cut down and the spring has dried up. His family has been orphaned, his students have been orphaned, his community has been orphaned, the entire House of Israel has been orphaned. "We are orphans without a father," laments Jeremiah.[114] Superficially, the end of the verse merely explains, tautologously, its beginning. However, it actually opens a new horizon for us. When a person in his time of trouble is in need of spiritual support, he seeks help by turning to his parents, and they provide aid and succor, encouragement and reassurance, and in this way, consolation and relief. Now, our time of terrible distress has come. "We are orphans" – but the father, the Rav ל"ז, from whom we could have expected to draw comfort and invigoration, is not available, for it is him we mourn.

"My father, my father, the chariots of Israel and its horsemen."[115] You have been taken from us. You returned your soul to the Creator of Lights. The verse from the Ne'ilah service, which you loved so much, has been fulfilled in regard to you, "Let Him hide me in the shade of His hand, under the wings of His presence." But for us, your family, your disciples, and your disciples' disciples, you will continue to be a father. Wherever your Torah insights are recited, whenever we discuss the complexities of your thought, as long as we live in your light and observe your image, whenever we strive to embody your values, you will live with us. You will impart to us of your spirit and will guide us. Our sages' statement will be fulfilled through you:

> R. Yehudah said in the name of Rav: "I will dwell in Your tent forever [lit., for worlds]":[116] Is it possible for a person to dwell in two worlds? Rather, [what is meant is this:] David said before the Holy One, blessed be He: Lord

of the World, let it be Your will that [my] halakhot be recited in my name in this world," for R. Yohanan said in the name of R. Shimon b. Lakish: Every scholar in whose name a Halakhah is recited in this world, his lips murmur in the grave.

And may the words of David be realized with respect to us:

"For my father and mother have abandoned me, but God has gathered me in."[117] Said Rabban Shimon b. Gamliel: It is a father's way to have compassion [on his children] – "as a father has compassion on his children";[118] it is a mother's way to console – "as a man whose mother comforts him."[119] Said the Holy One, blessed be He: I will fulfill both father's and mother's part: "I, even I, am your comforter."[120]

(Yalkut Shimoni, Yeshayahu 474)

Notes

1. Translated according to the requirements of the Rav's interpretation. More generally, the verse is rendered: "These are the generations of Adam."
2. A *talmid hakham*; see Makkot 22a.
3. An allusion to Nehemyah 8:8, which describes the Torah reading of Ezra the Scribe, and from which the gemara derives the essential Sinaitic requirements of aides memoires; see Nedarim 37b.
4. Literally: "the blow."
5. Used to describe David in II Shemuel 23:1.
6. Literally: "first-born."
7. II Shemuel 1:19, 23, 27.
8. Mo'ed Katan 8a. That is, the survivors should not hire someone to visit the deceased's relatives to urge them to mourn, nor should they hire professional mourners or a professional eulogist.
9. "Inyan Ha-Hesped," in *"Torat Ha-Adam,"* ed. Rabbi H. D. Chavel, *Kitvei Ha-Ramban*, vol. 2, p. 82.
10. Ibid., p. 88.
11. Berakhot 33b.
12. Quoting Bamidbar 12:7, God's praise of Mosheh.
13. Translated from the Yiddish.
14. "Mah Dodekh mi-Dod," in *Divrei Hagut ve-Ha'Arakhah* (Jerusalem, 5742), p. 69. I quote the Yiddish from memory, although I am not certain that those were his exact words.
15. Literally, "mosaic."

16. Bamidbar 12:7–8.
17. Devarim 34:10–12.
18. Literally, "its fullness."
19. Bereshit 1:4.
20. Kohelet 2:13.
21. Bereshit 1:17–18.
22. Berakhot 5b.
23. Bava Kamma 91a.
24. Vayikra 10:7, referring to the deaths by burning of Nadav and Avihu, two of Aharon's sons.
25. From the Ahavah Rabbah prayer in the Shaharit service.
26. Lit., "fetus and afterbirth."
27. Sukkah 28a, referring in general to the entire Talmud.
28. This assertion, which is here translated from the Yiddish, focused on a very specific element, and of course was not intended as a general comparison.
29. Lit. "he cast original coins."
30. An allusion to Bereshit 41:9.
31. See Rashi on Devarim 6:7.
32. Bava Batra 175b.
33. Megillah, chap. 3.
34. Tehillim 114:8.
35. The quotation is in Yiddish.
36. Literally, "what."
37. The reference is to the modern theory of light, which defines light as both a particle and a wave.
38. Vayikra 11:36.
39. Avot 2:8.
40. The so-called sixth chapter of Avot.
41. Avot 6:1.
42. Lit., "world."
43. The letter was published in *Sefer Ha-Yovel li-Kvod Morenu Ha-Gaon Rav Yosef Dov Ha-Levi Soloveitchik* shlit"a (Jerusalem, 5744), at the end of vol. 1.
44. Shemot 31:18.
45. Shemot Rabba 41:5.
46. Yode'ei hen, an expression that conveys overtones of kabbalistic knowledge of the "secrets of the Torah." Hen is an acronym for hokhmat nistar, "the science of hidden matters."
47. "Pelitat Soferim," *Divrei Hagut ve-Ha'Arakhah*, p. 139.
48. The Hebrew is reminiscent of the description of the high priest's Yom Kippur service in the Temple.
49. As did Orpah from Naomi; see Ruth 1:14.
50. "U-Vikkashtem Mi-Sham," *Ish Ha-Halakhah: Galuy ve-Nistar* (Jerusalem, 5739), end.

51. Yehezkel 1:14.
52. Lit., "intellectual greatness."
53. Lit., "childlike smallness."
54. *Be-Sod Ha-Yahid veha-Yahad* (Jerusalem, 5736), p. 412.
55. *Divrei Hagut ve-Ha'Arakhah*, p. 159.
56. Allusion to Shir Ha-Shirim 5:11.
57. A play on sofiyut and Ein Sof.
58. Hosea 11:1.
59. Yirmeyahu 31:20.
60. An echo of R. Yohanan's statement: "Wherever you find God's transcendence, there you find His humility entioned as well" (Megillah 31a).
61. Lit., "fear of heaven."
62. Tehillim 16:8.
63. *Ish Ha-Halakhah*, p. 31.
64. In Yiddish.
65. R. Shlomo Zalman, to our sorrow, has since passed away.
66. That is, stains caused by menstrual blood or the like.
67. After Shoftim 1:1.
68. "Nose'ei Ha-Tzitz veha-Hoshen," in *Divrei Hagut ve-Ha'Arakhah*, p. 192.
69. As halakhic decision-making.
70. Nose'ei Ha-Tzitz veha-Hoshen," in *Divrei Hagut ve-Ha'Arakhah*, p. 148.
71. Referring to R. Haym's comment, quoted above, that "lack of clarity in elucidation and exposition betrays lack of understanding." The Rav ל״ז demonstrated that clarity of elucidation is linked to clarity of understanding.
72. Mishlei 22:6.
73. That is, the fear of your master should be like the fear of heaven; see Pesahim 22b.
74. Lit., "his *shi'urim.*"
75. Hilkhot Talmud Torah 4:5.
76. Hilkhot Talmud Torah 5:12.
77. Tehillim 36:10.
78. Tehillim 91:1.
79. Tehillim 121:5.
80. Bamidbar 14:9.
81. Shabbat 130a.
82. "Peleitat Sofreihem," *Divrei Hagut ve-Ha'Arakhah*, p. 148.
83. Bamidbar 13:30.
84. Tehillim 91:2.
85. Shevuot 15b.
86. Shir Ha-Shirim 2:3.
87. *Hilkhot Teshuvah* 10:3.

88. Tehillim 57:2.
89. Tehillim 63:8.
90. Yeshayahu 4:6.
91. Zohar Emor, on Vayikra 23:42, and see Sukkah 6b.
92. See Gittin 62a.
93. An allusion to Shemot 23:8.
94. Doheket et Raglei Ha-Shekhinah. See Berakhot 43b.
95. Tehillim 16:9.
96. A reference to Avot 4:28.
97. Yeshayahu 57:15.
98. Allusion to Bereshit 1:26.
99. As mandated in Avot 1:15.
100. Tehillim 84:8.
101. Tehillim 87:2.
102. Melakhim II 25:9.
103. That is, converting a place dedicated to one to a place dedicated to the other.
104. Lit., "the *mizvah* of Torah and its study."
105. "Be-Inyan Birkhat Ha-Torah," *She'urim le-Zekher Aba Mari* ל״ז, vol. 2 (Jerusalem, 5745), pp. 5–6.
106. From an article initially published in *Hadoar* (5720), and reprinted in בסוד היחיד והיחד (ירושלים, תשל״ו), p. 420.
107. R. Shlomo Zalman of Liady, founder of the Lubavitch hasidic dynasty.
108. Lit., "flesh."
109. That is, the lament which the prophet Elisha made at the departure of his master Elijah; see II Melakhim 1:12.
110. Lit., "like blind men in a chimney," an expression found in Bava Batra 12b.
111. Berakhot 8a.
112. Berakhot 5b.
113. An allusion to Shir Ha-Shirim 2:3 and the discussion above.
114. Eicha 5:3.
115. II Melakhim 1:12.
116. Tehillim 61:5.
117. Tehillim 27:10.
118. From the liturgy.
119. Yeshayahu 66:13.
120. Yeshayahu 51:12.

Chapter 11

A Portrait of Rav Shlomo Zalman Auerbach זצ״ל[1]

That Rav Shlomo Zalman Auerbach זצ״ל was relatively unknown to the general Israeli public – the secular press was astounded by the attendance of a quarter of a million people at his funeral – was largely to his credit. The ignorance derived, in essence, from his studied lifelong avoidance of the confrontational arena. That he ought to be better known to the general American Jewish public goes without saying.

Reb Shlomo Zalman was, in effect, the Israeli Reb Mosheh Feinstein זצ״ל. This equation does some injustice to each, as it ignores particular qualities that energized and enriched their lives and beings. And yet it relates, surprisingly, to major elements regarding role, status, personality, and perspective that were critical to their position as *gedolim* of our generation. Both were Roshei Yeshiva for decades, and yet were preeminent as untitled *poskim*. Both fused humility and authority, and both sought, by precept and example – by what they did and what they refrained from doing – to promote harmony and diminish confrontation. In the specific area of *psak*, each dealt with the cutting edge of modern issues, particularly as regards medicine and technology; and each approached *she'eylot* animated by sensitivity to human concerns as well as fidelity to Halakhah. Finally, while both were deeply rooted in the haredi world throughout, they maintained genuine rapport with the full range of the Torah community.

Analogies aside, however, Reb Shlomo Zalman could certainly be appreciated on his own merits. Reb Shlomo Zalman was endowed, as a *lamdan*, with a set of qualities that served him ideally as a *posek*. He had encyclopedic knowledge – and he had it, as *mehudaddim befikha*, at his fingertips. His temperament was remarkably judicious, invariably level-headed, and never pedestrian. He was deferential to the views of others, and yet genuinely self-confident. He could be innovative, and even daring. His view, for example, contrary to that of the Hazon Ish, that the application of *lifnei iver*, the proscription against enabling others to violate an issur, needs to consider long-range effects rather than immediate concerns, has potentially radical implications.[2]

But his innovations do not bear a forced aspect and never appear improvised. Finally, he had a sharply honed sense of balance – of general principle as distinct from detail, of textual and logical analysis in juxtaposition to his rootedness in a specific tradition.

He brought to the interpretation and application of Halakhah a profound sensitivity to the human dimension. Along the continuum of *psak*, he was far from being amongst the most radical *mekilim*, and he worked within clearly perceived parameters. But an awareness of the human element was always a significant factor – and not only in deviant situations. Moreover, in many contexts, he regarded this as a halakhic interest, quite apart from the personal. Some of his *pesakim* concerning Shabbat, for instance, were informed by the sense that the day should be experienced as pleasant rather than as an obstacle course.

This element was no doubt related, in part, to his own personality. One saw no emotional extremes in him. He was a blend of composure and joy – and that, within the context of a remarkably integrated life. There was in him a streak of *temimut* in the sense of naivete. He could, for instance, express amazement over a report that in America there are people who regard themselves as wholly observant and yet cut corners with respect to income tax. An astute judge of people and situations, he yet combined innocence with perspicacity. Above all, however, he was a *tamim* in the best and fullest sense of the term, *hit'halekh lefanai ve-heyih tamim*, (Walk before Me and be whole) as commanded to Avraham. He led a wholly organic life, without fissures and devoid of conflicts, in the service of the

Ribbono shel Olam. It was not exceedingly dramatic, but it was manifestly joyous: *ule-yishrei lev simhah* (And joy to the upright of heart).

The human touch was manifest in yet another aspect – simplicity and, concurrently, accessibility. He lived in a very plain apartment, by no means ascetic but quite modest, where he would receive anyone who had a *she'eylah.* The line at the foot of the steps would form daily around two o'clock, and one did not need an introduction to enter. Every question, even if, from a certain perspective, it may have been trivial, was treated seriously. If it mattered enough to the person who presented it, it was important enough to Reb Shlomo Zalman as well. And above all, not just the questions but the people were treated with respect. He knew how to listen – and not just to halakhic inquiries. He communicated a sense of genuine respect to interlocutors; he gave you a sense of worth. In all my discussions with him, I found him reassuringly paternal but never condescending; and that was the typical response.

Finally, he was marked, quite strikingly, by a measure of openness. Let there be no mistake. He himself was deeply rooted – intellectually, emotionally, hashkafically – in the world of the *yishuv ha-yashan,* and its values and priorities guided his life and what he sought for his children and *talmidim.* But he could recognize and acknowledge the worth of those who were cut from different cloth and could appreciate their needs and their accomplishments. He not only abjured factional politics but abhorred it, and he judged people on their merits rather than by labels.

Cloistered in many respects, he was nevertheless very much in touch with others. He was, of course, grounded in the haredi world, living in Sha'arei Hesed, an area marked by the very best features of *harediyut* – intensive commitment to Torah learning and halakhic observance, and a deep awareness of tradition, classical and recent – and marred by none of the worst features. Its culture does not denigrate labor, and its walls are not plastered with hate-mongering posters. It is an area within which the impact of such figures as Rav Zvi Pesach Frank and Rav Yaakov Mosheh Charlop is still felt; within which Rav Kook's memory has always been very much esteemed. Reb Shlomo Zalman was inextricably engaged in this neighborhood for many decades and, indeed, left his imprint upon it.

Reb Shlomo Zalman was of this world and served to guide it. While not a philosophic devotee in the narrow sense of the term – he was, generally, not much involved in philosophical thought – he had great respect for Rav Kook. And beyond that, while certainly not an ideological Zionist, he had an intuitive appreciation for the significance of the enterprise of *shivat Zion* and the building of Eretz Yisrael. Hence, he related positively to the whole gamut of the religious spectrum, and *dati-le'umi Bnei Torah* turned to him no less than others. And they found a ready ear and an open mind.

Hence, precisely because he had an empathetic appreciation for much of the broader scene, he was saddened in more recent years by his feeling that much was going awry in that scene. His response was not so much anger as concern, disappointment – at times, even anguish. What troubled him primarily was the sociocultural scene rather than the political arena – the ongoing secularization and divisive polarization. He no longer felt fully comfortable on his Jerusalem streets. This concern cast a shadow. And yet, what is left with us, and what we shall so sorely miss, is the memory of a remarkable gadol, at once overawing and benign, who bestrode us like a Colossus, and yet related to us, great and small, at the core of our innermost being.

Notes

1 This article first appeared in the Fall 1995 issue of *Jewish Action*, the magazine of the Orthodox Union.
2 *Editor's Note:* For example, he permitted serving food and drink to a nonreligious person who would become upset if asked to wash and make the blessing because, in the long run, the negative impact of not serving him would result in a graver sin. He reasoned that there was no *mikhshol* in serving him because the sin created by serving was less than the future, anticipated sin. See *Minhat Shelomoh,* chap. 35.

General Index

251

Jew and Gentile, 164, 236
Jewish social ethics, 145
Job, 232
Jonson, Ben, 180
Joseph
  see Yosef
Joshua
  see Yehoshua
joy
  in Torah study, 223
  mizvah of, 225
Justinian, 11

K
Kabbalah, 84, 217
Kagen, Rav Israel Meir
  see Hafez Hayyim
Kahana, Yitzhak Zev, 187n21
Kant, Immanuel, 65, 94, 190
Kaplan, Rav Avraham Eliyahu, 60n47
Karaites, 69
Karelitz, Rav Avraham Yeshaya
  see Hazon Ish
Keats, John, 20, 114
kehunah, 61
Kezot Ha-Hoshen (Rav Aryeh Leib
  Hakohen), 51, 64, 73, 87n32
Kiddush Hashem and *Hillul Hashem*, 141
kiddushei ketanah, 176–177
Kingsley, Charles, 169
Kluger, Rav Shlomo, 60n40
Kook, Rav Abraham Issac, 53, 193,
  249–250
Kubla Khan, 127
Kuhn, Thomas S., 59n27

L
Langer, 112
Lebowitz, Rav Baruch Ber, 217
Levi, tribe of, 149

Levinas, Emanuel, 218
Lewis, C.S., 81
Lichtenstein, Dr. Yehiel, 113
Lichtenstein, Rav Yitzhak Abba, 215
Lieberman, Rav Saul, 48
light
  modern theories of, 216, 244n37
Lithuania, 41
literature, 108, 114–116, 217
  see humanities
Locke, John, 46
Lorenzo, 45
Louis-Phillipe, 94
love of Torah, 230
Luria, Rav Shlomo
  see Maharshal

M
MacLeish, Archibald, 45
Maharal, 95, 156n15
Maharam Schiff, 43
Mahari Mullen, 182
Maharsha (Rav Shmuel Eliezer Edels), 42
Maharshal (Rav Shlomo Luria), 47, 95
Maimonides
  see Rambam
Maimonides School, 191, 229, 230
Malakhi, 61
Mandeville, Bernard, 148
Marbury vs. Madison, 11
Marxism, 131
maskilim, 178
Mass'et Binyamin, 167
mathematics, 100, 108, 219
Rav Matya ben Harash, 20
Meiri, 62, 183
Meltzer, Rav Isser Zalman, 50, 217
mercantilism, 181
mesorah, 80, 83, 123
meta-history, 84

Source Index

II. RABBINIC SOURCES

A. *Mishnah*